Three Revolutions

Robert Crotty

National Library of Australia Cataloguing-in-Publication entry (pbk)

Author:	Crotty, Robert B.
Title:	Three revolutions : three drastic changes in interpreting the bible / Robert Brian Crotty.
ISBN:	9781921817489 (pbk.)
Notes:	Includes bibliographical references and index.
Subjects:	Bible--History of doctrines. Bible as literature. Bible--Criticism, Textual.
Dewey Number:	220.5

Cover design by Astrid Sengkey
Original artwork by Yvonne Ashby

An imprint of the ATF Ltd
PO Box 504
Hindmarsh, SA 5007
ABN 90 116 359 963
www.atfpress.com

Three Revolutions

Three Drastic Changes in Interpreting the Bible

Robert Crotty

ATF Theology

Adelaide
2012

I dedicate this book
to my granddaughter, Matilda.
She has brought joy
and light into my world.
May she bring much joy
and light into the world of others.

CONTENTS

LIST OF FIGURES

INTRODUCTION

For Roman Catholics and others the Second Vatican Council came somewhat as a surprise. There were wise Catholic scholars who, for a long time, had said adamantly that there would never be another Ecumenical Council after the First Vatican Council had ended in 1880. With the infallibility of the Pope declared at that First Vatican Council, why would another be needed? Could another Council say anything that an infallible Pope could not say more clearly and with more authority? Despite all that, the Second Vatican Council was convened in 1961.

At that stage I was studying theology within an Australian religious order. With avid curiosity, I followed every moment of the convocation, preparation and the opening days of the Council. This was to be a New Pentecost, Pope John XXIII had said. I expected it would be. Then, I went to Rome in order to further my studies in 1963 and was in the very hotspot of Council politics. I lived in a monastery where some thirty of the Council Fathers were lodged. I met with them and came to know some of them well, heard the inside stories about what was really taking place inside St Peter's Basilica, the meeting place for the Council. At first I could hardly believe what I heard about the differences of opinion and the squabbles.

I would leave Rome at the end of 1966, a very different person to the one who had arrived over three years earlier. I was by then desperately determined that the Council decrees would change the life of the Catholic Church in Australia. In particular, I would claim that the study and interpretation of the Bible was at the very crux of future change. I felt obligated to spread the word of change and newness.

This is the story of my life, including how it changed during the years of the Council, most of which I spent in Rome and Jerusalem. It includes my later disappointment when it became obvious that the Council's influence was being dumbed down. However, the story will centre on my study of the Bible during tumultuous years of change in the Catholic Church.

It is a fact that since the age of seventeen I have been studying the Christian Bible, which consists of the collections of both the Hebrew Scriptures and the Christian Scriptures. For a considerable part of this time-span of some sixty years, I have been a student of some sort, continually enrolled in one or other course; for the rest I have been a researcher and tertiary lecturer as well as a husband, father and grandfather.

Looking back at my life from the vantage point of rather more than the biblical three-score-and-ten years, I regard with considerable interest the chequered journey that I have travelled while interpreting the texts contained in the Christian Bible. Since the journey still interests me as the main participant, it may interest others. I am not particularly anxious to 'convert' anyone to a particular way of thinking about the Bible or, indeed, any particular perspective on life and events. I am content simply to tell my tale.

It might have been expected that, following my quite early initiation into the study of the Bible, I would have progressed in a straight line with an ever gradually deepening understanding of it as, over many years, I became more competent in the biblical languages and achieved a greater facility in handling and explaining texts. That was not in fact the case.

Instead, I am now able to see that my understanding of the biblical texts has advanced much more erratically by a series of quite drastic revolutions, which affected me very personally but which actually duplicated wider revolutions taking place in the (mainly Catholic) ecclesiastical world outside me. These revolutions have been life-changing, challenging and usually quite painful. This book is a chronicle of three revolutions, which have affected my thinking on biblical interpretation over so many years, together with an attempt to explain them.

In recording these revolutions in this book, I do not think for one moment that my path has been unique. What I underwent has been common to many others, both within the Roman Catholic tradition and in other Christian traditions. Nor was the trajectory of my path inevitable. It seems to me that there were certainly some other biblical interpreters, some quite close to me, who voluntarily avoided these revolutionary changes at one point or another, claiming that the changes were deviant or that to follow such a path would be hazardous. Who knows, perhaps they were correct?

I chose to allow myself to be carried onwards on a succession of tides that brought change to my life and my relationships.

Each revolution caught me up and forced me to make life-changing decisions. I still think this was the better strategy.

The Structure of Revolutions

The very language I have been just using about revolutions and revolutionary change evokes the academic work done on how progress takes place in the natural sciences by Thomas Kuhn in a book written in 1962 and with a revised edition in 1970, *The Structure of Scientific Revolutions*. In Kuhn's vocabulary, the word 'revolution' should be accompanied by 'paradigm', 'paradigm shift' and 'normal science', all of which require some explanation. Kuhn may not have invented the terminology but he certainly gave it currency.

The similarity of language is not by chance. I first read Kuhn's *The Structure of Scientific Revolutions* in the early 1970s and it explained a great deal for me not only about the study of science and scientific change but more particularly about religion (which Kuhn presumably never initially expected). In fact, Kuhn's thought swept me off my feet. As I read his text, I felt scales falling from my eyes; I understood much that had previously been opaque.

Kuhn wrote of natural scientists, such as physicists or astronomers, establishing a 'paradigm' and working together as an academic community within that paradigm. A paradigm, according to Kuhn, is the plan that an academic group adopts in order to solve a problem, using acceptable methods, standards and generalisations. One commentator has written:

> A paradigm is a fundamental image of the subject matter within a science. It serves to define what should be studied, what questions should be asked, how they should be asked, and what rules should be followed in interpreting the answers obtained. The paradigm is the broadest unit of consensus within a science and serves to differentiate one scientific community (or sub-community) from another. It subsumes, defines and interrelates the exemplars, theories, methods and instruments that exist within it.[1]

1. George Ritzer (sec ed 1980), *Sociology: A Multiple Paradigm Science*, Allyn and Bacon: Boston Mass.

Kuhn's paradigm is something like a pair of glasses which forces scientists to see reality only in certain ways and from a certain perspective when they wear those glasses.

How does a science, such as physics or astronomy, make progress according to Kuhn? His explanation was novel. He claimed that science advances not by a logical and progressive development of thought and practice (as most people thought and probably still think) but by a scientific revolution or a 'paradigm shift'. There is a scientific revolution when one paradigm is replaced by another. There have been such scientific revolutions at the onset of the pre-modern, the modern and the post-modern periods. In physics, final causality, the search for purpose in the universe, was replaced by mechanism, the Newtonian search for cause and effect; mechanism was subsequently replaced by quantum-mechanical randomness. And so it goes on.

Once a paradigm has taken its hold of a scientific community it is difficult to displace. It establishes what Kuhn called 'normal science' where all the assumptions and methods of the paradigm are taken for granted, and scientists proceed happily with their business of solving what they perceive to be problems. Scientists are usually comfortable within the 'normal science' in which they have been trained. Using the metaphor of a pair of glasses above, scientists actually want to use the same pair of glasses as their companion scientists; they have grown accustomed to them; they actually like the glasses.

A number of commentators, even in the early days of Kuhn's popularity, remarked that a paradigm shift in the natural sciences is something like a religious conversion. The paradigm shift usually does not happen of a sudden; it is rarely a purely intellectual affair; it can even be a very upsetting experience and is brought about only because there are increasing anomalies, observations or measurements that do not fit in with the paradigm, in the practice of 'normal science'. When sufficient anomalies occur, the normal science undergoes drastic change and adopts a new 'normal science'. This process does not happen in a necessarily logical manner.

This process can be indicated by a flow chart:

Paradigm A ('Normal Science')

➔Anomalies

➔Crisis

➔Revolution

➔Paradigm B (new 'Normal Science')

Thus, the astronomer Claudius Ptolemy, born around 90 CE, used instruments and measurements to work out the lay of the Earth relative to other bodies in the solar system. He concluded that the Earth is a perfect, static sphere. The other bodies (sun, moon, planets) orbit around the earth on concentric spherical shells of invisible crystal. He decided that there were eight of these shells. This was a revolution in astronomy. A new paradigm had been born and there was a new understanding of the solar system. However, this model of the solar system threw up anomalies. The bodies did not always move according to its pattern. Ptolemy explained the irregularities by epicycles or revolving spheres set into the shells. But that did not explain all the anomalies. So Ptolemy added 'eccentricity' to the mix, the observation that the Earth is not at the exact centre of all the shells.

After Ptolemy, as anomalies continued to raise their heads, later astronomers had to add more epicycles and varying eccentricities until the model became encumbered with some eighty shells and epicycles. Then, Nicolaus Copernicus (1473–1543) proposed an entirely new model, a new revolution, by which the planets orbit the Sun and not vice-versa. The anomalies disappeared. There was a new paradigm and a new normal science within which researchers could move forward.

As I said, even in the 1970s I saw the possibility of applying Kuhn's insights to the study of religion and specifically to the religious insiders' study of their own religion. It seemed to me that Kuhn's theory could explain what had happened to me, as an academic involved with the study of the Bible, in the same way as it could explain what happened to scientists who saw that science in their day had changed dramatically and taken a new path. Progress in my own study of the Bible, I felt sure, had come about by a series of revolutions, brought about by the accumulation of anomalies within the academic study of religion, and not by a neat progression of logical thought.

This book will detail three successive revolutions that have overtaken me in my study of the biblical literature up to the present day. There have been some people along the way who have condemned me for what I have said and written about the Bible, particularly, they would say, after I had been given significant opportunities to study it at depth. I do not intend this book to be an apology for any of that. It is simply an explanation as to how I have reached the mindset that I have today.

Have I come to the end of this intellectual journey and this exciting adventure? There can be no reason to think that a final revolution has taken place in my own experience or that what is generally accepted today about the study of the Bible among many of my academic peers is the best answer.

Perhaps there is yet another revolution ahead of which I am only vaguely aware at the moment. In my younger days, I never dreamt that I would believe what I believe today. I still find anomalies in the study of the Bible. Perhaps they will accumulate and bring about yet another revolution in my lifetime. If so, I hope to have the courage to allow myself to be carried to yet another place. Or perhaps I may have run out of time for any further revolution.

Before beginning my narrative, I need first define this particular area of study that has so engrossed me for so long a time: the Christian Bible that consists of the Hebrew Scriptures and the Christian Scriptures.

The Hebrew Scriptures

The object of my study over these many years has been, in the first place, the Hebrew Scriptures or what Christians have come to call the Old Testament.[2] It contains, in its present layout, three major sections. The first section is usually called the Torah (its Hebrew title and usually translated as 'Law') or the Pentateuch (which means 'five scrolls' or a 'five-part book' in Greek), the first five books of the Bible: Genesis, Exodus, Leviticus, Num-

2. The term 'Old' Testament (Latin, *testamentum*, 'covenant or treaty') was intended to imply that that the covenant or treaty between God and the Jews had been abrogated and that a 'new' covenant had been put in place. The books relating to the two covenants came to be known as the Old Testament and the New Testament. The religious doctrine inherent in this thinking is called supersessionism; Christianity is said to have superseded or displaced Judaism. While this may be acceptable terminology when some believing Christians talk between themselves, it is unacceptable in academic writing. In fact, many believing Christians are beginning to rethink the long-standing usage.

bers and Deuteronomy. The other sections of the Hebrew Scriptures are: Nevi'im (the Prophets) and Kethuvim (the Writings). Sometimes Torah or Law has been used traditionally to designate the whole corpus of writings; at other times the term denotes only the first five books. However, using 'Law' to describe these five books is rather misleading. There is as much narrative as law in them. A better translation would be 'Teaching' or 'Instruction'.

The second section of the Hebrew Scriptures, the Nevi'im or Prophets, include the following books: Joshua, Judges, 1 and 2 Samuel, 1 and 2 Kings, Isaiah, Jeremiah, Ezekiel and The Twelve Prophets. Not all of these would make up what we commonly understand as 'prophetic' books.

The third section of the Hebrew Scriptures, the Kethuvim or Writings include the following books: Psalms, Proverbs, Job, Song of Solomon, Ruth, Lamentations, Ecclesiastes, Esther, Daniel, Ezra-Nehemiah and 1 and 2 Chronicles.

But not all lists of the individual books making up the Hebrew Scriptures are the same. For example, the Catholic Church has its own list of those sacred books which it considers to be inspired by God. The final decision on which books were to be included in the list was only declared by the Catholic Church at the Council of Trent in 1546. Trent decided that there were 73 books in the Catholic Bible, neither more nor less: 46 in the Hebrew Scriptures and 27 in the Christian Scriptures. This collection of sacred books is known as the *canon* or 'rule, measure', those books which have a regulating or ruling value for faith and morality.

Of the 46 books accepted into the Hebrew Scriptures there were several over which there had been longstanding debate in the early Christian Church. These were Tobit, Judith, 1 and 2 Maccabees, Wisdom, Sirach, Baruch and parts of Esther and Daniel. They were called 'deuterocanonical' to distinguish them from those books over which there had never been any debate, known as the 'protocanonical' books. The distinction between 'proto (first)' and 'deutero (second)' referred only to whether serious debate had taken place; both groups of books were regarded as equally sacred by the Council of Trent.

However, the Jews had recognised over time a smaller collection for their Hebrew Bible. By the end of the second century CE they had come to accept only what Christians would later call the 'protocanonical' books, mentioned above. The Protestant churches also produced a different canon for the Hebrew books. When Martin Luther broke away from the Church in the sixteenth century he placed great emphasis on the Bible. However, he preferred the Jewish canon and placed the deuterocanonical books in an appendix as 'books which are not held equal to the Sacred Scriptures and yet are useful and good for reading'. Protestant Bibles eventually excluded these deuterocanonical books, although today they are usually once again included in a separate section and regarded as important by Protestant scholars at least for the academic study of early Christianity.

That covers broadly the scope of the Hebrew Scriptures; the Christian Scriptures had a similar history.

The Christian Scriptures

After much debate, at times quite acrimonious, the Christian Scriptures had been gathered into a definitive collection by the end of the fourth century CE, twenty-seven books in all. These were: the four gospels of Matthew, Mark, Luke and John; the Acts of the Apostles also attributed to Luke; fourteen letters of Paul, although there was always doubt about his authorship of at least one of them (the Letter to the Hebrews), and today there is general agreement that some others are not by his hand; the Catholic letters, so-called because they were presumed to be not addressed to particular communities but to the universal (*catholica*) church —the letter of James, two letters of Peter, three letters of John, one letter of Jude; finally, the book of Revelation.

Most Christians accept these same twenty-seven books as forming the Christian Scriptures.[3] We have seen that there is no Christian unanimity about the Hebrew Scriptures, with Catholics having the extra deuterocanonical books included, while Protestant Bibles place them in an appendix and call them 'The Apocrypha (hidden (books)'. This is always confusing since Catholics use the term Apocrypha to describe certain books which were never accepted by any Church as belonging to the Sacred Scriptures proper, such as the Gospel of Thomas.[4]

These two collections, the Hebrew Scriptures and the Christian Scriptures, together comprising the Bible of the Christian Church, have been the subject of most of my study for over fifty years. They have been tumultuous years and, as I have intimated, years during which I have been overtaken by three drastic revolutions.

3. Some of the smaller Eastern Churches either remove certain books or add some.
4. The *New Revised Standard Version* of the Bible lists them as 'apocryphal/ deuterocanonical'!

I hope that the story of these revolutions, insofar as they affected me over so many years, will be helpful and instructive to some readers, perhaps even at times entertaining.

Note

Thomas Kuhn wrote *The Structure of Scientific Revolutions* (University of Chicago Press: Chicago) in 1962. It aroused enormous interest in the areas of history of science and sociology of science. After adding a postscript to answer his many critics, he published a second edition in 1970. Kuhn was dealing with development taking place within the natural sciences. Soon, others applied his ideas to the social sciences, law, art and many other areas of human endeavour. I (and others) have applied his thinking to religion.

PART 1:
AS THINGS WERE—BEFORE THE REVOLUTIONS

Chapter 1
BEGINNINGS

Born in 1937, I was brought up in a Roman Catholic home in Melbourne during the 1940s and 1950s. In those days, Roman Catholics in Australia were a very tribal group. For the most part their ethnic roots were in southern Ireland, Eire. My grandparents on my father's side had come from a small community in County Clare. We knew those people who belonged to our tribe, who were sympathetic to us; we also knew the 'other'. A few discreet questions (what school did you go to? Where were you married? Is your surname English or Irish?) would usually determine religious allegiance. As a boy, I was able to distinguish among shopkeepers, neighbours and play-friends those who were Catholic and those who were not. Being Catholic or non-Catholic was a primary distinguishing characteristic, certainly more important than the demographics of gender or ethnic origin. Those who were not Catholics were usually lumped under the general designation of 'Protestants', although I did know some non-Catholics who were Jews.

Knowing Jews was unusual and due to the fact that my mother, before her marriage and having children, had been employed by a Jew whom she admired greatly. She sent her ex-employer a Jewish New Year card every September and I used to look with wonder at its Hebrew script. He reciprocated with a Christmas card and present to her. While I knew from my parents that there were individually good non-Catholics, I also became convinced by my religious education that the Non-Catholic Group, as a whole, had gone astray from the path of truth and correct action. They were self-deceived and they were, at least as a Non-Catholic Group, against all that Catholicism, Truth and Right Action stood for.

Church and School

The tribal centre for us Catholics was the suburban parish church. Many of the parish priests in the Melbourne of the 1940s and 1950s were Irish, the surplus of a never-ending supply of priests who would be sent out yearly from Eire to the English-speaking world. Just as there were not sufficient farms for the multiple sons of large Irish families to work, so there were not sufficient Irish parishes to occupy the never-ending stream of newly-ordained Catholic clergy.

On Sunday, all Catholics were obliged to attend Mass at the suburban parish church. All the ritual action was performed by the priest in a brogue-laced Latin. Few of the attendees had any idea of what was symbolised by the Latin ritual and language, apart from the fact that it was a mysterious and fearful event. It was on this mainly social Sunday occasion and within the parameters of the Catholic school that most of my early social relationships were formed.

In those days, all Catholic children belonging to practising Catholics went to a Catholic school as I did, usually a parish school run by one of the religious orders of nuns for primary education and a more central secondary school run by male religious for boys (such as the Christian Brothers) or nuns for girls. This was not by choice; Roman Catholics in Australia were at that time strictly required, by local church law, to send their children to a Catholic school, if it was physically possible, under threat of mortal sin and eternal damnation. The religious orders made what could only be described as valiant efforts to provide this relatively cheap education to ever growing numbers. In retrospect, however, particularly the male religious teaching orders became havens for a minority of misfits, although the female religious orders were not exempt from this problem. There were certainly honourable and exemplary exceptions in both male and female religious orders who were not social misfits.

Co-education was unknown in Catholic secondary schools. Any relationships between boys and girls had to be forged outside the secondary school boundaries. There was, both in the social life associated with the local church and in the school, a determined attempt to forestall in the bud 'mixed marriages', a marriage between a Catholic and a non-Catholic. Such marriages were considered to be headed inevitably for disaster. Since friendship might lead to marriage, non-Catholic friendships even for younger Catholics were seen as less desirable.

As a result, church and school encouraged us to form our social circle among like-minded Catholics: there were exclusive meetings for a Catholic scout group, a Catholic tennis club and Catholic dances.

Within this tribal society there were fixed ways of thinking (ideas about the world, about the authority of the Catholic Church, about the powers and authority of the clergy) and defined ways of acting (moral attitudes, particularly about sex, and a social etiquette). The Christian Brothers even had their own book on manners and etiquette with a distinctive Catholic leaning, written by an anonymous 'A Christian Brother'; it was obligatory for the Brothers' students to buy this. These ideas, activities and values made up a separate Australian Catholic culture. This culture was not questioned; indeed, there was no avenue provided for engaging in any questioning.

This common way of thinking, acting and valuing was thus upheld by the school, promoted in the Catholic home and practised in the parish church. At its core was a religious body of knowledge that sustained it.

Religious Education

From about Year 2 at school we were introduced to the Catechism, a question-and-answer compendium of Roman Catholic belief and practice. This rote-learned belief system introduced Catholic youth, first of all, to a distant, fearful God who yet could see and organise everything on earth including the weather (and 'he'—in those days, he was definitely male—was sometimes asked to reorganise meteorological conditions to suit school events), secondly to a wonder-working Jesus who could heal the sick, raise the dead, change water into wine and quell storms, next to angels and saints who invisibly intervened in human lives and, finally, to a grim foreboding about what awaited after death. Death would be followed by one of the following: Heaven, Hell, Purgatory (a state of purgation, the most likely first stop after death for the majority of people) or Limbo (for unbaptised babies). Even if Heaven was not terribly attractive, it was far better than the alternatives.

Within the confines of the Catechism's 'world', humans were weak beings, prone to sin because they had been born sinful, who lived in a 'vale of tears' and could only realistically look forward to death as an entry to a better life. To ensure that the reader would be ready at any time to face death, the Catechism instilled practices, some obligatory and some recommended, such as daily prayer, at least Sunday attendance at Mass and reception of Communion and frequent confession of sins. It also provided a comprehensive list of sins in case there was any doubt about the details of human weakness.

This Catechism had to be learned by heart in school and accepted as it stood; it was not up for critical discussion. The very best students were those in the primary school class who could recite prodigious amounts of it from memory. Later in life, when I came across Jewish children who could recite reams from the Hebrew Bible and Muslim children who could repeat the text of the Qu'ran, I could understand their zeal to do so.

The Catechism and its religious commentators (the priests, nuns and religious brothers) were able to delineate a Dreamtime in the past which incorporated wondrous events associated with the Creator-God, the wondrous events that took place during the life of the Man-God, Jesus, and these were expanded by a recitation of medical and nature miracles associated with saints in more recent times and visions of the Virgin Mary particularly to children at Lourdes and Fatima.

My introduction to the Bible in the form of biblical stories began in Grade 2. There was a wooden stand about a metre and a half tall in the classroom with a number of large, gaudily-painted pictures on a sheaf of sheets. They depicted various events from the Christian gospels and the nun, Sister Celine, would turn over the pages until she found a particular one and then describe it in detail and derive some religious lessons from it. We would be drawn imaginatively into the picture and its lessons.

Those pictures are still very much before my mind's eye today: for example, the picture of the Annunciation to Mary (looking very much like a nun with a blue veil) by an angel (with wings, wearing a dress and having long hair yet, incongruously, supposed to be male!) that she was to become the Mother of God; the Visitation of Mary to her cousin Elizabeth; the birth of Jesus in a stable; Jesus throwing the money changers out of the Temple; Jesus dead on the cross. Each image was embedded into the imagination visually, and lessons appropriate to Catholic teaching and practice were linked to the details of the picture. This was a very clever indoctrination of the young.

In Year 4 I transferred schools (because we moved house) and I went to a Christian Brothers College in East Melbourne. Being taught by men was a new and rather daunting experience. They were, in the main but with some exceptions, harsh men who lived an austere and demanding life. Having been brought up in a family that did not condone physical violence, this exposure to violent men acting in the name of the Christian religion was all the more confusing. The Catechism, learned by heart, remained the mainstay of religious teaching in the Brothers' school.

A year or so later, we were first introduced to *The Illustrated Bible History of the Old and New Testaments.* Its author was a Dr Ignatius Schuster, although others had added to it. He has fortunately long disappeared into the mists of time. In the book's Introduction, he outlined its purpose:

> Bible History is not the foundation on which religious instruction rests, nor the centre around which it revolves, nor the goal towards which it tends. Our religion centres in our faith, which is not a condensed extract from Bible History, but comes from the Church. Not Bible History, then, but the teaching of the Church must, on Catholic principles, be at once the beginning, middle, and end of religious instruction. Hence, Bible History, to claim a place in religious instruction, must do so only inasmuch as it bears on the doctrines of faith . . . Bible History becomes an object lesson in faith, a veritable pictorial Catechism.

I am not sure for whom this Introduction was written. The child readers were not capable of understanding it. In fact, I am not sure that many adult Catholics at that time were capable of understanding it. However, the statement described the book precisely for what it was: a pictorial Catechism. That was also the way in which it was used in the classroom.

The Introduction then went on to state:

> A Bible History should serve as a simple introduction to the Book itself, and Catholic teachers will not be fulfilling their duties as religious instructors unless they lead the children to a devout reading of the Scriptures, especially the Gospels.

The theory was that this course in Bible History was intended only to supplement the teachings of the Church, found succinctly in the Catechism, although it might lead to a reading of the Bible text itself, mainly the gospels. Dr Schuster considered that reading of the Bible to be a good thing. However, the teachings of the Church were not, in any way, dependent on the Bible or on Bible History. Even if the student was motivated to go on and actually read the biblical text, this could only provide a further confirmation of what was already being taught in the Catholic doctrine of the

Catechism's question-and-answer format. It was Protestants who went to their Bibles to seek out information about what to believe and what to do and they ended up, according to Catholic wisdom, with a host of disparate answers, mostly misguided. We Catholics had the teaching Church to give us accurate information in a ready-made form.

But my present memory of that Schuster book no longer focuses on its text. It was the illustrations, admittedly an advance on those used in Sister Celine's classroom, which caught my imagination. The Introduction had concluded:

> The illustrations to this edition have been specially prepared with a view to increasing the educational value of the book.

The illustrations were woodcuts and they starkly presented remarkable Biblical pictures on every other page. There were pictures of God chatting with Adam and Eve (whose nakedness was meticulously hidden) in the Garden, of Moses striking the rock in the desert, of the wise Solomon threatening to have a naked baby (unsurprisingly minus any genitals) carved in two and, in the Christian Scriptures section, of Jesus changing water into wine and later being crucified. When bored in class, I would flip through the pages and devour these illustrations. Even now, I can close my eyes and still see them.

Looking back at Schuster's text, which continued to be used in the classroom for several successive years of my primary schooling, I can now perceive that there was one particular underlying argument, rather subtle but repeatedly put forward. The argument maintained that the Hebrew Scriptures had contained hints and fore-tellings about who Jesus was and what would happen to him. For that reason alone we Catholics read the Hebrew Scriptures.

Dr Schuster made these fore-tellings prominent in his written commentary in case there was any mistake. For example, a chapter on Abraham ends with the enigmatic statement: 'Circumcision was a figure of the Sacrament of Baptism.'[1] Likewise, the chapter on Moses' construction of the Tabernacle in the desert ends:

1. This was supposed to be a text for children; circumcision was never described other than as 'a Jewish rite'.

> As the tabernacle was divided into two parts, so our churches have two parts; one for the priests, called the sanctuary, the other for the faithful, called the body of the church. Hence, the tabernacle was a pattern of our Christian churches.

The author craftily added a chapter to the end of his Bible History which contained tales about the apostles never recorded in the New Testament. It came as a shock to me much later on to find that some of my knowledge about this era had no foundation in the Bible. We learned, for example, that John 'had been thrown into a cauldron of boiling oil, and was miraculously preserved' and that Peter had been crucified 'with his head downward'.

However, there was another important message in the final pages. After the apostles died, we were told that

> The bishops continued with unwearying zeal the work which the holy apostles had commenced. And as the faithful were obedient to their bishops, so the bishops were obedient to the successor of St Peter, that is, the Pope of Rome, who is the chief pastor of the Church. In this manner there was a bond of union and unity between the faithful and their priests, between the priests and their bishops, and between all the bishops and the Pope.

I am sure that Dr Schuster, if he really was an historian of any calibre, never believed that his survey of the biblical history had proved anything like this conclusion. Anyone who read historical sources could tell that this idea of apostles giving way to bishops who were obedient to the successor of Peter was sheer fantasy. This was the pattern for a later Catholicism (a pyramid of Pope, bishops, priests and, at the bottom of the pile, lay-Catholics) that Schuster doubtless wanted to see firmly established in his own time but it was not a description of anything that had ever happened in the past. Even a cursory knowledge of Church History would have shown that.

His triumphant concluding words were:

> Thus was established the One, Holy, Catholic, and Apostolic Church, which, built by Christ upon the rock of Peter, and guided by the Holy Ghost, has now existed for twenty centu-

> ries, and shall exist till the end of time, in spite of all that the infernal powers can do against it. Happy are they that belong to the Church, who believes as she believes, and who do the works which she prescribes.

By the time I reached secondary school my mind was firmly in this groove; it all seemed neat and logical. The argument inherent in Schuster's text with its illustrations was quite convincing: everything before Jesus had pointed to him as the divine Saviour; his life, death and resurrection from the dead had demonstrated that he was the Son of God come to save all humanity. Jesus had established the Church by his choice and instruction of Peter and the Apostles; Peter (as first Pope) and the Apostles had been succeeded by Popes and bishops, with priests under the bishops ministering to the lay faithful, of which I was one. I could even identify Schuster's above-mentioned oblique reference to 'infernal powers'—they were the Non-Catholic Group, especially the Protestants.

There was thus little need in my schooling for any in-depth study of the Bible. The teaching of the Catholic Church was contained in the Catechism, and the Bible stories simply illustrated and substantiated its unassailable truth. In church of a Sunday, during the course of the Mass, there was a set sequence of Christian Scripture readings, one from the gospels and one from the other writings, usually the letters of Paul but sometimes from the Hebrew Scriptures. These readings were arranged on a yearly cycle. They were read by the priest in Latin and then, but only on Sundays, read again in English translation.

The Pauline letters were normally incomprehensible even in English, but the gospel stories of Jesus' healings, exorcisms and parables were part of that imaginative religious world view that existed alongside the more visible, surrounding world. The religious world had been constructed by the words and stories provided by priests, teachers and parents. Both worlds were equally real to me. Certainly, the religious world was more important and it was unchallengeable.

During our final three years of secondary school we were actually introduced to some texts from the Christian Scriptures: in successive years we were supposed to read and study the gospel of Mark, the gospel of John and the Acts of the Apostles. This was an innovation at the time. However, we never progressed far into any of the three texts and there was never any systematic reading of them or commentary on them. Following Schuster's theory, the biblical readings were, after all, only an illustration of the doctrinal teaching of the Church.

On later reflection I am convinced that reading and studying biblical texts did not suit the Christian Brothers' pedagogy at that time. The Brothers' educational philosophy extolled the rote-learning of useful knowledge: handy lists of mathematical formulae, chemical formulae and the laws of physics, the rules of grammar and vocabulary lists for foreign and ancient languages. This rote-learning routine would stand the student in good stead in any public examination. However, there were no such formulae or rules evident in these biblical texts and, besides, they were not material required for any public examination.

One Brother, desperate to find something in the gospels that could be rote-learned, had us commit to memory the Prologue to the Gospel of John and then one of the lengthier parables in Mark, the Parable of the Sower. This was the limit of his pedagogical skill as regards teaching biblical texts and thereafter he too lost interest. The religion period in these latter years of our education was often turned over to other pursuits such as career education.

The Catholic Worldview

Having been well socialised into the Catholic tribe, by the time I was sixteen and in my last year of school, I unquestioningly accepted the cultural worldview of the Catholic. This worldview might have had some reference to the symbolic terminology of the Bible, but there was little reference to the Bible itself. The more significant and extraordinary events of the Christian Scriptures with its description of miracles, cures, raisings from the dead performed by a Man-God, who spoke and ate like humans but was endowed with supernatural powers, populated this worldview.

However, I was convinced that even in the present-day world there were many, similar extraordinary events: the appearances of the Virgin Mary at Lourdes and Fatima, saints with the stigmata (the wounds similar to Jesus' crucifixion wounds), the Shroud of Turin with its wondrous image of the dead Jesus occasionally displayed in the Cathedral of Turin, illnesses being readily cured by the application of saints' relics. At certain times and in certain places, I was convinced, the religious Catholic world intersected with the everyday world. The obvious point about all of these unquestionably wondrous events was that they only occurred within a Catholic context. It had seemed to me that non-Catholics would have had to be intellectually challenged if they did not see what was so patently obvious.

What was obvious? Protestants did not have visions and were not miraculously cured of their ills (unless one believed the deluded tales of Salvation Army people and Christian Scientists). None of them received the stigmata (this would no longer be the case today!) and none of them possessed a Shroud of Turin, which seemed to me the ultimate proof of divine approval of the Catholic Church. If there was any further need for confirmation of the total Catholic worldview, these solid facts supplied it.

By the end of my secondary schooling I accepted the Bible as a history of Dreamtime stories. It contained accounts of wondrous events that had taken place in the history of ancient Israel and in the life of Jesus and his first followers. However, these events were not that much more wondrous than the stories of cures and visions that occurred sporadically within the contemporary Church and not more wondrous than the regular changing of bread and wine into the body and blood of Jesus at Mass. I was the firmest of true believers, and certainly a biblical fundamentalist.

Note

I recently came across a 2011 bookseller's advertisement for Ignatius Schuster's book, *Illustrated Bible History of the Old and New Testaments:*

> Newly rebound edition of a famous Bible History used in Catholic schools for years. Covers the most important events narrated in the Bible. With 80 beautiful drawings of biblical events. For sixth through eighth grades. New full color cover! Imprimatur.

It still survives!

Chapter 2
TAKING RELIGION SERIOUSLY

Spurred on by this youthful, religious dedication, I decided to enter a monastery at the completion of my schooling and thereafter to become a priest. Soon after my seventeenth birthday, having completed my Matriculation certificate, I bade farewell to my now widowed mother and left home at the beginning of 1955, never to return, for a Juniorate run by the Passionist religious order in Sydney. The Passionists were a very strict religious order that had been founded in Italy in the eighteenth century by a Christian mystic, Paul of the Cross.

The Passionists

The Passionist order was regarded in the Catholic world as demanding a total commitment and as being extremely austere. I had no doubt at the time that this would be the best thing to do with my life. Based on my Catholic worldview I measured my life as a transitory thing; real living would take place after my death. I did not see any great value in doing anything in this world that was not preparatory for the eternal life beyond death. Hence, I chose what was considered by many to be as hard a life as could be imagined. In addition, the priesthood was considered to be the highest Catholic calling and so being an ascetic monk and a priest at the same time would add to the quality of the calling.

The Juniorate was a preliminary year in a religious college that was not quite a monastery. There, I met up with a small group of nine other aspirants. All of us would finish off our schooling in a very religious setting. For some of the others it meant preparing for the final year State exams;

for me, having already matriculated in Melbourne, it was mainly devoted to learning Greek and working on Latin, English and French.

One of the requirements listed for each entrant was to bring a Bible to the Juniorate. I bought a new one (there was no complete Bible in our Catholic home) with a few maps and appendices in it, and during that year I looked through some of its contents. However, it received little use. There were no specific classes in the study of the Bible; there were, on the other hand, classes in Christian Doctrine that plumbed much deeper than what had been studied in secondary school. The readings from the Scriptures used in the daily Mass were considered sufficient direct contact with the Bible and we were encouraged to prepare the gospel reading that would be used the next day.

I lived happily as part of this semi-monastic world, where strangely black-garbed men were our role models. In many ways, as I look back, we newcomers were slowly being indoctrinated into a Christian sect. Deprivation of sleep, deprivation of the senses, long periods of silence and meditation ensured that we were efficiently inducted into that sect. We were confronted by the *periti,* those who had passed through the initiatory rituals and had proved their worth and had been made religious priests or brothers. They were presumed by us neophytes to have achieved some peak of secret knowledge.

Presumably, in our estimation, these men inhabited yet higher realms of the Catholic religio-cultural world, more exclusive than the cultural world of common Catholicism, a secretive world where the more important communication was done in Latin, the English language being reserved for less important matters or for communicating with the more lowly lay-Catholics in the pews.

The Juniorate was a new experience. Liturgical services surpassed any secular interaction in this new cultural world and we heard the priests celebrate Mass, chant the hours of the Office and recite long prayers in Latin, presuming that they were conversing in a sacred discourse with their God, a discourse from which we were still largely excluded. These *periti* made forays into the outside world to give spiritual assistance to secular Catholics, seemingly with reluctance, performing acts of charity for the lay-Catholics' spiritual benefit not their own, since their preference was presumed to be the silence and prayerfulness of the monastery.

So the first year in the Juniorate passed. During the course of that time I was changing in myself, becoming more introspective and mystical, even more idealistic than previously. I had no doubt that my choice of this way of life, this exclusive, monastic world, was the best thing that I could possibly do. That choice, I was sure, would make the world a far better place, even if I should have little contact with it. I did not care what work I might be given in the future.

Unlike some of my companions, I did not see myself as a future great preacher, counsellor or teacher. Opportunities for a teaching role would be limited and I did not consider that my oratorical or counselling skills were highly developed. Yet, feedback that I received from those in charge was all positive. Everyone seemed to think that I was a good person who studied hard and achieved well. I was told that my request to go the following year to the Passionist Novitiate to begin my formal training over a year as a monk had been accepted. There, I would be fully inducted into the monastic world.

The Passionist Novitiate

I took my newly purchased but largely unused Bible with me when I entered the Novitiate, on the outskirts of the New South Wales town of Goulburn at the beginning of the next year, 1956. Mary's Mount, set apart in many acres of farmland from contact with the outside world, was a real monastery. Everyone was a monk or preparing to become one. Six of us arrived together as newcomers, four from the Juniorate group and two who had entered directly.

Each of us was assigned a room in the monastery, called a cell. There was a bed made of wooden planks on which lay a thick, straw mattress. For the rest, there was a table, chair and cupboard. We were given a tour of the monastery with its chapel (called a choir by the monks) for liturgical worship, the refectory with wooden tables around the perimeter of the walls where silence was always enjoined, the library (which was reserved for the use of the professed monks) and separate recreation rooms for the professed monks and the novices.

Every day began at 2am when we made our way to the choir. There we chanted the beginning of the Divine Office and meditated. We returned to bed about 3.30am to be awakened again at 6am to chant two further parts of the Office. Then we attended in silence two Masses and received communion.

During the morning there were classes on the practice of the religious life and its duties and on the text of the Rule by which the monastic order was run. There was a class in which we were taught the intricacies of reciting the Office and, as happened on major feast days, of singing it. In another class, we were introduced to the Book of Psalms in Latin, which made up the bulk of the Divine Office. Our task in this class was mainly to translate them. The rest of the day was taken up with chanting the remainder of the Divine Office, meditation, spiritual reading and some manual labour.

The classes on the Psalms during the Novitiate were my first real introduction to anything resembling biblical studies. The only other use of the Bible, apart from its extensive usage in the Office, during this year was an introduction to the 'prophecies' of the Passion and Death of Jesus in the Hebrew Scriptures (a more formal treatment than that included in Dr Schuster's tracing of 'fore-tellings' in biblical history).

The Novice Master was keen on these 'fore-tellings': excerpts from Isaiah, Zechariah and the Psalms that seemed to be literally alluding to the events that had transpired in the suffering and death of Jesus. I recall him saying that while the Christian Scriptures could be mined for spiritual direction and personal benefit, the Hebrew Scriptures was something we would, as religious professionals, have to study in the future but in fact only these prophetic texts and the Book of Psalms were of any substantial and lasting value.

This method of finding prophecies about Jesus embedded in the Hebrew Scriptures, with the implication that the inspired Hebrew writers and prophets had actually known in advance just about everything about Jesus (his birthplace, miracles, preaching, entry into Jerusalem on a donkey, rejection by the Jews, death by crucifixion, resurrection, ascension and his eventual acceptance by non-Jews) had been well established in the early centuries of Christian Bible study. It was claimed by those early writers that the Hebrew Scriptures were an encoded text that told in allegorical style the future gospel narrative. Such was my own understanding of the Hebrew Scriptures at this point in time.

The Novitiate year, so far distant as it was from normal living, had a profound effect on me. In the first place, I learned from the beginning that the aim of the religious life was nothing less than a search for human perfection. That word 'perfection' became a rallying call. I felt that devoting the entire day to sacred duties and doing everything out of obedience to my superiors would undoubtedly lead me to this perfection. I had never been exposed to any great moral temptations in my earlier life. I had never known a desire for wealth or power, and therefore this simple life of healthy food, sufficient if broken sleep and exercise in the country air suited me. My sexuality had been subtly controlled by the religious culture of Catholicism, implanted at home and nurtured at school and in the local church, and it was even more subdued by the regularity of this monastic regime.

After one year in the Novitiate I was formally accepted into the Passionist Order and was allowed to profess vows of poverty, chastity and obedience binding me to the Order as a poor, celibate and obedient monk for three years. Immediately following the profession ceremony, together with the three others who had survived the year, I travelled by train from Goulburn to Adelaide to begin my formal studies for the priesthood. I took my Bible, still largely unused and certainly not understood, with me.

We were collected at Adelaide railway station by the Superior of St Paul's Monastery, the Passionists' House of Studies in Adelaide, who had obtained cars and drivers for the morning. That day in January 1957 as we drove up to the new monastery, nestling in the foothills of what was then only a small provincial city, I did not realise that I would be meeting the person who would begin the process of changing my thinking about biblical studies in a first drastic revolution.

Among the group of welcoming monks was a young Passionist priest called Jerome Crowe.

PART 2: THE FIRST REVOLUTION

Chapter 3
THE FIRST REVOLUTION BEGINS

At this point in time when I arrived in Adelaide in January 1957 my firm belief was that the Scriptures, both Hebrew and Christian, were history, a unique history, the most defensible history that could be imagined. I accepted literally the stories about the Creation, Adam and Eve, the Ancestors (Abraham, Isaac, Jacob and Joseph plus their almost invisible wives) and the subsequent history of the Israelite people beginning with the Exodus out of Egypt, together with the gospel stories about Jesus' life and death and the accounts of the establishment of early Christianity. Every word, as far as I was concerned, was historically accurate.

The Hebrew and Christian Scriptures were both inspired writings, their truth guaranteed by the Spirit of God. They could not be questioned as far as reliability and historical accuracy were concerned. The text was inspired and inerrant, incapable of error. I also believed that the Hebrew Scriptures included coded messages concerning the future for the astute Christian reader.

From this perspective, it seemed clear that studying the Bible, which I knew would be one of my major tasks over the next six years, could only mean respectfully studying the texts in depth and expanding my understanding of their deeper meaning. I knew nothing of any theory of interpretation apart from a literal reading of the texts. I expected to further my study of Greek for a deeper literal understanding of the Christian Scriptures, and to learn Hebrew for a literal understanding of the Hebrew Scriptures. However, I expected that this study of the Scriptures would simply give me a deeper knowledge of what the Catholic Church had always taught.

Jerome Crowe

As I said at the end of the previous chapter, I met Jerome Crowe for the first time on the day of my arrival in Adelaide. He was the newly-appointed lecturer in Biblical Studies at the monastery. His progress had been similar to mine, leaving school and joining the Passionist Juniorate, passing through the Novitiate and then studying six years prior to ordination as a priest. Then, he had been sent to Rome to do further study for three years. He had that very same month as my arrival in Adelaide returned from overseas where he had been studying first in Rome, doing a degree in Theology and one in Biblical Studies, and then travelling to Jerusalem to attend the École Biblique et Archéologique Française. There, he had studied under Roland de Vaux, the Editor-in-chief of the Dead Sea Scrolls.

I knew Jerome already by repute. I had read in a Passionist journal, published in America, of his scholarly talents (written, I later found out, by one of his fellow overseas students who had another agenda—to stir up the local American Passionist monks—in his lavish praise for him). His fame had preceded him and we students were already in awe of the tale of his academic achievements. Later, I would find that Jerome was basically conservative and socially shy and would remain so until his premature death.

We began an elementary class in biblical studies with him in the first year of our study, which was otherwise mainly devoted to the study of philosophy. This course consisted of a general introduction to the Bible and dealt with some of the broad issues of the meaning of biblical inspiration and biblical inerrancy. What did it mean when one claimed that God had written the Bible through human agents and that the Bible could not contain any error? The question was pertinent because there seemed to be some obvious inaccuracies and clear evidence of human authorship in the texts—although these instances had to be pointed out to us. We went on to further study—how had the Hebrew, Greek, Latin and other versions of the Bible come to be written and gathered together? How could one establish the original text of the Scriptures?

This was all new and, I found, extremely interesting without being too challenging. I had never before even thought of how the biblical texts might have come into being and then been handed on. I must have presumed that they had fallen from the heavens, with extraordinary human authors writing in rapture. However, to our amazement, Jerome showed us that there had been great arguments over the texts in the past and, even more amazingly, that there were recent developments within the Catholic

Church relating to biblical scholarship, and that the Church was demanding that priests and seminarians like us bring ourselves up to date in a hurry.

For the first time, we heard of an encyclical letter written by the reigning Pope Pius XII called *Divino Afflante Spiritu* in 1943, over a decade earlier. It had urged Catholic scholars to further their understanding of the Bible and to make use of some of the modern methods to do so. We studied this encyclical in depth.

Jerome's presence caused some disturbance in the monastery. There were rumours circulating among the senior group of students that he was teaching that some of the biblical stories were merely myths and legends and, above all, that he had vital information on the mysterious Dead Sea Scrolls (discovered in 1947 but not brought to public notice until the 1950s) which challenged solid Catholic doctrine. Students began to divide between those who thought Jerome was leading them along a dangerous path and those who thought that Jerome's new thinking was the way to go.

In particular, there was also a furtive whisper, attributed to one of the older priests in the monastery, that Jerome was close to the heresy of Modernism dating from the turn of the twentieth century. This priest was sure that Jerome would soon be condemned by the Roman authorities for his opinions and removed from his teaching post. All of this talk about Modernism fascinated me and, never having heard of it previously, I set myself the task of finding out some of the facts about it.

For the first time there were anomalies gathering in my mind regarding the Christian Bible. Perhaps it was not the narrative of the Dreamtime that I had thought.

The Modernist Heresy

My study took me back to the nineteenth century and the beginnings of what was known at the time as the Search for the Historical Jesus. Somewhat to my own discomfit I found that some of what Jerome was teaching was certainly on the fringes of what I interpreted Modernism to be.

Nineteenth century scholarship, following the Enlightenment in European intellectual circles, was interested in what could be proved by science and history. It was the age of Darwin and the theory of evolution, the time when archaeology and geology developed and there was a passionate interest in ancient history. At a time when the events recorded in Homer's *Iliad* and *Odyssey* about the Greek expedition to destroy Troy were being seriously questioned and fact was being separated from traditional story in such matters as the founding of Rome by Romulus and Remus by Roman historians, scholars had naturally raised doubts concerning the historical character of the events recorded in the gospels. In the mentality of the time this was serious business for Christians: if Jesus had not been an historical figure, then it would seem he should be disregarded as a teacher and saviour; if the foundation of the Christian church could not be mapped historically, the Church could not be given credence for any moral and spiritual authority.

Academic Christians in the nineteenth century had been left with the task of constructing a history of Jesus and of early Christianity on the basis of texts whose reliability was constantly under scrutiny. Many from the Christian academic community attempted, throughout the nineteenth century, to construct a 'Life of Jesus' that would be acceptable according to the canons of history and yet faithful to the gospel texts. Often eschewing the 'supernatural' in the gospels—such things as miracles, exorcisms and healings—scholars focussed more on the sayings of Jesus in order to construct their portraits of him. Many different versions of an 'historical Jesus' resulted. Each had repercussions for any subsequent discussion of the history and character of the early Church.

Known at the time as The Search for the Historical Jesus, this fevered research during the nineteenth century later became known as the First Search for the Historical Jesus (because there would be other Searches at a later date). As I studied these matters, I became enthralled with this new world of research.

The formal onset of the First Search has usually been attributed to a German, Hermann Reimarus (1694–1768), who wrote an essay on the life of Jesus, published posthumously in 1778 as *Von dem Zwecke Jesu und seinen Jungen* ('The Aim of Jesus and his Disciples'). In it Reimarus tried to recover a human Jesus from what he saw as many centuries of overlaying Christian dogma. He presented his Jesus as a failed leader who thought that he was the Messiah[1], the deliverer of the people of Israel.

As far as the basic gospel texts were concerned, some common ground was being established among the scholars. Even a cursory survey of the gospel texts showed that Matthew, Mark and Luke were interdependent. They became known as 'the Synoptics' since they had a 'common view-

1. The word 'Messiah' is English for the Hebrew *mashiah* and Greek *christos*, 'anointed one'. This word had many meanings in the Hebrew Scriptures. For Reimarus it meant a political leader.

point'. They told more or less the same story, sometimes in identical or near identical words. But sometimes there were significant differences. For example:

Matthew 9:9	Mark 2:14	Luke 5:27
As Jesus was walking along, he saw a man called Matthew sitting at the tax booth; and he said to him, "Follow me." And he got up and followed him.	As he was walking along, he saw Levi son of Alphaeus sitting at the tax booth, and he said to him, "Follow me." And he got up and followed him	After this he went out and saw a tax collector named Levi, sitting at the tax booth; and he said to him, "Follow me." And he got up, left everything, and followed him.

There are significant overlaps in language; there are also some significant variations in the name of the principal person. This constituted what was known as the Synoptic Problem. Taking many such instances into account, with the three gospels laid out side by side, various theories were contrived to account for such similarities and differences. Surely, two of the evangelists had cribbed from another? Perhaps the three had copied from another, now lost, gospel. The paramount question was: who had copied from whom? In the case above it would seem Matthew and Luke have adapted the Markan text which they must have had in front of them in something like the form it has today.

After performing many such comparisons across the three Synoptics, two original sources were eventually recognised by the scholars in the three texts—Mark and what was called 'Q'. Mark, because its text was short and pithy, was generally accepted as the first gospel to have been written, somewhere in the 60s CE. Q, a shorthand for *Quelle* or 'source' in German, accounted for those Jesus-sayings which were contained almost word for word in Matthew and Luke but did not occur in Mark. Presumably Matthew and Luke had access to this Q, but Mark did not know anything about it. An example of Q would be this parallel passage in Matthew and Luke:

Matthew 6:22-23	Luke 11:34-36
"The eye is the lamp of the body. So, if your eye is healthy, your whole body will be full of light; but if your eye is unhealthy, your whole body will be full of darkness. If then the light in you is darkness, how great is the darkness!"	"Your eye is the lamp of your body. If your eye is healthy, your whole body is full of light; but if it is not healthy, your body is full of darkness. Therefore consider whether the light in you is not darkness. If then your whole body is full of light, with no part of it in darkness, it will be as full of light as when a lamp gives you light with its rays."

Thus the scholars had a text for Q, which could be artificially put together from what overlapped in Matthew and Luke, but they did not have, and even today still do not have, any corresponding manuscript for a Q.

Since Matthew and Luke were said to be largely dependent on Mark and Q, they were discounted as historical sources themselves (see figure 1). They were secondary, dependent on the more original sources. In current terminology, they were plagiarists. The only original sources were therefore Mark, Q and John (whose gospel was quite different from the Synoptics in its language, style of writing and its sequence of events).

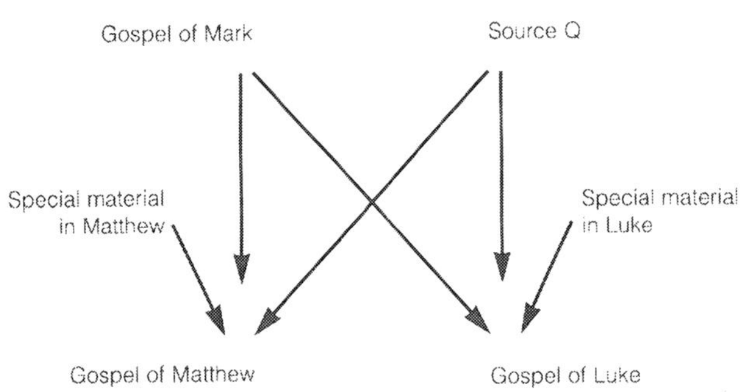

Figure 1: Historical-critical outline of the Gospel sources.

Next, John's long Jesus-speeches (for example his Final Discourse continues for four chapters, cc 14-17 of the gospel) and his more elaborate chronology for Jesus' life raised suspicions that its text had been tampered with by later writers. Hence, the First Searchers also abandoned John as an historical source. That left Mark and Q as the only reliable witnesses on which any history could be written. And even these two would be eventually suspected of being tainted by early Christian preaching. Nevertheless, many liberal Christians continued to write 'Lives of Jesus' during the rest of the nineteenth century, with due *caveats* about bias in the gospels that they were using as sources. Roman Catholic scholars, however, were warned by the authorities in Rome not to have anything to do with this new trend.

In 1901, Wilhelm Wrede published his *Das Messiasgeheimnis in den Evangelien* ('The Messianic Secret in the Gospels') in which he claimed it was absolutely impossible to write any substantial history of Jesus, even on the basis of Mark and Q. This work shattered the hopes of those liberal Christians who had hoped to be able to find an historical Jesus who would be acceptable to the historical profession and who would also provide a reasonable basis for Christian teaching.

Soon after, Albert Schweitzer, who as an old man would receive the Nobel Peace Prize for his work as a medical missionary among lepers, reviewed the many 'Lives of Jesus' from the previous century in the light of the new developments which Wrede foreshadowed. He demonstrated the subjectivity employed in these various Lives. Each Life of Jesus, he said, revealed more of the nineteenth century author than of an historical Jesus. Schweitzer concluded that the historical Jesus had been a shadowy figure, a fanatic, preaching the coming end of the world and dying under the delusion that his death would actually bring about the collapse of the contemporary world order.

Schweitzer claimed that his own historical Jesus never intended to found a Church and never intended to leave behind any lasting program for future Christians—since this Jesus foresaw no future for the world after his death. As for the details concerning Jesus, Schweitzer was convinced that the gospel texts were so overladen with the early preaching of the church and the theology of those who handed on the traditions, that it was impossible to reconstruct anything more than the vaguest outline of the life of an individual called Jesus.

For many scholars, Schweitzer's work signalled the end of any further searching for an historical Jesus. It was certainly the end of the First Search.

I was enthralled by all this, but regarded it as forbidden fruit. This critical study of the Bible had hardly made any impression on Roman Catholic study until shortly before we students were exposed to it in the late 1950s. Why had it taken so long? It had been the Enlightenment of the eighteenth century which had given rise to the 'historical-critical method' among

Protestant scholars and they accordingly endeavoured to explain how the Bible had been produced and should be understood in historical terms.

In the eyes of the Catholic Church, on the other hand, the American Revolution of 1776, the French Revolution of 1789 and particularly the movement towards Italian unity were all spawned by these ideas of the Enlightenment and the Church was opposed to these revolutionary movements. After all, the Church had widespread land holdings in Italy (the Papal States) and the Pope was more like an absolute monarch than a president. The Church refused to accept the new Enlightenment thinking whether it dealt with distribution of land or the historicity of the gospels.

In the few instances where Catholic biblical scholars emulated their Protestant counterparts there had been swift official action. Perhaps the clearest example was Ernest Renan (1823-1892), who had began his study for the priesthood in France. He was introduced to Hebrew and Syriac and to the study of the Bible. Discontented, he left the Catholic seminary and became an orientalist and archaeologist, proving himself to be an outstanding scholar. While on an archaeological expedition to Syria in 1860 he began his *Vie de Jésus* (Life of Jesus) which he published in 1863 and in which he claimed that Jesus was an eminent human being but not divine, that Jesus' message in Galilee had won over a large following and that his simple but powerful message had been distorted by the later church. It became a best-seller and aroused furious passions for and against it.

Renan was subsequently appointed to the professorship of Hebrew at the Collège de France and, in his opening address, he called Jesus an 'incomparable man', intimating that he might not have been God. Amid cries of scandal he was dismissed and he did not regain a university post for another eight years. Renan wrote in a clear, attractive and almost rhythmic style, making full use of the new biblical methodology. This methodology, he claimed, led him to deny the supernatural in the gospels and even the existence of a transcendent God. For many Catholic authorities Renan demonstrated only too well to what a dire end meddling with the Protestant methods of biblical interpretation would lead.

In 1867 Pius IX (1792-1878), universally regarded as the most autocratic Pope ever, showed his intransigent opposition to any of these new strains of thought. He was struggling to maintain his political control over the Papal States; the last thing he wanted were challenges to the *status quo.* He issued a document entitled *The Syllabus of Errors* in 1864. In it he condemned propositions which would seem perfectly reasonable to us today.

Some examples of the *unacceptable* propositions are:

> 15. Everyone is free to embrace and profess that religion which is considered to true according to human reason.
>
> 17. There is at least a good hope that all those who do not belong to the true church of Christ (ie the Catholic Church) will find their eternal salvation.
>
> 77. Today it is no longer proper that the Catholic religion should be regarded as the sole religion of the state, to the exclusion of all other forms of worship.
>
> 78. In some Catholic countries, wise legislation has decreed that people coming to reside therein shall enjoy the public exercise of their own peculiar worship.
>
> 79. The Roman Pontiff can and should reconcile himself, and come to terms with progress, liberalism and modern civilisation.[2]

The *Syllabus* was a strident claim that there should be no freedom of conscience, no freedom of the press, no free parliamentary systems, no equality before the law. Employing the modern historical-critical method to interpret the Bible would not even have crossed the horizon of this Pope's mind. The content of the *Syllabus* was the typical reaction of the nineteenth century papacy to modern thinking and the modern worldview. [3]

At the time we are talking about in the 1950s, when I first studied these things, I would have broadly agreed that the Church had a monopoly on truth. After the publication of the *Syllabus*, Pius IX had convoked the aforementioned First Vatican Council, which met at the end of 1869 and lasted to 1870. It was brought to an abrupt close by the Franco-Prussian

2. The Latin text is in H Denzinger and A Schönmetzer (1965), *Enchiridion Symbolorum*, thirty-third ed, Herder: Rome, pp 576–584.
3. It needs to be said that the *Syllabus* has to be read in its context. The Pope believed that the Catholic Church was the perfect society, that it had a complete grasp of truth, that it contained in itself all the resources required to achieve its own spiritual goal. Within that mindset, the document does make some sense.

war which consequently led to the loss of the Papal States, the event most feared by Pius IX. This loss seemed to justify all his earlier anathemas.

One of the central decrees coming from the Council declared that the Pope had supreme authority in the church and was infallible when he taught under certain conditions. This decree bolstered his spiritual power just when he had been bereft of temporal power. The Pope emerged from Vatican I with supreme and unchallengeable ecclesiastical authority which he delegated to bishops and they, in turn, delegated it to their priests. Worship, teaching and government were completely in the hands of the clerical hierarchy. This had made sense in the earlier pre-modern worldview where the world was a finished product of unchanging essences with an inbuilt order which was directed to a fixed purpose. It no longer made sense in the modern period. Given the Catholic Church's pre-modern worldview, the new advances in biblical research would not be accorded a welcome reception.

It must be realised that the Catholic Church had not been really engaged in the study of the Bible since the time of the Reformation in the sixteenth century. The Protestant reformers had insisted on the Bible as the source of their teaching and also the basis for their differences with the Roman Church. In defending themselves, Catholics, from the time of the Council of Trent in the sixteenth century, had insisted on Tradition, the teaching authority of the popes and the bishops, and the sacramental system as the sources of divine revelation.

As Dr Schuster had pointed out to us youngsters in his Introduction to the *Illustrated Bible History of the Old and New Testaments*, the Bible was used by the Catholics merely as a means of proving already established doctrines and of substantiating established practices, providing a 'mine' from which proof-texts could be extracted to prove the rightness of what were already existing Church teachings and practices. This was precisely what I had been exposed to at school and up to this point in my biblical education.

By the time of Pius IX's death in 1878 and the accession of Leo XIII (1810–1903), by contrast a very learned and cultured person, the new methods of biblical interpretation were, however, beginning to infiltrate even into academic Catholic circles. Roman Catholic biblical scholars had divided into three uneven groups. There were those conservatives who, following Pius IX, refused to accept any new worldview and any new way of thinking. As a result they saw no future for a new literary theory applied to the Bible, since they did not consider the Bible was literature in any ordinary sense of the word.

A second group were progressives who saw the possibilities inherent in the new methods and the necessity to go further cautiously for the betterment of the Christian Church. Finally, there were radicals who claimed that the new developments in biblical interpretation heralded the very end of Christianity, Catholic or otherwise, as it had been known.

The leader of the progressives was acknowledged by many to be a Dominican priest, Marie-Joseph Lagrange (1855–1938). It was a name with which I would later become very familiar. Eventually, I would stand by the grave of Lagrange in Jerusalem and applaud his achievements. Lagrange was well grounded in higher education, having obtained his doctorate in law prior to joining the Dominican order. Because the Third French Republic had outlawed religious orders from France, he had to go to Salamanca in Spain to study for the priesthood. It happened by chance that Salamanca at that time was a centre for a Catholic revival in biblical studies, using the new methods with discretion, and Lagrange imbibed the changing ethos.

Following his ordination to the priesthood he was sent by the Dominicans to the University of Vienna where he studied in the Oriental Faculty and then in 1890 he set up the École Biblique et Archéologique Française in Jerusalem as a Catholic teaching centre where the Bible could be studied as divinely revealed truth but also as a literary work. The École Biblique was where Jerome had studied and where, at a later time, I would go. It would have a profound effect on my thinking.

Lagrange was one Catholic scholar who was willing to meet the new methods of interpretation on their own ground. He always held that the Scriptures were not homogeneous, that development and even change in theological thought and teaching became apparent as the biblical books were read in chronological sequence. In order to trace this development he insisted that the historical-critical method needed to be employed. In 1892 he set up the *Revue Biblique,* a journal that would show how the new methods could be put into practice.

The Catholic Church at this stage was in turmoil, as we saw above, not knowing which direction to take as The Search for the Historical Jesus took hold. In an endeavour to provide such direction Leo XIII issued an encyclical letter on biblical study in 1893 called *Providentissimus Deus.* While it showed an awareness of what was happening in the world of biblical scholarship and allowed Catholic scholars to investigate the Bible as literature, it was fearful of going too far:

> There has arisen, to the great detriment of religion, an inept method, dignified by the name of the 'higher criticism', which pretends to judge of the origin, the integrity and authority of each book from internal indications alone . . . It will not throw on the Scripture the light which is sought, or prove of any advantage to doctrine . . . seeing that most of them (the biblical critics) are tainted with false philosophy and rationalism, it must lead to the elimination from the sacred writings of all prophecy and miracles, and of everything else that is outside the natural order.[4]

Leo XIII made it clear that a valid interpretation of Scripture should be a wholly Catholic affair:

> For although the studies of non-Catholics, used with prudence may sometimes be of use to the Catholic student, he should, nevertheless, bear in mind—as the Fathers also teach in numerous passages—that the sense of Holy Scripture can nowhere be found incorrupt outside the Church, and cannot be expected to be found in writers who, being without the true faith, only gnaw the bark of the sacred Scripture and never attain its pith.[5]

The same words would hopefully start a religious riot today but at that time Leo XIII was siding with the progressives. Towards the end of his long reign in 1902, he set up the Pontifical Biblical Commission. He intended it, first of all, to assist Catholic biblical scholarship and appointed forty-one consultors, many of them progressives from the second group mentioned above. As I became aware of the Commission's constitution as a young student, I did not know that one day I would sit before its modern-day consultors for my final examination in biblical studies.

Leo was aware that the Holy Office, the doctrinal watchdog of the Church and the direct successor to the Holy Inquisition, had been passing

4. *Rome and the Study of Scripture*, Grail Publications: Indiana, pp 20–21.
5. Ibid p 17.

its own decrees in answer to biblical questions and they were an embarrassment because of their blatant display of ignorance and lack of scholarship in the biblical area. According to his plan, the Biblical Commission, with its consultors who were more expert in biblical studies, would offset the Holy Office.

I had set out to learn about Modernism and had been drawn into the First Search and Catholic participation in it. Besides the progressives such as Lagrange in the second group, I was intrigued by the radicals in the third group. These would eventually be dubbed the 'Modernists' by the Church. In particular, I wanted to know more about a particular Modernist, Alfred Loisy, a name that in some dark way attracted me.

Around the turn of the century the heresy of Modernism was born or perhaps it should be said it was invented by the Catholic Church. It was the most elusive of all church heresies, a catch-all term constructed by the collective mind of the Church authorities to cover all those challenges in the current scholarly world of biblical and theological research that dismayed them. The person who was guilty of the biblical phase of Modernism was said to have been this Alfred Loisy (1857–1940), a French priest and professor of biblical studies.

Loisy had been attracted by the liberal Protestant historical-critical method and had made use of it in his own doctoral research. However, in reaction to those critics who maintained that the institutional and visible church was superfluous and that only an interior and personal Christian response was required for salvation, Loisy upheld the Catholic Church as the true mediator between God and humanity, even if he denied that the historical Jesus had actually founded it. His famous dictum was: 'Jesus proclaimed the coming of the Kingdom, but what came was the Church'. He accepted the then popular distinction between the Jesus of History (a history that could be established by historical methods) and the Christ of Faith (the Church's teaching about the deeds and words of Jesus) and submitted that the early Christian community was an impenetrable barrier standing between the believer and the historical Jesus.

Loisy and other Modernists had been treated with some sympathy by the aged Leo XIII, but Leo died in 1903. The incoming pope, Pius X (1835–1914), was someone different. He had been a pious and zealous country priest, with no pretensions to academic ability and no interest in intellectual pursuits, who had been advanced, despite his own protestations, through the ecclesiastical ranks to become the Patriarch of Venice. From there he was elected to the papacy on the death of Leo XIII. It is said that he retained his unused return train ticket to Venice throughout his reign.

Confronted with Alfred Loisy and other Modernists, the pope panicked. He did not understand that there was a new world on his doorstep. There was no choice in his mind between protecting what he saw as his vulnerable, faithful Catholic flock and dallying with new biblical theory.

In 1903, the year of Leo's death, Loisy had published a book summarising his ideas on Jesus and the early church, *L'Évangile et l'Église* (The Gospel and the Church). Pius X immediately placed it on the Church's Index of Prohibited Books. Pius' own naïve biblical method can be seen from an encyclical which he published in the following year to commemorate the fiftieth anniversary of the Catholic Church's declaration that Mary had been 'immaculately conceived without original sin'. It betrays the literalistic and simplistic method of interpretation of the new pope and of the whole pre-modern era.

> Adam wept in his punishment but he perceived Mary crushing the serpent's head. Noah in the safety of the Ark looked forward to her. So did Abraham as his hand was stayed. Likewise Jacob when he saw a ladder standing on the earth, with its top reaching up into heaven; a stairway for the angels of God to go up and come down. Moses saw her in the bush that was alight and did not burn. David sang of her as he danced before the ark of the covenant. Elias saw her in the little cloud rising up out of the sea. But why go on? [6]

Indeed, Loisy, reading such fundamentalist and pious nonsense, must have wondered—why go on? Nevertheless, he sent a conciliatory letter to Pius. It was never answered. Instead, Pius sent a message to the Archbishop of Paris ordering Loisy 'to burn what he adored and adore what he had burned'. Being a realist, Loisy acknowledged that he could not continue within the Catholic Church.

In 1908 he was excommunicated by Pius X. In what might be interpreted as a vindictive action he was declared *vitandus:* he was henceforth to be personally avoided by all Catholics. He left his professorship and the Catholic Church with great bitterness and took up a university post. He died in 1940 and he left a Latin epitaph to be engraved on his gravestone:

6. The Latin text is to be found in *Acta Apostolicae Sedis* 36 (1903–4), pp 453f.

Tuam in votis tenuit voluntatem ('He kept your will in spirit'). Perhaps it was some measure of my changing attitude in later times that I used this as my personal motto. Only years after his death would Loisy's considerable contribution to biblical studies be unofficially recognised by scholars within the Catholic Church.

Meantime, in Jerusalem, the more moderate Lagrange was in difficulty too. He had read a paper to an international congress in Fribourg in 1897 in which he had applied the historical-critical method to the Pentateuch, the first five books of the Bible, and argued that it had been composed from a variety of sources. Reports of this paper filtered back to Rome and he was vindictively attacked. The common view was still that Moses had written the Pentateuch *verbatim*. There were many who waited for Lagrange to go too far before they pounced.

By the early 1900s, after he had published a book in 1903 entitled *La Methode Historique* ('The Historical Method'), there was a growing demand from the conservatives that he be silenced. The ever-prudent Lagrange, realising that he was being hunted by powerful enemies, turned from the study of the Hebrew Scriptures to the study of the Christian Scriptures where he excelled and achieved much of his life's work. It was ironic that his last journal article was on the sources of the Pentateuch, the very topic where his troubles with the Church had begun, and he is reported to have sat up on his deathbed in 1938 correcting the proofs.

Pius X had virtually wiped out a generation of budding Catholic scholars. He had encouraged a network of ecclesiastical espionage units to report to Rome on academic deviants who preached or taught anything that seemed to be in any way unorthodox. It was a dark era for Catholic biblical scholarship. Possibly the only redeeming feature of his pontificate was his establishment in 1909 of the Pontifical Biblical Institute in Rome as a centre for higher biblical studies, using methods approved by the Catholic Church. The Pontifical Biblical Institute would eventually become a focal point for the very best in Catholic biblical studies and itself be threatened with closure by Roman authorities in the 1960s.

Leo XIII's innovations did not last. Progressive consultors on the Biblical Commission were soon replaced with conservatives and between 1905 and 1915 the Commission took on a menacing front, issuing a series of very fundamentalist decrees. These stated for example that Moses was the sole author of the Pentateuch and that the first three chapters of Genesis, which told of the creation of the world and Adam and Eve, were to be understood by Catholics in a literal and historical sense. Another decree announced that there was insufficient evidence to warrant the prophecy of Isaiah being assigned to more than one author, when it was obvious to anyone who could read Hebrew that there were several hands at work in its composition.

In dealing with the Christian Scriptures, the Biblical Commission decreed that Matthew, not Mark, had been the first gospel to be written, composed in Hebrew or Aramaic and then translated into Greek without any substantial changes. The authorship of the fourth gospel was attributed to John the apostle, an eyewitness to the events he narrated. On all these points the Commission took up a stance starkly at odds with the historical-critical method; the decrees were not based on reputable scholarship.

The Catholic Church that I knew as a boy in the 1940s and 1950s had been led by priests educated in this thought-world, fundamentalist and negative. These priests were too often limited and fearful men whose academic training had been poor. Their biblical knowledge was literalist and unsophisticated. They could do little more than re-state a biblical text so as to back up what the Catholic Church was already teaching.

Anomalies were controlling my thinking. The Bible was a very human document. It had flaws. It had inconsistencies.

Against the mediocrity of the scholarship I had been subjected to in school and in the Catholic parish church and in the monastery so far, here was Jerome Crowe in 1957 declaring that a new day had dawned. He was announcing in the small monastic community in Adelaide that drastic change was afoot in Catholic biblical studies. As I listened to Jerome and did my own reading and study I was well aware that a great change was indeed taking place and that I wanted to be part of it. Jerome was introducing into a small group the historical-critical methodology. This was the start of the first revolution in the study of the Christian Bible in which I was involved and the following two chapters will explain that revolution more in detail.

Notes

The reader interested in the actual texts cited in this chapter will find the originals in Denzinger , H and Schonmetzer, A (eds), *Enchiridion Symbolorum*. This book has gone through many editions and is always being updated. It is now online. An English version of the papal documents relative to the study of the Bible, cited at various points in these chapters, is found in *Rome and the Study of Scripture* (Grail Publications, Indiana, 1962).

Some of this material and various other general matters pertaining to the Christian Scriptures have been published in a different form in my book *The Jesus Question. The Historical Search* (HarperCollins Religious, Melbourne, 1996). Other materials pertaining to both the Hebrew Scriptures and Christian Scriptures were covered in my subsequent book *Beyond the Jesus Question. Confronting the Historical Jesus* (PostPressed, Flaxton, Qld, 2003).

Chapter 4
STUDYING THE HEBREW SCRIPTURES: AUSTRALIA

I completed the introductory course in biblical studies over two years. I could see the edges of the first revolution but my real induction into it took place when I began the first year of a four year course on Biblical Studies in 1959. In that year we were formally introduced to the historical-critical approach to interpreting the Bible.

The Hebrew Torah

Our initial study was of the Pentateuch or Torah, which had been the battleground for Lagrange and so many others. I recall that when we started this study, the lines were being drawn. There were students who could not stomach Jerome's teaching. They felt that their very faith was being challenged and, after all, their perseverance in this austere life was undertaken on the basis of that faith. There was also a fear that their hopes of attaining the priesthood might be compromised if they followed what Jerome was putting before them.

Jerome outlined for us the old and the new. Both Judaism and Christianity had long held that the original author of the Torah was Moses, just as David was considered to be the author of the Psalms and Solomon the author of all the Wisdom Literature. Since there are explicit references to Moses being the author of law codes, it was relatively simple to maintain that he had also written the narratives accompanying those law codes. But such a simple solution flew in the face of the many anomalies in the text of the Torah, not the least being that at its conclusion there is an account of Moses' death ('He wrote that in prophecy', the stalwart defenders answered!).

There were anachronisms (for example, Genesis 26 mentions the Philistines long before they would ever have arrived in Palestine; there are seventeen references to domesticated camels in the book of Genesis, relating to times before camels were domesticated), changes in style (sometimes there is vivid and colourful narrative, in other places the style is dry and concise, delighting in lists and genealogies, and again there is sometimes a distinctive preaching style) and vocabulary (for example, sometimes the mountain on which Moses received the Torah was called Sinai and sometimes Horeb), inconsistencies (for example, Exodus 19:25 states that Moses goes down and 'spoke these words . . . '—but no words follow) and repetitions (there are two creation stories side by side in Genesis 1–2, two Flood stories intricately interwoven in Genesis 6-9, Moses receives his call from God twice in the book of Exodus) and inconsistent variation in the use of the divine names of Yahweh and Elohim[1]. A more complex hypothesis than Mosaic authorship seemed to be needed to explain this Hebrew text.

None of this was new in biblical scholarship; however, it was certainly new in twentieth century Catholic biblical scholarship. The first real challenge to Mosaic authorship had actually come from a French Catholic priest, Richard Simon, in 1678. He claimed that Jewish scribes had played a major part in writing the Torah, and the Hebrew text had been compiled from a number of pre-existing documents. While certain documents derived from Moses, it was Ezra, after the Babylonian exile, who actually produced the final version. Simon's conclusions were considered sufficient grounds for his book to be placed on the ever expanding Index of Prohibited Books, and for the scholarly priest to be banished to a rural parish in Normandy.

In the next century, Jean Astruc, a member of the French royal court, published a study on the Torah in which he discerned two major sources (identified by their use of different divine names—Yahweh and Elohim), together with other minor sources. He thought that Moses himself (and

1. 'Elohim' is a plural form of 'god' in Hebrew. It is used as a personal name but in fact it is a generic term. 'Yahweh' is the personal name of the God of Israel. Its origin and meaning is disputed. The older Hebrew text of the Bible has only consonants with some markers for vowels. In the Christian period vowels were added to the consonants. Because at a later date the Jews did not pronounce this name in their religious services, the text left only the consonants for Yahweh (Y-H-W-H). In those religious services, instead of 'Yahweh' the reader would say 'Adonai or 'Lord' and so the vowels of 'Adonai were linked with the consonants of Yahweh to give the impossible word Jehovah. Yahweh and YHWH became alternate writings for the divine name.

here he disputed the claim of Simon that Moses was not the author) had used these sources and arranged them like the Synoptic gospels, but that subsequently the pagination of the text had become confused.

An important addition to the study of the Torah was made by the German scholar, Wilhelm de Wette (1780–1849), who concluded in 1805 that the book of Deuteronomy, or something similar to it, was the book discovered by the high priest Hilkiah in the Temple when it was being renovated and handed to Josiah the king. There is a text in 2 Kings:

> The high priest Hilkiah said to Shaphan the secretary: 'I have found the book of the law in the house of Yahweh.' When Hilkiah gave the book to Shaphan, he read it. Then Shaphan the secretary came to the king, and reported to the king, 'Your servants have emptied out the money that was found in the house and have delivered it into the hand of the workers who have oversight of the house of Yahweh.' Shaphan the secretary informed the king. 'The priest Hilkiah as given me a book.' Shaphan then read it aloud to the king. (2 Kings 22:8–10)

After these initial forays, the nineteenth century seethed with energetic attempts to identify and date more completely the sources for the Torah. Julius Wellhausen (1844–1918) provided the classical solution. Wellhausen was the son of a Protestant pastor and achieved well in his own work in theology and biblical studies. Interestingly, as a professor of theology he realised that his teaching was causing some of his students destined for the Protestant ministry to give up their calling. He resigned and transferred to a secular university as professor of oriental languages.

In his research on the Hebrew Scriptures, Wellhausen also identified two early sources, the Yahwist and the Elohist, which were each distinguished by their use of the respective divine names—Yahweh and Elohim. This followed Astruc's theory. For shorthand Wellhausen used the sigla J (since in German the divine name was written as *Jahve)* and E. He agreed with de Wette that a first edition of Deuteronomy had appeared in 622 BCE under Josiah, but it had been expanded by later additions. This source, identified by the siglum D, had been combined with the J and E materials.

The latest editorial stage came with the addition of a priestly source, called P by Wellhausen, written during the Exilic period. The end result was the sequence J-E-D-P, the so-called four source documentary theory, with the final editing of the Torah attributed to Ezra in the fifth century BCE.

To understand what this theory entails we can take an example. Exodus 13:17–14:2 has been divided by some experts between three of the sources which were said to have successively added to the same text.

E: When Pharaoh let the people go, Elohim did not lead them by way of the land of the Philistines, although that was nearer; for Elohim thought, 'If the people face war, they may change their minds and return to Egypt.' So Elohim led the people by the roundabout way of the wilderness toward the Red Sea. The Israelites went up out of the land of Egypt prepared for battle. And Moses took with him the bones of Joseph who had required a solemn oath of the Israelites, saying, 'Elohim will surely take notice of you and then you must carry my bones with you from here.'

J: They set out from Succoth, and camped at Etham, on the edge of the wilderness. Yahweh went in front of them in a pillar of cloud by day, to lead them along the way, and in a pillar of fire by night, to give them light, so that they might travel by day and by night. Neither the pillar of cloud by day nor the pillar of fire by night left its place in front of the people.

P: Then Yahweh said to Moses: Tell the Israelites to turn back and camp in front of Pi-hahiroth, between Migdol and the sea, in front of Baal-zephon; you shall camp opposite it, by the sea.

Wellhausen claimed that the comprehensive legal and ritual system which the Torah attributed to Moses was in fact not extant in that early period of Israelite religion, but had only developed in post-exilic Judaism (after the sixth century BCE), when the clerical priesthood rewrote the past and made it appear that Israel had always been an ecclesiastical society. It needs to be said that his theory was grounded on a quite distorted and prejudiced view of that period of Judaism, which he perceived as dominated by a stifling, legalistic system that had restrained the free religious spirit of earlier times.

Wellhausen was confident that his literary analysis of the Torah would provide a sufficient basis on which to reconstruct an historical schema: from a primitive period marked by henotheism, the worship of a number of gods, Israel had progressed to a more sophisticated monotheism during the time of the prophets in the eighth and seventh centuries BCE, then faltered by favouring the narrow sectarianism propagated by priestly legislation after the exile in the sixth century.

As time passed, Wellhausen's theory was considerably refined and the criteria for identifying sources in the Torah were multiplied. This led to sources being discovered within sources, a virtual multiplicity of strands, and brought about a ludicrous situation in which a limited piece of Biblical literature would be divided into an ungainly number of separate 'sources', each with its characteristic siglum. Thus, for example, in commenting on Genesis 14, a well known biblical scholar, Otto Eissfeldt, could present the academic community with the following unreal dissection:

> With this narrative it is quite clear that it presupposes the already complete compilation L+J+E+B+D+H+P, and that it has been inserted into it. For it is dependent not only on the L narrative of Lot and Abraham (Gen xii, 6-8 + xiii, 2, 5, 7-11a, 12bβ-18) . . . [2]

This presupposes that successive editors had made myriad, miniscule additions to an original text.

Under Jerome in the late 1950s, we were drilled in the JEDP theory, which had developed since the time of Wellhausen. We learned to recognise the sources in the biblical text. By this stage I had also begun learning Hebrew, necessary for this sort of work and continued, in a smaller class, to study the language in more depth. In fact, my companions and I were catching up with progress in the Catholic Church.

The Popes and the Bible

I now began studying the more recent past in the Catholic attitude to the Bible. In 1920 Benedict XV had issued an encyclical letter, *Spiritus Paraclitus,* which took an even more defensive stance than that of Leo XIII some twenty-seven years earlier regarding the modern methods of biblical interpretation. The letter was particularly conservative regarding history in the Bible and it is clear that there would be little opportunity for orthodox Catholics to question the factuality of the gospels. One paragraph read:

> If Jerome were living now, he would sharpen his keenest controversial weapons against people who set aside what is the

2. Otto Eissfeldt (1965), *The Old Testament. An Introduction,* Blackwell: Oxford and New York, p 211.

> mind and judgement of the Church and take too ready a refuge in such notions as 'implicit quotations' or 'pseudo-historical narratives' or in 'kinds of literature' (*genera quaedam litterarum)* in the Bible such as cannot be reconciled with the entire and perfect truth of God's word, or who suggest such origins of the Bible as must inevitably weaken—if not destroy—its authority.[3]

From that point in time there had been an eerie silence from the Vatican as regards biblical scholarship. Two decades later, in 1941, the Biblical Commission, which had issued no decrees since the days of Benedict XV, suddenly sprang back into action and condemned a pseudonymous brochure, whose author was later known to have been an obscure Italian priest, Dolindo Ruotolo. Unbelievably, Ruotolo's brochure was condemned by what was regarded as a very conservative Biblical Commission because it was too conservative!

Ruotolo had attacked the scientific study of the Bible and had stated that, in the first place, any study of the biblical text should be restricted to the Latin translation which was presumably more reliable than the original languages—Hebrew, Aramaic and Greek. He proceeded to promote a spiritual meaning derived from the biblical text, one which God directly revealed to the believing reader, rather than any literal meaning. Over time he had written a thirteen volume treatise on the Bible extolling this spiritual meaning. In an earlier age, poor Ruotolo would have been lauded by the Church that now condemned him in 1941.

Ruotolo's 'spiritual meaning' was neither better nor worse than the allegorical method proposed by Augustine in the pre-modern worldview. It was on a par with the authoritative writings of the untutored Pius X. But the Commission was not allowing Ruotolo to go back in time. His condemnation established two principles for Catholic scholars in the 1940s: that the interpretation of the Bible requires scientific study and that the literal meaning of the text (not some spiritual sense that fell from on high) is the primary one. Had it not been that a Catholic world involved in a World War had more pressing matters on its collective mind, the decree from the Commission would have come as a bombshell.

Two years later in 1943 the real turning point came for Roman Catholic scholars. Pius XII (1876-1958) published a new encyclical on biblical

3. *Rome and the Study of Scripture,* p 54.

studies, *Divino Afflante Spiritu* mentioned earlier. It built on the condemnation of Ruotolo. The Pope stated that the Catholic interpreter of the Bible should be skilled in the use of all relevant scientific methods, making use of the original languages of the Bible and concentrating on the literal meaning:

> What is the literal sense of a passage is not always as obvious in the speeches and writings of the ancient authors of the East as it is in the works of our own time. For what they wished to express is not to be determined by the rules of grammar and philology alone, nor solely by the context; the interpreter must, as it were, go back wholly in spirit to those remote centuries of the East, and with the aid of history, archaeology, ethnology and other sciences, accurately determine what modes of writing (*litteraria genera*), so to speak, the authors of that ancient period would be likely to use, and in fact did use.[4]

In short, the Pope was saying that the Bible was not to be read naively as history. It is interesting that this statement almost pointedly abrogates what Benedict XV's encyclical *Spiritus Paraclitus* had stated in 1920 regarding literary forms, although Pius called them *litteraria genera* out of deference to Benedict who had used the term *genera quaedam litterarum.* The terms meant the same, but it could be said that they were not identical in order to defuse any claim that one Pope had countermanded his predecessor. The statement about literary forms meant that the Bible contained not only history, but poetry, parables, legends and so on.

After *Divino Afflante Spiritu,* Biblical scholars in the Catholic Church felt moderately safe for a while. In 1948 the forward thinking Cardinal Emmanuel Suhard of Paris put a test question to the Biblical Commission concerning the early chapters of Genesis and the Mosaic authorship of the Pentateuch, matters which seemingly had been definitively decided for Catholics at the turn of the century by the decrees of the same Commission. It was a set-up, a Dorothy Dixer, to ensure that earlier decrees be no longer enforced. In a letter of reply the Commission, through its Secretary General Athanasius Miller, noted the vast changes that had taken place over the previous forty years. It stated that Moses could no longer be con-

4. *Rome and the Study of Scripture,* p 97.

sidered the author of the Pentateuch in the normal sense of 'author' and that the Pentateuch was dependent on written sources and oral traditions.

Dealing specifically with the first eleven chapters of Genesis Miller claimed that their literary forms corresponded to no classical categories and could not be described as 'history'. The Genesis narratives reported, the letter stated, fundamental truths in a simple and figurative language and gave a popular description of the origin of the human race and the Hebrew people. The words were liberating to an upcoming generation of biblical interpreters.[5] They were mind-boggling to me.

The avenues opened by the encyclical and the 1948 letter of the Biblical Commission to biblical research, however, were soon to be closed again in 1950 by yet another encyclical from Pius XII called *Humani Generis*. This encyclical reflected the growing fear in Rome that theologians and biblical scholars were getting out of hand and was the result of religio-political machinations afoot in Vatican circles. It generally denounced what were considered to be theological deviations, but some of those denunciations impinged on the biblical domain. For example, polygenism, the theory that the human race began from more than one ancestor, was censured in this way:

> It is in no way apparent how such an opinion can be reconciled with that which the sources of revealed truth and the documents of the Teaching Authority of the Church propose with regard to original sin.

The subtext here seemed to be that the story of Adam and Eve had to be taken literally. Then, returning yet again to the debate over the literary forms of the first chapters of Genesis, the encyclical partially retracted what had been stated in the Biblical Commission's reply to Suhard only two years earlier:

> Therefore whatever of the popular narrations have been inserted into the Sacred Scriptures must in no way be considered on a par with myths or other such things, which are more the product of an extravagant imagination than of that striving for truth and simplicity which in the Sacred Books, also of the Old Testament, is so apparent that our ancient

5. The text is in *Rome and the Study of Scripture*, pp 150–153.

> sacred writers must be admitted to be clearly superior to the ancient profane writers.

This to-ing and fro-ing on the part of official documentation was no cause for great wonder. While the reign of Pius XII had allowed Catholic scholars to catch up with their non-Catholic peers, the last few years or so of his pontificate were disastrous. He was gravely ill, possibly mentally unstable, and had lost control of church politics in the ever volatile Roman ecclesiastical scene. The reactionary forces gathered together and devised a strategy which was to be put in place after the death of Pius. The jovial John XXIII, supposedly to be a caretaker Pope, would take over the papal throne.

This was the context for us as students. Pius XII was still reigning but it seemed that, from a study of *Divino Afflante Spiritu*, the way was open to new thinking. *Humani Generis* was recognised but it was overlooked. So it was that Jerome felt empowered to introduce us to JEDP, to literary forms and to a historical questioning of the Bible. There were a few books that landed in our meagre library, such as the newly arrived Bruce Vawter's *A Path through Genesis,* that clearly upheld Jerome's stance. Seeing new ideas in print and written by a priest gave credibility to what we were hearing in class and allayed fears that we were straying from Catholic truth.

In the monastic classroom, from being an appendage to support and bolster Church teaching, the Bible had become instead the prime source of Church teaching. However, we immediately found that what we were learning in the Biblical Studies class could contradict what we were learning in the Theology class. And often it did just that. It was a testing time.

If it was difficult for some to accept the new trend in the study of the Hebrew Scriptures and to agree that Adam and Eve were mythical stories, that there had never been an historical Jonah swallowed by a great fish, that the prophecy of Isaiah had been written in three stages, centuries apart, by three different 'Isaiahs'; it would be much more painful for those same students when we came to the Christian Scriptures.

A revolution had certainly taken over our thinking as far as the study of the Hebrew Scriptures was concerned. This was the historical-critical approach. The fact was that the these Scriptures did not contain primarily history. They contained a variety of literature and while the general outline of the history of Israel could be discerned, certainly not all biblical narratives were historical.

But the first revolution, the historical-critical method, had not only affected the study of the Hebrew Scriptures. It had even more effectively changed the study of the Christian Scriptures.

Note

Bruce Vawter's *Path through Genesis* (Sheed and Ward: London, 1956) was a book that stirred the English-speaking world of biblical scholarship. It went through thirteen editions in English and Spanish from 1956 to 1976. He introduced many younger students to the idea that in the first eleven chapters of Genesis there was no history and in the remainder of Genesis there were only broad historical allusions. Vawter came to Australia in the late 1950s and was invited to speak to Catholic seminarians. I attended his addresses in Adelaide and remember feeling a sense of exhilaration at what I heard.

Chapter 5
STUDYING THE CHRISTIAN SCRIPTURES: AUSTRALIA

The Christian gospels had been considered sacrosanct by Catholics even if they had put them to little use. Up to the 1950s, most observant Roman Catholics accepted, as I had done, the gospels as strictly historical documents, inspired by God and free from any error, whose apparent discrepancies could be explained away with a little ingenuity. But now the same historical-critical approach used in the study of the Hebrew Scriptures was applied to the gospels and we students were exposed to it. Whereas the Hebrew Scriptures seemed a little distant, the Christian Scriptures were at the heart of what we saw as our Catholic faith.

Already we knew that there were stalwart Catholic apologists who upheld the literal exactitude of the gospels stories. The four gospels all told the same story, or so we had been told. Thus, scholars in the Catholic camp tried to reconcile the trials of Jesus. Matthew and Mark have a trial before Caiaphas and the Sanhedrin at night. Luke and John have Jesus taken before Annas at night and then before Caiaphas and the Sanhedrin in the morning. The scholars invented a sequence that harmonised all four accounts: the trial before Annas was 'informal', the real trial taking place in the morning before Caiaphas and the Sanhedrin. This could be combined with the fact that Caiaphas and the Sanhedrin began their trial at night but it proceeded until the morning. With these two provisos, all four gospels are relating the same story.

Further, John wrote that Jesus' body had to be removed from the cross on the Friday since it was the eve of the Passover; however, the Synoptics had described Jesus preparing a Passover meal on the previous Thursday evening. Was the Passover on the Friday or the Saturday? There is some evidence that there were at least two Jewish calendars and that different groups of Jews dated the Passover either on the Friday or the Saturday that year. Hence, it could be said that the Synoptics and John were both correct. In fact, they were saying quite different things.

But this naivety could not go on forever. There had already been new developments and we were soon exposed to them. After the end of the First Search, a number of Christian (but non-Catholic) theologians and historians, accepting the scepticism of Albert Schweitzer, expressed their doubt that anything substantial about an historical Jesus could be known, apart from the fact that he had existed. They consoled themselves by rejecting any theological requirement for an historical Jesus.

Formcriticism

Thus, Rudolf Bultmann (1884–1976), a Lutheran and one of the great Protestant biblical scholars, who was the longstanding professor of New Testament at Marburg University in Germany, strenuously maintained that Christian faith required only the brute fact of Jesus' existence and death, not the historical details. The Christian would find salvation, he maintained, by the proclamation of the first Christian community, not by understanding actual historical events.

While Bultmann's nineteenth century predecessors had concentrated on the words of Jesus in the gospels in order to reproduce the authentic teaching of the founder of Christianity, he held that very few if any of the Jesus-sayings could be traced back to an historical Jesus. However, the preaching of the early Church community as recorded in the Christian Scriptures, whether historically reliable or not, was a salvific force. In short, history did not matter. His method of interpreting the Scriptures was called *Formgeschichte* or Form Criticism.

This method first identified literary forms (such as parable, miracle story, Jesus-saying) in the gospel texts, then it identified the typical *Sitz im Leben* or life-situation in which such forms would have flourished. It distinguished between the *Sitz im Leben Jesu* (the life-situation of Jesus), the *Sitz im Leben der Kirche* (the life-situation of the early church) and the *Sitz im Evangelium* (the life-situation of the written gospels). A saying or the narration of an event, which had occurred in the life of Jesus, might even have changed its form as it was handed on in the life-situation of the early church and then changed again when it came to be recorded by an editor in the written gospels.

We could take as an example the narrative of Jesus allowing his followers to pick corn on the Sabbath in Mark 2: 23–28. When challenged by the Pharisees for this activity, Jesus cites the case of David who, when he and his followers were hungry, took sacred bread from the house of God. The story ends with the Jesus-saying: 'The sabbath was made for humankind, not humankind for the sabbath'. A Formcritic might analyse this story on the three levels mentioned above;

> Level 3, *Sitz im Evangelium*: Mark has incorporated a story of Jesus' debate with Jewish adversaries into his narrative sequence of healings and exorcisms in order to demonstrate that he was the Jewish Messiah, able to overcome the encroaching forces of evil represented in human illness, demon possession and ignorance. In this context, 'Messiah' means the leader of the people of Israel, sent by God to overcome the forces of evil.
>
> Level 2, *Sitz im Leben der Kirche*: In the early church community there had been problems over the issue of Sabbath observance. Did Christians still have to obey the Sabbath regulations with the rigour of other Jewish sects? This saying and the related action of Jesus were used to instruct converts that such rigorous observance was not required.
>
> Level 1, *Sitz im Leben Jesu*: Formcritics could debate whether Jesus had actually said these words and had actually been involved in a confrontation with other Jews. They might propose that it was likely they he had spoken more or less the stated words in the course of a discussion or, on the other hand, they might propose that the 'event' had been constructed in good faith at Level 2. This would have been what Jesus would have said, had the occasion arisen.

However, for Bultmann, Christian faith was based on the 'Jesus' reflected at Level 3 in the gospel story of Jesus. Whether this Jesus ever existed as at Level 1 and whether he actually was responsible for the gospel sayings were considered immaterial. Bultmann was to write:

> I do indeed think that we can now know almost nothing concerning the life and personality of Jesus, since the early Christian sources show no interest in either, are moreover fragmentary and often legendary; and other sources about Jesus do not exist. [1]

Further, Bultmann maintained that the gospel proclamation was enveloped in a mythical world image that thought in terms of a three-tier natural world where miracles, cures and exorcisms took place. The interpreter had to become a 'demytholigizer' and strip away those mythical elements, replacing them with the language of the modern day in which scientific thought predominated. He wrote:

> A blind acceptance of New Testament mythology would be simply arbitrariness; to make such acceptance a demand of faith would be to reduce faith to a work.[2]

Redaction History

In the 1940s the Bultmannian methodology as applied to the gospels was refined by a procedure that became known as *Redaktionsgeschichte* in German, and in English as Redaction History. It emphasised the role of an anonymous 'editor' in the formation of the gospel tradition, and it maintained that four editors had each constructed a distinctive and personal portrait of Jesus from pre-existing material in the gospels of Matthew, Mark, Luke and John. These were not eye-witnesses recounting history from memory. They were literary people who worked on existing traditions to produce a religiously meaningful text. Each text carried the literary imprint of its author.

While Formcriticism was concerned with the different literary forms in the biblical text and the particular rules that applied to them, Redaction History was concerned with the way these pre-existing snippets of literature had been used by the compiler or editor.

According to Redaction History, no matter what the origin of the original traditions, no matter what stages the material had passed through, the

1. Rudolf Bultmann (1934), *Jesus and the Word*, C. Scribner's Sons: New York and London.
2. *New Testament and Mythology and Other Basic Writings* (1984), edited by Schubert M Ogden. Philadelphia: Fortress, p 3.

vital formative feature of the gospels was the redactional or editorial activity of this final editor who would have modified and shaped the available material until it reached its present format. Hence, attention turned to 'the theology of Mark' or 'the theology of Luke' and, by consequence, to the 'Jesus of Mark' or the 'Jesus of Luke'. Redaction History seemed to distance the historical Jesus even further from the gospel text than had been done previously. The scholar might be able to retrieve the Jesus of Mark but not necessarily an historical Jesus.

By the time that I had become more involved in my biblical studies, I discovered that the First Search for the Historical Jesus had actually been bypassed. It was over. There was something new afoot. Jerome introduced us to texts that had taken up this new development.

The Second Search for the Historical Jesus

Already by the mid 1950s, around the time I first became involved in this study, some scholars, particularly in Germany and the United States, had begun to react disconcertedly to the negative results of the First Search. They undertook the Second Search (at the time it was called the 'New Search') for the Historical Jesus. The principal proponents were a German, Ernst Käsemann and James Robinson, an American. I remember reading Robinson's *The New Search for the Historical Jesus*, one of the main texts of the Second Search, around this time. I felt that I could accept his sophisticated understanding of Jesus as it was transmitted through the gospels.

These Second Searchers were certain that they were more in control of the gospel texts than some of their sceptical predecessors had been, and that much valuable new information had been learned in the preceding fifty years about the history and culture of the times in which Jesus had lived. They were well versed in the methods of Form Criticism and *Redaktionsgeschichte*. With all of this behind them, they felt they could present a more fleshed-out and credible history of Jesus.

While they would not venture to give historical details about Jesus' birth, they could identify that an important turning point had occurred in his life when he met with John the Baptist and was baptised by him. This event led to Jesus' ministry in Galilee, where they identified him as a teacher, an exorcist and a healer who ministered primarily to the poor and marginalised. This period of ministry culminated in a journey to the capital city of Jerusalem and his execution by crucifixion on the orders of the Roman governor, Pontius Pilate. The Second Searchers were circumspect regarding any specific historical details related to the resurrection of Jesus. Certainly they acknowledged that it was part of the early tradition but they did not try to describe it in any detailed, literal fashion.

I had come to the study of the Scriptures during the time of the Second Search. Having recovered from the study of the Hebrew Scriptures, my companions and I were virtually thrown headfirst into that Second Search, with Jerome Crowe to guide us. We looked for literary forms in the gospels, we tried to imagine life-situations, the *Sitze im Leben,* that might have given rise to sayings of Jesus, we discussed the editorial activities of gospel writers. We reconstructed a basic life of Jesus that could be proved by the evidence.

The Second Search was a great relief to many practising Christian scholars. It proved for them that there was continuity between the historical Jesus and the preaching of the early church. There seemed, therefore, to be sufficient reliable historicity on which to base the faith claims of Christianity and its ethical practices.

However, the New Searchers, soon after they had begun to publish the results of their research, had been stopped in their tracks by two discoveries: the chance discovery of scrolls in caves down by the Dead Sea and the discovery of Gnostic codices in Egypt. They had taken place earlier but by the mid-1950s the full exposition of the Dead Sea texts became public knowledge. These extended the boundaries of the normal science of biblical studies at the time.

We students came to know the Dead Sea Scrolls very well from Jerome. Of the discoveries in Egypt I would be ignorant for some years.

The Dead Sea Scrolls

Jerome had come back from Jerusalem, having studied under Roland de Vaux, the first editor of the Dead Sea Scrolls, highly enthused to spread the news of their discovery. It was due to him at this time that I read my first book on the Dead Sea Scrolls, Millar Burrows' *The Dead Sea Scrolls.* At age 19, I already knew that in some way the history of the Scrolls would affect my thinking in a profound way.

The real story of the discovery of the scrolls might never be told. In so far as the story was related by De Vaux it ran as follows. In the spring of 1947 three young Bedouin cousins were minding goats by the Dead Sea, in an area that would later be named as Qumran (see figure 2). This had originally been the Arabic name of a nearby watercourse, dry except in winter. They realised that one of their herd was missing. Goats sometimes sought relief from the intense summer heat in caves. The boys began searching in the many caves in the area and threw stones into a small cave hoping to disturb the goat. They heard the sound of something smash. They were afraid and they fled. Their fear was due to the fact that, as Muslims, they believed in *djinn* or spirits, some good and some malevolent, who inhabited caves and jars. It was best to give these *djinn* a wide berth.

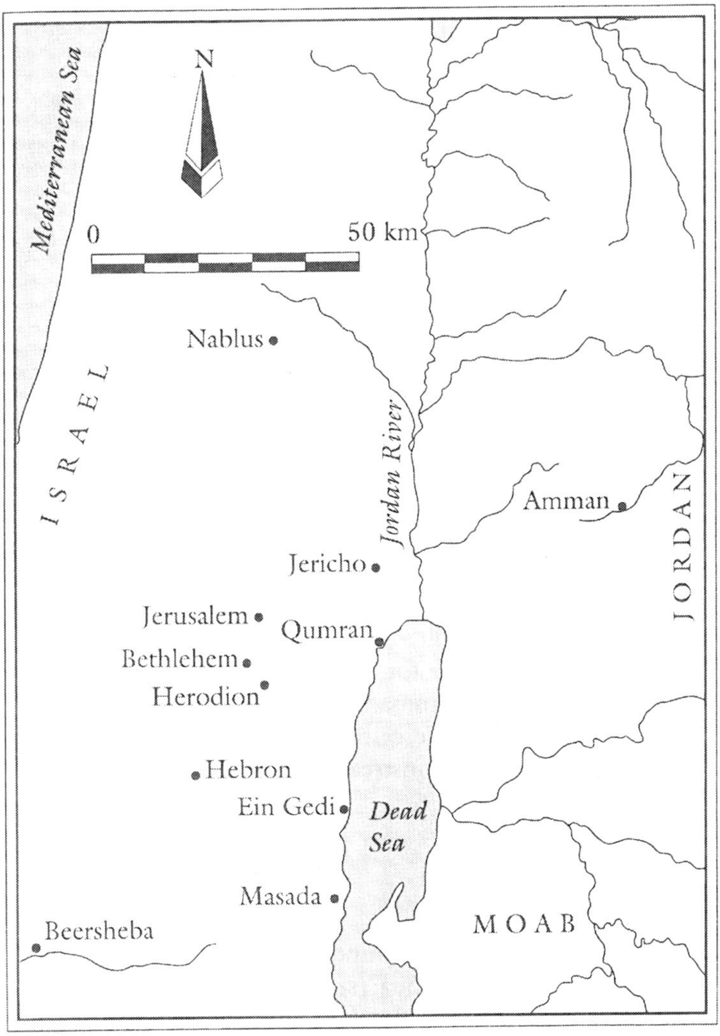

Figure 2: Qumran and the Dead Sea area

Some time later, one of the three, Muhammad ed-Dhib ('Muhammad the Wolf'), overcoming his fear, returned to the cave. He climbed in and with the aid of a cigarette lighter investigated the cave. He found that it contained pottery jars, some intact and some already shattered, one by the initial stone. Some of the jars contained manuscripts written on leather skin. The boy removed three leather rolls wrapped in frayed linen and took them back to the Bedouin encampment. The leather was inscribed with text but these Bedouin were illiterate. Details of the original story might have been lost forever as one of the possibilities was that the Bedouin were involved in illegal activity, perhaps smuggling or perhaps antiquity hunting, and not primarily goat minding.

When the tribal group came to Bethlehem, the scrolls were offered to an antiquities dealer called Khalil Iskander Shahin, known familiarly as Kando, a Syrian Christian. Subsequent events are difficult to trace but possibly a Syrian merchant from Bethlehem, George Shaya, and two Bedouin returned to the cave and recovered four more scrolls. The merchant took one scroll, a damaged and decomposing one, while the two Bedouin sold the other three to another antiquities dealer in Bethlehem called Feidi al-Alami. Muhammad ed-Dhib was not included in this second foray and almost fades from the scene at this point. It is reported that he obtained enough from his transaction to buy a rifle and finance a wedding dowry. Later, he appeared as hired help at the excavation site at Qumran.

Kando suspected that the three scrolls in his possession were valuable and set out to sell them in Jerusalem. He offered them first to two young American scholars at the American Schools of Oriental Research. They could not raise the money to buy them, although they recognised their value. But they were allowed to keep the scrolls for a day and to take photos of the texts. Overnight they realised that one of the scrolls contained the Hebrew text of the prophecy of Isaiah. These photos were sent to W.F. Albright, the famed biblical archaeologist in America, who recognised immediately their significance, claiming that this was the most important archaeological find of the twentieth century.

After some misunderstandings, Kando did manage to sell his three scrolls to a Syrian Orthodox archbishop, Mar Athanasius Yeshua Samuel, for £24 sterling. Later the archbishop acquired a fourth, the decomposing one taken by Shaya from the second find in the cave. The archbishop was a collector of ancient manuscripts, although he was not able to read these particular scrolls, and seemed to sense that the scrolls were genuine.

Kando was a member of his Syrian denomination which must also have raised his confidence that this was no scam.

The other three scrolls also came on to the market. The head of the Department of Archaeology at the Hebrew University of Jerusalem, Eleazar Sukenik, was alerted to the fact that Feidi al-Alami had ancient scrolls. Sukenik made the rather dangerous trip to Bethlehem to meet with the dealer. It was late November 1947 and the future of Palestine was in the balance. Relationships between Jews and Arabs were hostile and Bethlehem was in Arab hands. Sukenik was shown the three scrolls and allowed to take two back to Jerusalem to study them. While doing so the news of the United Nations' decision to create a separate state of Israel as a homeland for Jewish people was declared over his radio.

It all seemed providential. Sukenik decided to buy the scrolls. These were what today are known as the War Scroll and the Thanksgiving Psalms. Later he managed to acquire the third scroll, a second copy of the prophecy of Isaiah, not in as good a condition as the one retained by the archbishop.

Sukenik was a dedicated Zionist. Largely self-educated, he had excavated synagogues and Jewish tombs on the Mount of Olives. By familiarising himself with the early Jewish inscriptions on ossuaries (burial boxes for human bones) he had become an expert in the palaeography of early Hebrew script. Hence he was no amateur when it came to assessing the scrolls. From the onset he knew that they were ancient and important.

Meanwhile Palestine had erupted in violence. On 14 May, 1948 the Jewish People's Council met in Tel Aviv and declared the creation of the State of Israel. Immediately, Arab forces from Egypt bombed Tel Aviv. They would be joined by Saudi Arabia, Transjordan, Syria, Lebanon and Iraq and the war would continue until January 1949.

In that same month the archbishop, Mar Samuel, flew to America to take up a position ministering to Syrian Orthodox communities there and, if the legend can be trusted, carried his four scrolls on to the plane under his flowing robes. His efforts to sell the scrolls in Jerusalem had fallen through. From the photographs taken at the American Schools of Oriental Research it was now certain that the four manuscripts included the prophecy of Isaiah (a much better preserved copy than that obtained by Sukenik), a commentary or *pesher* on the prophecy of Habakkuk, the Rule of the Community (a collection of regulations and doctrinal statements belonging to some Jewish sect, which at that stage could not be further identified) and the dilapidated scroll containing the Genesis Apocryphon (a commentary on and paraphrase of the book of Genesis written in Aramaic).

The four scrolls were lodged in a bank vault in New York. Negotiations by Mar Samuel over a sale fell through. No-one was willing to meet his price and there was still some suspicion among scholars that the scrolls were fakes. In 1950 the prophecy of Isaiah was published from the photographs taken by the American scholars in Jerusalem, and in 1951 the Rule of the Community (originally known as the Manual of Discipline) and the Habakkuk *pesher* were published, all of them under the auspices of the American Schools of Oriental Research. The fourth scroll, the Genesis Apocryphon, because of its poor state of preservation, still could not be opened.

On June 1, 1954 Mar Samuel, impatient for a buyer, offered his four manuscripts for sale by advertisement in the *Wall Street Journal:*

> **THE FOUR DEAD SEA SCROLLS**
>
> Biblical manuscripts dating back to at least 200 BC are for sale. This would be an ideal gift to an educational or religious institution by an individual or group. Box F 206, The Wall Street Journal.

They were purchased for $US250,000 by a New York banker who was acting as intermediary for an unknown buyer. The unknown buyer, in fact, was the State of Israel and the four scrolls were returned promptly to Jerusalem on an El Al flight.

By 1954, therefore, the seven manuscripts originally on the market were in the hands of the newly established State of Israel. The Israeli government built a magnificent museum, called the Shrine of the Book, in the grounds of the Israeli Museum, to house their treasure. From the start it was conceived as a sacred place to house relics of the new State's religious past. It was built in the shape of the lid of the first earthenware jar found shattered in the cave. Within this modern construction a tunnel likc passageway leads to a central hall. There the scroll containing the prophecy of Isaiah was displayed, wound around a gigantic Torah handle. Up until the 1980s the original remained on display but, due to deterioration, it has been replaced with a good facsimile.

But during this time more scrolls had been discovered near the Dead Sea in an area, after the conclusion of the War of Independence, belonging to the Hashemite Kingdom of Jordan. The area in which the original manuscripts had been found had been systematically combed by both Bedouin and archaeologists and ten more manuscript-bearing caves were found. In one of these, cave 4, there were some fifteen thousand fragments, some no larger than a fingernail, which had originated from an estimated trove of 584 texts. Although it was the richest of all the finds there was not a single intact scroll recovered from the debris in cave 4. Altogether, about 818 texts were discovered in all eleven caves. The number cannot be given with exactitude since there is ongoing debate as to whether some fragments should be combined into one or more texts.

There were three types of scrolls: biblical texts, Jewish religious texts and texts which reflected the life style and beliefs of a Jewish group or sect (or perhaps plural groups/sects), sometimes called sectarian texts. Among the two hundred odd biblical scrolls and scroll pieces, all books of the Hebrew Bible apart from Esther were represented although the Isaiah scroll is the only complete biblical text found. Esther may have not been esteemed since it does not mention the name of God. These biblical books are dated to 200-100 BCE and were approximately 1000 years older than any other existing Hebrew manuscript.

There were also some four hundred Jewish religious texts, such as the Book of Jubilees and the Assumption of Moses. The two hundred or so sectarian writings included several Rules intended for the guidance of the life style of a community or communities. Most of these sectarian texts were completely unknown to scholars prior to the discoveries.

The Qumran Excavations

Naturally the scroll finds around the Dead Sea raised questions: Who had placed the scrolls in the caves? When and why? Not far from the general area of the eleven caves there was a small ruin or *tell* in the region known as Qumran. Only passing interest had been paid to it previously. In late 1951 Roland de Vaux, a staff member at the École Biblique et Archéologique Française in Jerusalem, and G Lankester Harding, an agnostic who loved all things oriental and was in charge of the Department of Antiquities in Jerusalem, made a preliminary examination and they began excavating the ruin on a full scale in 1953.

The ruins, when uncovered by de Vaux, revealed a tower, presumably for defence or use as a watchtower, a long room which was positioned next to a kitchen-pantry and was presumed to be an eating hall, a pottery workshop with two pottery kilns and about a thousand storage jars nearby[3], a scriptorium with writing tables (although their identification has been recently challenged as well as the identification of the room as a scriptorium) and two inkwells, storerooms, workshops, a mill, a cattle pen and an intricate water system linking up large water cisterns (see figure 3).

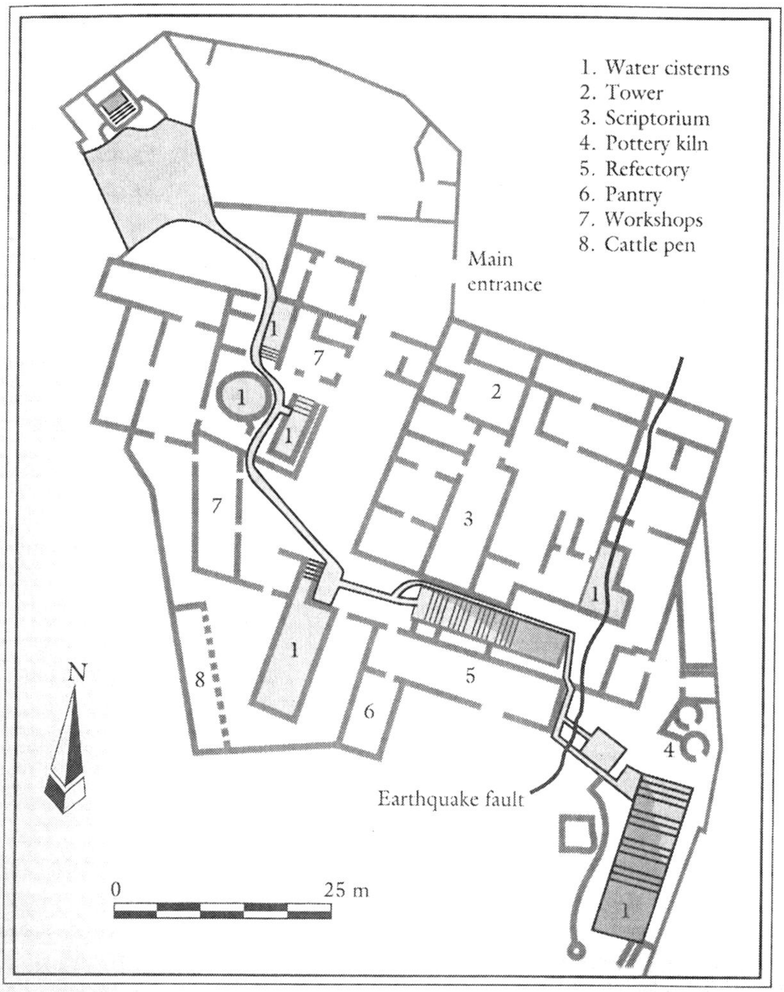

Figure 3: The layout of the Qumran ruins according to De Vaux

3. Why there should have been so many jars has always tested interpreters. A recent theory has suggested that Qumran was a centre for perfume making and these were the perfume containers.

What follows is the broadly accepted account of the history of the ruins according to de Vaux. It needs to be said that this account, sometimes known as the consensus position, has been under consistent attack by historians and archaeologists for some time. However, whether right or wrong the consensus position has had tremendous influence on the interpretation of the Qumran event and also on the interpretation of the individual scrolls and deserves an airing.

This theory holds that the ruins at Qumran go back to a military outpost constructed by one of the kings of Jerusalem, possibly Uzziah in the eighth century. The settlement at that time consisted of a simple rectangular building with a cistern for water attached. It was destroyed and abandoned in the next century.

A fresh occupation would have taken place around 150 BCE with a restoration of the main building and the addition of new rooms. Next, during the reign of John Hyrcanus 1 (134-104 BCE) there would have been a substantial increase in building activity with the addition of the two-storeyed tower, presumably for defence but perhaps only for vigilance, an assembly hall, the dining hall, kitchen, store rooms, the scriptorium, workshops and intricate water installations. Outside the perimeter of the main building was their cemetery.

This phase of occupation came to a dramatic close when some disaster overtook the monastery, caused a fire, and brought about abandonment of the site. The date and cause of the disaster is disputed. It could have been an invasion by Romans in the 60s BCE or Parthians in the early 30s BCE. However, de Vaux was confident that it was the earthquake described by the historian Josephus 'in the seventh year of Herod's reign' which would place it in 31 BCE.[4] In any case the building was covered with ash and there was a deep layer of mud, presumably from cracked cisterns, in many places.

The settlement, from de Vaux's understanding of the strata, was then abandoned until the beginning of the Christian era. During the first decade of that era a second major phase of building and occupation could be detected, continuing to the final destruction of the building by the Romans in 68 CE. For a period after the destruction, the ruined building at Qumran may have been used by Roman troops.

4. The date is established by reference to Flavius Josephus, *Antiquities*, XV, 121:

> Meanwhile the battle of Actium took place between Caesar and Antony, in the seventh year of Herod's reign, and there was an earthquake in Judaea, such as had not been seen before.

According to this interpretation of the ruins, the copying of the scrolls, their seclusion and all events related in them, must have taken place before 68 CE when the building was destroyed. References to persons and events connected with the actual foundation of the sect, such as are recorded in the sectarian texts, would have to be situated in the second century BCE since the interpretation of the strata dates the foundation of the building around 150 BCE. What now follows is the consensus position's view on the events leading to Qumran's foundation and the identification of its inhabitants.

To the amazement of the academic world, de Vaux identified these ruins as a monastery belonging to the Essenes, a Jewish sect, mentioned by some of the early writers like Pliny and Josephus. Other major sects were the Pharisees and Sadducees. But no Jewish monastery had ever been found previously. He claimed that these Essenes were responsible for copying the manuscripts and eventually for storing them in the adjacent caves.

The organic connection between the archaeological site and the scrolls was proven, for de Vaux, by the scriptorium, by the presence of the pottery kiln and jars (since similar jars had been found in the caves), by the water cisterns which complied with the mention of ritual immersion in the sectarian scrolls. That the sect was Essene (a suggestion already made by Sukenik in 1948) seemed to be proved by the description of an Essene presence in the Dead Sea area, to the north of Engadi, by Pliny the Elder in his *Natural History:*

> On the west side of the Dead Sea, but out of range of the noxious exhalations of the coast, is the solitary tribe of the Essenes, which is remarkable beyond all other tribes in the whole world, as it has no women and has renounced all sexual desire, has no money, and has only palm-trees for company. Day by day the throng of refugees is recruited to an equal number by numerous accessions of persons tired of life and driven thither by the wave of fortune to adopt their manners . . . Below them lies Engadi (*infra hos Engada*). [5]

5. *Natural History,* 5.15.73. Josephus also made mention of the Essenes, describing them as one of the three main 'philosophies' within Judaism in *Antiquities,* 18:20.

We will see that the final phrase in this statement, taken to prove the geographical location of Essenes at Qumran, would become a matter of great debate.

The Qumran Community

The origins of the Qumran community, according to the consensus position, are to be sought in the middle of the second century BCE when a group of Essenes went out into the desert and began rebuilding the ruined Jewish fortress. Their founder and leader was a figure mentioned prominently in some of the sectarian documents, the Teacher of Righteousness, a priest. At this stage the group would have numbered some fifty persons.

The desert-dwelling group was confronted by a 'Wicked Priest', also mentioned in sectarian documents, a renegade who sought to kill the Teacher. The consensus view identifies the Wicked Priest with one or other character of the Hasmonean period, usually Jonathan (160–142 BCE) but sometimes Simon (142–134). These two had assumed the role of High Priest, and there were many who maintained that neither had the right to do so. The sectarian texts relate that the Wicked Priest died a horrible death at the hands of the Gentiles. This could fit in with Jonathan who was executed by the Seleucid general, Trypho, after his imprisonment, but also with Simon who was murdered by his brother-in-law, Ptolemy.

Another important figure mentioned in the same texts in this founding period was the 'Man of the Lie', usually distinguished from the Wicked Priest. He caused a schism in the sect. Various attempts have been made to identify this person.

From the text of the Community Rule, found in the first cave, the sort of life lived by the sectarians at Qumran was reconstructed. The building uncovered by the archaeologists would have been their communal centre and they would, at their high point in the final phase of their occupation, have numbered a hundred or more. They would have carried out communal activities in the centre although there do not seem to have been any dormitory arrangements. Presumably they slept in huts or tents or perhaps in the caves. Some of the caves showed signs of ongoing habitation. Those who joined the community had to be Jewish and they underwent an initial scrutiny by the 'Supervisor' of the monastery, who is also mentioned in the sectarian texts. The Hebrew word for supervisor in the texts is *mebaqqar* which, if translated into Greek, would give *episkopos* or 'bishop' in English.

In a ceremony to mark their admission the Essenes took an oath to observe the Torah as it was interpreted by the Teacher of Righteousness. There was also a baptism, a bathing ritual. It was made clear however that the exterior bathing meant nothing if it was not accompanied by a purification of the heart. This baptism was repeated at regular intervals. Another prominent ritual was a sacred meal of bread and wine shared by all the monks.

During their first year the novices took no part in sacred meals nor in the frequent ritual bathing ceremonies. At the end of that year there was another scrutiny in the presence of the Supervisor and they handed over their personal possessions to be kept in store. Only after a second year were they fully initiated and allowed to join the other members of the sect.

These Essene monks would have carried out tasks such as farming, weaving, pottery making, copying manuscripts, cleaning, cooking. They also had religious duties which included common prayer, the ritual bathing and the participation in sacred meals of bread and wine. These sacred banquets were held in anticipation of the end-times when the sectarians expected to be joined by two messiahs, a Messiah of Aaron, a priestly messiah, and a Messiah of Israel, a lay messiah. It was presumed that the two Messiahs would come from the desert regions and that event would bring life in the monastery to its final climax. Presumably, the final battle against the forces of evil and darkness, described in the War Scroll, also found in the first cave, would then take place.

Whether celibacy was enforced or esteemed at Qumran was a debatable point. A few skeletons of women and children were found in the cemetery on the periphery of the building but the majority of those uncovered have been male. Not all graves have been excavated up to today (mainly because of problems with orthodox Jews who object to disturbing bones). While the life-style described in the texts suits an all-male environment, the priestly members must have intended their lineage to continue and this could only have been achieved by marriage. Possibly an elite group would have practised celibacy.

Once a year on the Jewish festival of Weeks, the 'Session of the Many', a council of all the full members of the community, met. They renewed the covenant or treaty between the Qumran community and God and they received new members. However, the normal running of affairs and the regulation of the life of the group was deputed to a supreme council which consisted of twelve members and three priests. There is uncertainty whether the text implies twelve in total, of whom three were priests, or fifteen in total. The whole community was divided into smaller groups, perhaps as small as ten.

There are many obvious structural similarities between this description of the Qumran group, as given by the consensus position, and the early Christians. The meal of bread and wine, baptism as a rite of initiation, the council of twelve lay members and three priests, leadership under a 'bishop', the messianic expectation (even if two messiahs were expected), esteem for celibacy and the practice of communal poverty are the more striking. Their attitudes towards wealth and divorce were also similar to those of the Christians.

More than that, when the actual wording of the sectarian texts is examined we find that there are conceptual similarities between the sectarians and Christians. The sectarians referred to themselves as 'The Way', 'The Sons of Light', 'the New Covenant', 'the Light of the World'. They were exhorted to 'walk in the light' and to await the 'Spirit of Truth'. There is a clear distinction between the Light where the sectarians live and the Darkness outside their particular world. These phrases are reminiscent of the terminology used in the Christian gospels, particularly the gospel of John, and the usage of 'The Way' as the earliest title for Christians in the Acts of the Apostles.

On the basis of such comparisons the case for some sort of contact, perhaps close contact, between Qumran and early Christianity was an obvious deduction for scholars to make.

Broadly, among Christian scholars who followed this mainstream interpretation three positions on the scrolls were taken up. A minority saw the scrolls as the literature of proto-Christians, a group who existed before the Christian era and in some way transmogrified into the Christian church at a later date. This position made some Christians uneasy since it challenged the uniqueness of Christianity and the role of Jesus.

Other scholars recognised in the scrolls the literature of a Jewish group from whom some of the early Christian disciples had come. This would particularly have applied to John the Baptist and his followers. A much larger group, the majority view, maintained that the scrolls belonged to a Jewish sect which flourished at the same time as early Christianity, although there was no direct contact between the two groups.

The Dead Sea Scrolls were a constant source of wonderment for us students in Adelaide in the late 1950s and into the 1960s. Those of us who read the literature and the texts belonged to the third group: we held that the Essenes lived at the same time as the early Christians but were not directly related to them. Even so, for some of those in our monastery the Dead Sea Scrolls were seen as a threat. Were Jesus and the first Christians somehow caught up with this mysterious monastery? Did the scrolls reveal that Christianity was not unique? We did not know enough at that stage to come to any firm conclusion. Jerome exposed us to the documents, to his slides of the Qumran area and to his personal communications from De Vaux. We drew our own conclusions.

The Second Search, *Redaktionsgeschichte*, the Dead Sea Scrolls—these were the outward symptoms of the first revolution in its impact on the Christian Scriptures. The Bible could be seen as human, capable of mistakes, needing literary analysis. It had been the 1943 Encyclical that gave the revolution some sort of official validity. No subsequent retraction by the Popes or other Vatican officials could undo what we believed to be a new way of thinking. We students no longer believed the Bible to be a wholly historical record. It was no longer the record of Dreamtime events and sayings. Both the Hebrew Scriptures and the Christian Scriptures were very human documents.

We did accept that there had been an historical People of Israel who had left behind clever writings. However, in order to understand their narrative texts it was, we considered, necessary to accept the theory of JEDP or something like it. We understood that this People of Israel had undergone a number of historical phases: the Ancestors, the Exodus from Egypt, the Conquest of Canaan, the United Kingdom of David and Solomon, the divided kingdom of the kings of Israel and Judah, the Exile in Babylonia and the Restoration of Israel after the Exile. How much of the details of these phases in the biblical text were historically accurate was a matter of conjecture. Certainly not all of the biblical texts were historical.

Something similar obtained with the Christian Scriptures. While we held to the broad outline of the 'facts' of the life of Jesus as told in the gospels, we certainly realised that there were significant discrepancies. Jerome had written a series of articles for the *Australasian Clergy Review* in which he toyed with the opinion of a female French Biblical scholar, Annie Jaubert, who largely relied on evidence about calendars in the Dead Sea Scrolls to conclude that the Last Supper might have taken place on Tuesday of the week Jesus died. Today, this would not raise an eyebrow; then, it was enough for Archbishop Matthew Beovich of Adelaide, a most conservative man and no scholar, to remark menacingly to Jerome that he certainly hoped that Thursday would be reinstated for the Last Supper before the series of articles concluded.

To some extent the requirement for double thinking was going. We had become used to having textbooks for Theology where biblical passages were treated as if they were proof texts and where all events in both Scriptures were accepted as historically literal. Now, lecturers in Theology bypassed the text books as outmoded. The anomalies had accumulated and the revolution had taken place. There was a new paradigm in place.

By the end of our six years of study in the Adelaide monastery we were rather circumspect Second Searchers using the sophisticated tools of historical criticism on the biblical texts and taking note of the anomalies thrown up by the Dead Sea Scrolls. We realised that we students were looked at askance by some of the other monks and by some of the older clergy in the parishes; as far as they were concerned we had been led astray. For our part, we felt that there was a certain obligation not to reveal all that we actually believed about the gospels to the local Catholic populace.

In 1962 I was ordained a priest at the age of twenty-four. As was usual, this took place a semester before the completion of theological studies. Jerome persuaded me during this final stage of my studies to try my hand at writing. I wrote four articles on the meaning of the Temple in ancient Judaism and the spiritual usage of the idea of Temple in New Testament writings. They were published in a theological journal, *Sursum Corda*. While they were not great articles and I would not at all stand by them now, they showed the interest I had in the biblical text and the fact that I was sufficiently confident to manipulate it.

At this point in time I felt that I had accomplished a rather difficult intellectual feat. I had lived for over six years through a drastic change - from firmly believing in the Bible as an historical document to being able to decipher between history and other literary forms such as myth, poetry and legend in that Bible. I still held the biblical text in high regard but I did not think for one moment that it was entirely either a divine text or an historical text although, in the end, history was very important. There had been an historical Israel and there had been a Jesus who lived and died in more or less the way that was described in the texts. I was convinced that I could continue in the same vein and find an ever deepening understanding of the texts of the Hebrew and Christian Scriptures, which I could now read in the original languages, and for which I had the requisite historical-critical methods to analyse.

That was not how it would turn out. It would not be a matter of following the 'normal science' and moving forward along the same path forever. The literary advances, archaeology and the Dead Sea Scrolls were producing a growing list of anomalies that threatened the paradigm of the historical-critical approach and presaged another revolution.

Notes

For historical interest, an overview of the Second Search is detailed in

Robinson, J (1959), *A New Quest for the Historical Jesus,* AR Allenson: Naperville, Ill.

There is a vast literature on the Dead Sea Scrolls and many translations of the texts. Two can be recommended for the general reader:

Martinez, FG and Tigchelaan, E (1997-8), *The Dead Sea Scrolls (two vols),* Brill: Leiden and Eerdmans: Grand Rapids
Vermes, G (1997), *The Complete Dead Sea Scrolls in English (complete edition),* Allen Lane Penguin: London

There are also some general introductions that fill in much of the background:

Schiffman, L, Tov E and Vanderkam, J (eds) (2000), *The Dead Sea Scrolls: Fifty Years after their Discovery,* Israel Exploration Society: Jerusalem
Shanks, H (1998), *The Mystery and Meaning of the Dead Sea Scrolls,* Random House: New York
Vanderkam, J (1994), *The Dead Sea Scrolls Today,* Eerdeman: Grand Rapids

On the archaeology of Qumran, the original consensus position can be found in:

De Vaux, R (1973), *Archaeology and the Dead Sea Scrolls: The Schweich Lectures of the British Academy 1959,* OUP: London.

More recent archaeological accounts are found in:

Golb, N (1995), *Who Wrote the Dead Sea Scrolls?,* BCA: New York and London.

Martinez, FG and Barrera, J (1993), *The People of the Dead Sea Scrolls*, Brill: Leiden
Schiffman L (ed), *Archaeology and History in the Dead Sea Scrolls*, Sheffield University Press: Sheffield

There have been a myriad number of interpretations of the scrolls and the excavations. The following are broad treatments:

Charlesworth, J (ed) (1992), *Jesus and the Dead Sea Scrolls*, Doubleday: New York
Cook, E (1994), *Solving the Mysteries of the Dead Sea Scrolls*, Zondervan: Grand Rapids
Silberman, N (1995), *The Hidden Scrolls*, Griffin Paperbacks: Melbourne
Stegemann, H (1998), *The Library of Qumran. On the Essenes, Qumran, John the Baptist and Jesus*, EJ Brill: Grand Rapids and Leiden
Thiede, C (2000), *The Dead Sea Scrolls and the Jewish Origins of Christianity*, Lion Publishing: Sandy Lane West

The following are much more speculative and need to be read with caution:

Baigent, M and Leigh, R (1991), *The Dead Sea Scroll Deception*, Corgi Books: London
Betz, O and Reisner, R (1993), *Jesus, Qumran and the Vatican*, SCM: London
Eisenman, R (1996), *The Dead Sea Scrolls and the First Christians*, Element: Shaftesbury, Dorset

From time to time references will be made to some of the Roman historians. Material has been taken from Pliny in Rackman, H. and Jones, W. (1938-42), *Pliny: Natural History*, London. There will be even more use made of the Jewish historian Josephus who was regarded as a traitor by many in his own time because he went across to the Romans. His works can be found as below and they are readily available online:

Whiston, W (trans) (1987), *The Works of Josephus*, Hendrickson Publishers Inc.: Peabody, MA.

Chapter 6
LEAVING AUSTRALIA

The following year, 1963, I went back to Sydney to do pastoral studies in preparation for my future life as a priest. For six months I lived in yet another Passionist monastery in the Sydney suburb of Marrickville. However, these studies were truncated by my religious superior's decision to send me to Rome to do further academic work in theology and biblical studies. I never did get to be a pastor or use my pastoral studies. The intention was that I should eventually return to Australia and take up a position as a lecturer in a proposed new theological seminary in Melbourne.

In August of that year I booked on a ship, the *Fair Sky*, travelling from Melbourne to Sydney, Auckland, Singapore, Colombo, Aden, Suez, Port Said and thence to Naples. It took six weeks and I used the opportunity to further my studies. I would have spent up to seven or eight hours a day, with a few rare breaks, working mostly on Hebrew and Greek grammar and texts in very pleasant surroundings, sometimes sitting on the deck (since I shared a very small cabin on the lowest deck without natural light) and enjoying the sun and the sea. While many on board went close to stir-crazy with the monotony of day after day without sight of land, I was in my element.

Living in Rome

Having landed in Naples, I arrived in Rome by train and went to the Passionist mother house of Sts. John and Paul on the Celian Hill, where I would live for over two years. The mode of life was similar to that in the monasteries in Australia except that we spoke Italian in daily interaction. The plan was that I would first go to the Angelicum University, run by the

Dominican order, to study for a Masters degree in Theology and then go to the Pontifical Biblical Institute, run by the Jesuits, to begin a Masters degree in Biblical Studies. A Masters degree in Theology was a pre-requisite for the Masters degree in Biblical Studies.

The degree in Theology entailed a massive bulk of work. Lectures were in Latin and all exams were in Latin. Practically everything depended on final written and oral examinations. For the greater part the curriculum was based on a study of medieval texts and thinking and, in the end, the intense discipline of study did not do me any harm. I also had to write a minor thesis. I chose to do one on a biblical topic, supervised by a very competent biblical scholar, and pursued an idea that had been festering in my mind during my last year of study in Australia. Where did the people of ancient Israel's ideas about life beyond death, about retribution for the good and evil for which they were responsible, come from? This gave me a chance to do some work on Hebrew texts.

I took time during the course of the year to take up biblical languages (Hebrew, Greek and Syriac) more seriously with the best of tuition. I studied Hebrew under a Dutch Dominican and an advanced course under a Maltese Dominican. I took one Greek course with an English Jesuit (who actually ran the course in English) and another course that dealt with ancient Greek papyrus texts with a Spanish Dominican who also introduced me to Syriac.

Living in Rome also gave me the opportunity to imbibe the Italian culture and the ecclesiastical world of the Vatican in the era immediately following the death of John XXIII, an event that had happened only a few months before I arrived, when the course of the second Vatican Council still hung in the balance. I discovered the situation in the city to be very tense.

Indeed, the Catholic scene in the early 1960s had changed yet again as far as biblical scholarship was concerned. Conservative forces had decided that the time had come to put down the threat perceived in the modern Catholic biblical movement. The spark for an open warfare waged by the conservatives against biblical scholars was a popular but well written article by a Jesuit academic, Luis Alonso-Schökel, who would become a scholar of world repute and one of my future lecturers at the Pontifical Biblical Institute.

His article was written in 1960 and entitled 'Dove va l'esegesi cattolica?' (Where is Catholic exegesis going?).[1] It set out to explain the recent changes in the study of the Bible and virtually documented the revolution that we had experienced in Adelaide. This article was very soon answered by another, written by a conservative Roman identity, Antonio Romeo, in the periodical *Divinitas* (published by the conservative Lateran University in Rome) which was called 'L'enciclica *Divino Afflante Spiritu* e le 'opiniones novae' ("The Encyclical *Divino Afflante Spiritu*' and the 'New Opinions').[2] This was a long rambling diatribe lacking logic and scholarship and attacking any novelty in biblical studies.

Romeo denied there had been any new direction in the Church's thinking and denied that the 1943 Encyclical had given any permission for biblical scholars to move away from former methods and positions. With abrasive zeal he dubbed Catholic biblical scholars as 'a whole swarm of termites working away incessantly in the shadows'. In particular the article viciously attacked the Pontifical Biblical Institute and its professors. This was to be the very Institute where my second year in Rome was to be spent.

What should have been an ecclesiastical storm in a teacup became serious. Rumours and denunciations circulated. Two leading professors from the Pontifical Biblical Institute, Maximilian Zerwick and Stanislaus Lyonnet (who were learned men but actually happened to be also rather staid and conservative), were removed from their teaching positions.

In the midst of such a disturbance, John XXIII had unexpectedly convoked a new Council, to be called Vatican II. He hoped, he said, that it would open up some windows and allow the Spirit of God to breathe on the church. Having expected that the appointment of the aged and retiring John XXIII would quieten things down, shock ran through the upper echelons of the Vatican hierarchy. In 1961 the Holy Office issued a *Monitum,* an official warning, deprecating the fact that Catholic biblical scholars were calling into question 'the genuine historical and objective truth of the Holy Scriptures'. It only added to the pessimism rampant among those scholars.

By the time Vatican II began, the year before I arrived, there were two factions in Rome—the arch-conservatives and the progressives—and they both endeavoured to sway the minds of the bishops gathering for the Council. Representatives of both factions actually handed out leaflets to

1. *Civiltà Cattolica* (1960), pp 449–460.
2. *Divinitas* 4 (1960), pp 385–456.

bishops on the steps of St Peter's Basilica as they arrived for the start of the Council proceedings. One faction denounced Catholic biblical scholars and the Pontifical Biblical Institute; the other defended biblical scholars and called for understanding regarding the Pontifical Biblical Institute.

The Council had already appointed a committee to work on a number of documents, including one on Scripture and Tradition as the two ways by which God communicated with his people. Understandably, among Catholic biblical scholars there was grim foreboding when a draft proposal was presented to the assembled Fathers of the Council on the Sources of Revelation. This draft confirmed the scholars' worst fears when it appeared in 1962. It incorporated the *Monitum* of 1961 and called for restrictions on biblical research. It was a document that could have been written for the Council of Trent in the sixteenth century rather than a Council in the 1960s.

On a portentous day in the Council the voters met to discuss this document. The draft was put to the vote: is this draft unsuitable as a basis for further discussion? A two-thirds majority was needed to remove the document. Voting was as follows: 1368 yes; 822 no; 19 null. It was not the two-thirds required, but the next day John XXIII personally intervened and removed it from further discussion anyway.

It would be 1965 before an alternative appeared. By then John XXIII had died and had been replaced by Paul VI. In the meantime changes had been made in favour of the biblical scholars. The Rector of the Pontifical Biblical Institute had met with the new Pope and asked why two of his professors were still suspended from teaching. Paul VI claimed to have no knowledge of the matter. The suspensions were immediately lifted. The two men had never been formally charged, so they could not be asked to retract anything. It was one of the unexplained anomalies of John XXIII's reign that the visionary who convoked Vatican II and brought warmth and humanity to the papacy could have allowed such a situation to continue throughout his incumbency.

These were exciting times for me to be living in Rome. Academic Rome was in a state of flux and I happily joined in the conversations among my peers and superiors. It could be said that for the most part, my theological studies at the Angelicum reflected a scholarship that revered the past and did not foster innovation. The studies were, I would still maintain, good discipline for the mind and a good foundation for the future but they were not at the cutting edge of research and newness. In particular, this Catholic Theology still had not incorporated the new developments in biblical studies. We were required to concentrate on the Latin text of Thomas Aquinas from the thirteenth century and to study historically the way in which the main Christian teachings had led up to the point where he manipulated them and the way these same teachings had developed down to the present day.

The final examinations, some written and some oral, required us to know a great deal about one hundred broad theological topics or theses. For one exam, I had to write for four hours non-stop in ecclesiastical Latin on one sole topic bringing in Aquinas, the Hebrew and Christian Scriptures, the early Church Fathers and modern opinions.

With this foundation in historical theology, and with a much better grasp of the biblical languages, in September 1964 I went to the Pontifical Biblical Institute, the one founded by Leo XIII, to start my Baccalaureate in Biblical Studies. Any progress in my skills in biblical interpretation had practically been on hold during the year at the Angelicum. Now I would extend the boundaries of the normal science of the revolutionary historical criticism I had learned in Australia.

Chapter 7
STUDYING THE HEBREW SCRIPTURES: ROME

My year at the Pontifical Biblical Institute included several very important learning experiences. In the first place there was a heavy emphasis on languages. Entry into the Baccalaureate was based on passing the Masters degree in Theology (which to that point had taken me seven years full time including the Baccalaureate in Australia) together with passing entry exams in Hebrew and Greek plus one foreign language from English, French and German. It was presumed that students should be competent in the three foreign languages and, since the lectures and examinations were in Latin, fluency in that was a given.

The first revolution was taken for granted at the Institute. We were expected to work within the historical-critical paradigm. However, we were expected to use the best of tools to do so, particularly the linguistic tools.

Having completed the earlier Hebrew and Greek courses, I found that under excellent tutelage I had reached the highpoint of my linguistic abilities. I could read Hebrew and Greek texts with some fluency. I sorely wish today that I could have been able to maintain the momentum I achieved then. During the course of the year, besides advanced studies in Greek and Hebrew, I was also required to learn Aramaic. After two classes we were translating Aramaic texts (since the alphabet is the same as Hebrew and the grammar similar) from the book of Daniel.

Not all the teaching at the Biblical Institute was good. On the negative side, for example, was a course in Biblical History taught by a Jesuit, Vilam Pavlovsky. He was a Pole, a humourless man and a boring lecturer. For him, history was based on quasi-mathematical principles. He worked out biblical dates by logical deduction. He maintained that the kings of Judah and Israel sometimes had a period of co-reign during which a son would rule side by side with his father, that there were different ways of calculating the regnal years of a king in different historical periods, that sometimes the biblical text giving a particular date had been corrupted, but that always the biblical text, using these correctives, gave a reliable sequence of the kings' periods of rule. In this way we worked out the supposed exact dates of all the kings of Israel and Judah. While I admired his ingenuity when, with a blackboard full of figures, he triumphantly showed that the Bible's dates were right, I knew that this was not the way to go.

The Book of Deuteronomy

Of more importance to me was the course run by the late William Moran, an American Jesuit, on the book of Deuteronomy. Moran was a hard taskmaster who ran tutorials on the Hebrew text during which we students were berated and pushed to our limit. However, his lectures and class notes demonstrated that Deuteronomy was a superb piece of writing with complex literary structures incorporated into its text.

For example, very early on we studied the first chapter of Deuteronomy. It contains 46 verses. From this first chapter we removed verses 1-5. This excerpt was, Moran explained, simply an introduction giving notice of the persons involved and the places visited and would have been a late addition to the original text. Then we were shown that the style of writing in verses 9-18 also betrayed a later hand that had added some details to an already existing text. It was also removed. We were left with the remnants of the chapter up to verse 36, where a new section obviously begins. The part of the chapter we were set to study, after the later additions had been removed, read as follows in English with Moses speaking to the people of Israel:

> YHWH our God spoke to us at Horeb, saying: 'You have stayed long enough at this mountain. Resume your journey, and go into the hill country of the Amorites as well as into the neighbouring regions—the Arabah, the hill country, the Shephelah, the Negeb and the seacoast—the land of the Canaanites and the Lebanon, as far as the great river, the river Euphrates. See I have set the land before you; go in and take possession of the land that I swore to your ancestors, to Abraham, to Isaac, and to Jacob, to give to them and to their descendants after them.'

I said to you, 'You have reached the hill country of the Amorites, which YHWH our God is giving us. See, YHWH your God has given the land to you; go up, take possession, as YHWH, the God of your ancestors, has promised you; do not fear or be dismayed.'

All of you came to me and said, 'Let us send men ahead of us to explore the land for us and bring back a report to us regarding the route by which we should god up and cities we will come to.' The plan seemed good to me, and I selected twelve of you, one from each tribe. They set out and went up into the hill country, and when they reached the Valley of Eshcol they spied it out and gathered some of the land's produce, which they brought down to us.

They brought back a report to us, and said, 'It is a good land that YHWH our God is giving us.'

But you were unwilling to go up. You rebelled against the command of YHWH your God; you grumbled in your tents and said, 'It is because YHWH hates us that he has brought us out of the land of Egypt, to hand us over to the Amorites to destroy us. Where are we headed? Our kindred have made our hearts melt by reporting. "The people are stronger and taller than we; the cities are large and fortified up to heaven! We actually saw there the offspring of the Anakim!"'

I said to you, 'Have no dread or fear of them. YHWH your God, who goes before you, is the one who will fight for you, just as he did for you in Egypt before your very eyes, and in the wilderness, where you saw how YHWH your God carried you, just as one carries a child, all the way that you travelled until you reached this place. But in spite of this, you have no trust in YHWH your God, who goes before you on the way to seek out a place for you to camp, in fire by night, and in the cloud by day to show you the route you should take."'

When YHWH heard your words, he was wrathful and swore: 'Not one of these—not one of this evil generation—shall see

> the good land that I swore to give to your ancestors, except Caleb son Jephunneh. He will see it, and to him and to his descendents I will give the land on which he set foot, because of his complete fidelity to YHWH.'

This seemed at first sight a rather pedestrian narrative, peppered with some nondescript dialogue. With enthusiasm, Moran pointed out to us that if we identified the speakers in the text and divided the text according to what they each had to say, an interesting structure would emerge. So, in class, he did just that. He showed us the list of speakers:

YHWH speaks
Moses speaks
The people speak
The scouts speak
The people speak
Moses speaks
YHWH speaks

More importantly, he deftly demonstrated that there was a concentric pattern in this list:

YHWH speaks
  Moses speaks
    The people speak
      The scouts speak
    The people speak
  Moses speaks
YHWH speaks

This is a chiasm, we were told, where the beginning of the text corresponds to the end, the second part to the second last part, the third to the third last and so on. It would have been constructed with full deliberation by some scribe. The isolated centre is the vital key to understanding what a chiasm is about. In this case, it is the announcement by the scouts:

> They brought back a report to us, and said, 'It is a good land that YHWH our God is giving us.'

In other words the extended text was a very clever way of depicting the interaction between a good God and his rather stubborn people of Israel, upon whom he wanted to bestow a good land. In order to understand the tenor of the passage, the isolated centre needed to be understood and then the rest falls into place. Taking sentences piecemeal out of this elaborate pattern would have led to errors of understanding.

There were innumerable patterns like this, some small and some overarching, in the book of Deuteronomy. Continually, slabs of text were placed aside by Moran as being later additions by scribes who had amended the book for any number of reasons. He showed us how some of the text had to be corrected because the transmission of the Hebrew had clearly been faulty.

Gradually, as we worked on the text day after day in class and in our private study, the book of Deuteronomy in all its complexity began to fall into place. In the end I was able to see a complete structure underlying the Hebrew text. I was amazed at the beauty of its literature, at the rather simple but solemn message that it delivered: when the People of YHWH were obedient and followed the mandate of YHWH, they prospered; when they were disobedient, they suffered.

I was also less and less convinced that the events related in this literature were historical. In fact, Moran never brought up that issue.

Biblical Archaeology

One of the other subjects required at the Biblical Institute was Biblical Geography. This was taught by another American Jesuit, the late Robert North. He was a 'dirt archaeologist' who had worked at a number of sites in Jordan in the 1950s and 1960s. An erudite man, he brought a good deal of archaeological experience into his coverage of the geography of the Bible.

For the first time I now confronted the growing anomalies in the revolutionary method I had adopted. It was North who introduced me, in a serious way, to the writings of an important American archaeologist, William Foxwell Albright (1891–1971) whose works I had become vaguely familiar with in Australia. Although I would today reject practically all the conclusions drawn by Albright, his influence on my thinking at that time was significant. He was considered to be the doyen of the historical critical methodology.

Because Albright influenced so many of us in that era of biblical study and provided us with an intellectual basis for pursuing the new revolution of biblical criticism, I think that it is important that we see what his main argument was. Archaeology, in the way Albright understood it, has become known as Biblical Archaeology, the study of the Palestinian past in so far as it impinged on events in the biblical narrative. It was established in the nineteenth century by those interested in Biblical literature and church history and it was largely funded at that time by church-affiliated groups. It set out initially to prove that the Bible was correct in every detail, but later this Biblical Archaeology was content with the lesser task of confirming that the principal characters and events identifiable in the biblical texts were substantially historical.

The earliest explorers in Palestine were quasi-archaeologists and, at the same time, rather literal biblical scholars like Edward Robinson (1794–1863), a professor from Union Theological Seminary in New York, who cursorily examined sites in 1838 and endeavoured to match them with apposite biblical place names and events. This was a maximalist approach which presumed *a priori* that it should be possible to parallel most biblical texts with archaeological findings.

The German liberal Christians of the late nineteenth century, however, saw it the other way: there was little correlation to be found between the physical, archaeological remains in Palestine and the biblical text, since the biblical text was 'mythical'—by which they meant non-historical. This was where liberal Christian scholarship working on the Hebrew Scriptures had reached at the same time as the First Searchers were working on the Christian Scriptures.

A forceful attempt to bridge the divide between the two camps of the literalists and the liberals was undertaken towards the middle of the twentieth century by Albright. His teaching affected a whole generation of mainly English-speaking biblical scholars. Between the 1940s to the 1960s when scepticism over the historicity of biblical texts was rife in Europe, Albright stood firm. Basically, the Hebrew Scriptures, he claimed, reflected historical realities. He was looked up to by an admiring generation of students and they formed themselves into the Albright School.[1]

This Albright School raised hopes for a reconciliation between history and the biblical story, as against what it saw as the subjective and speculative findings of the German scholars. It sought to anchor the Ancestor

1. This School included principally Albright's stalwart disciples John Bright and GF Wright. There seemed to be unanimity even in the alliteration of their names.

period (it was usually called the Patriarchal period in those days) and the Exodus, in particular, as part of the historical record by somewhat uncritical, even if at times ingenuous, harmonisations. This was the sort of scholarship I had been searching for.

First, we need to see what was meant by the Ancestor period and the Exodus. Abraham, the supposed father of the people of Israel was said, according to the Torah, to have left his native city of Ur (presumably in Mesopotamia) and journeyed, at God's command, with his family to the land of Canaan. He had settled there and had a son, Isaac. Isaac would eventually have a son Jacob, also known as Israel. Jacob-Israel had twelve sons by four wives who became the twelve founding fathers of the twelve tribes of Israel.

ABRAHAM
↓
ISAAC
↓
JACOB-ISRAEL

Rachel	***Leah***	***Bilhah***	***Zilpah***
*Joseph**	*Reuben*	*Dan*	*Gad*
Benjamin	*Simeon*	*Naphtali*	*Asher*
	Levi		
	Judah		
	Issachar		
	Zebulun		

*Joseph was the father of Ephraim and Manasseh who were sometimes counted as founders of tribes rather than Joseph. In that case, either Simeon or Levi were omitted from the Twelve Tribes list.

The stories concerning Abraham, Isaac and Jacob (together with stories about their wives who are mostly invisible) are called Ancestor Stories.

The Torah also relates that the sons of Jacob, during a second phase of the story, went down to Egypt in a time of famine. The events are recorded in the latter part of the book of Genesis, a section identified as a novella about Joseph. They were at first welcomed by the Pharaoh, whom the Torah does not further identify. This was because Joseph, one of the sons of Rachel, had established himself as vizier to the Pharaoh.

At some later date, however, the growing number of descendants, who became known as the Israelites, was seen as a threat to national security and persecution broke out. The Israelites were subjected to slave labour in order to build supply cities and were required to expose their male offspring as a form of infanticide. On the very verge of annihilation the people were led to freedom by a leader, Moses (see figure 4). He led the people on a circuitous route through the wilderness of Sinai accompanied by wonders such as the crossing of the Sea of Reeds, the provision of miraculous food and drink and columns of cloud and fire to point the right direction in the desert. This event has become known as the Exodus (the Greek word for 'exit') and there is a protracted account of this Exodus in the books of Exodus, Leviticus, Numbers and Deuteronomy.

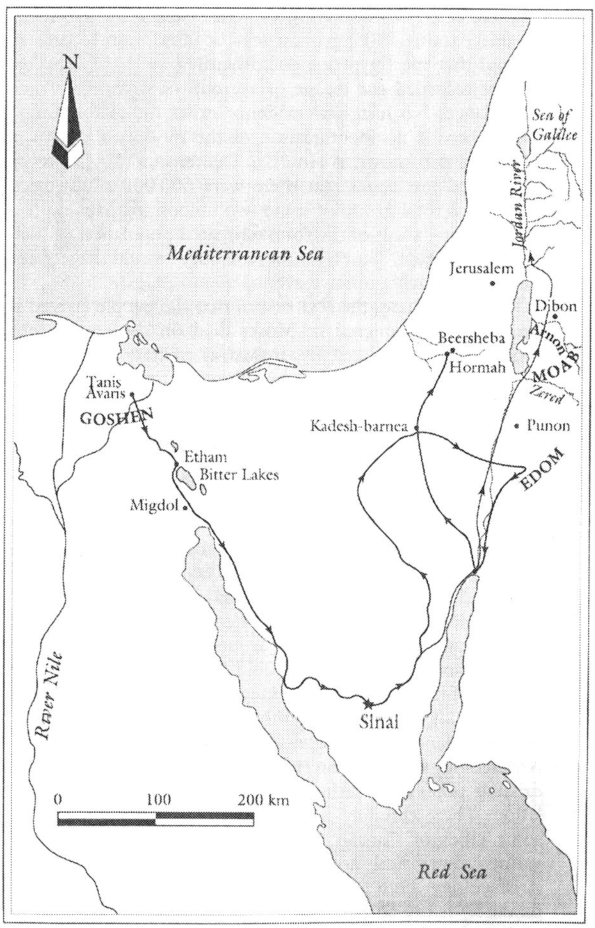

Figure 4: The supposed path of the Exodus following the biblical text

At an unidentified sacred mountain, somewhere in the Sinai peninsula, the group was said to have met its God, whose personal name was YHWH. This was the name revealed first of all to Moses and interpreted in the text of Exodus as meaning 'I am Who am', although its real meaning and origin is undoubtedly shrouded in past history. There at Sinai, the people of Israel made a covenant or treaty with YHWH. According to the terms of this covenant he would be their God and they would be his people.

In a third phase, the text relates that the people arrived in Canaan and conquered it. Moses had died on the eve of their entry and was replaced by Joshua as military commander. Under Joshua the people miraculously crossed the Jordan river (with the waters halting and allowing a dry passage) and immediately took the cities of Jericho and 'Ai in the very heartland of Canaan. From this central staging area they moved first south and then north, destroying cities, receiving submissions, occasionally making treaties. Soon the land was theirs and they parcelled it out among the twelve tribes. This story is recounted in the book of Joshua and part of Judges.

Faced with these Ancestor stories and the Exodus story, the Albright School attempted to bring the biblical story into line with historical fact. There was one clear date: the biblical text's forthright statement that there had been 430 years spent by the Israelites in Egypt.

> The time that the Israelites had lived in Egypt was four hundred and thirty years. At the end of four hundred and thirty years, on that very day, all the companies of YHWH went out from the land of Egypt. (Exodus 12:40)

Subsequently, the text stated that there were 480 years from the Exodus to the building of the first Temple which it said took place in the fourth year of Solomon:

> In the four hundred and eightieth year after the Israelites came out of the land of Egypt, in the fourth year of Solomon's reign over Israel, in the month of Ziv, which is the second month, he began to build the house of YHWH. (1 Kings 6:1).

Scholars were able to add the lengths of reigns of the kings of Judah given in the biblical text up to the destruction of Jerusalem by the Babylonians in 586 BCE and work out that the fourth year of Solomon would have been around 1016 BCE. These dates seemed to supply sufficient data, therefore, on which to establish a reliable chronological grid for major events in the biblical story.

Using other chronological notations in the Hebrew text, the descent of Jacob and his family into Egypt had been earlier dated to 1926 BCE, with 2216 BCE being given as the date of the birth of Abraham. The sojourn of the People of Israel in Egypt would therefore have begun at the end of Egypt's Twelfth Dynasty, and would have continued through the entire Thirteenth Dynasty, the Hyksos occupation (more will be said about these people later) and part of the reign of the female pharaoh, Hatshepsut.

The Exodus would have taken place in 1496 BCE and the conquest of Canaan, after forty years of wandering in the desert (also mentioned in the biblical text), would have taken place in 1456 BCE following Thutmosis III's victorious campaigns. At that stage, Canaan belonged to Egypt. The period of the Judges, as recounted in the Book of Judges, could then be dated to 1456–1080 BCE and would have coincided with the Egyptian empire's control over Palestine.

For some historians these dates were sufficient. But, the Albright School was intent on removing any perceived discrepancies and they devised subtle stratagems to reconcile biblical dates even further with known historical facts. The biblical text's 480 years from the Exodus until the building of the temple seemed too long and was therefore interpreted as a symbolic number representing twelve generations—each one being approximately forty years. But, the Albright School claimed, the average span of a physical human generation of that time was not forty but more like twenty years. Hence 480 years in the biblical text should be read as 240 actual years (12 x 20 instead of 12 x 40). The Exodus could thereupon be dated from the time of the building of the Temple at 1256 BCE (1016 + 240) rather than 1496 BCE.

That was a great relief as the new date brought the chronology of the Exodus into line with the reign of Rameses II. Because of this, the reference to 'Rameses' in Exodus 1:11 was adequately explained: 'They built supply cities, Pithom and Rameses, for Pharaoh.' This Rameses was, the Albright School said, Rameses II of whom quite a deal was known in the historical record.

Next, the Albright School looked askance at Genesis 15:13-16:

> Then YHWH said to Abram, 'Know this for certain, that your offspring shall be aliens in a land that is not theirs, and

> shall be slaves there, and they shall be oppressed for four hundred and thirty years; . . . and they shall come back here in the fourth generation.

Since the text referred to the sojourn of the Israelites in Egypt lasting four generations, the Albright School maintained that the 430 years mentioned in the biblical text should be abbreviated to 80 actual years (ie 4 x 20, on the same assumption as above) and the descent of the Ancestor Jacob into Egypt should therefore be placed in the fourteenth century (1256 + 80 = 1336 BCE).

Having situated the Ancestor period neatly in the early second millennium by this historical sleight of hand, it then seemed fortuitous that archaeological information from contemporary periods at sites such as Mari on the Euphrates, Nuzi in Iraq, Alalakh in Syria and Ugarit on the Syrian coast were coming into the public domain. These sites provided names, customs and other parallels that corresponded to similar traditions as found in the book of Genesis dealing with the Ancestor period and verified that the chronology they had espoused must be correct.

For example, equivalents were found for names like 'Abraham' and 'Benjamin' in these texts; parallel customs were found for the Genesis story of Abraham's adoption of a male heir and the provision of a substitute wife for an infertile one. However, many of these parallels have since been questioned and there does not seem to be any evidence that the stock of Semitic names or customary law can be isolated to any single ethnic group or any particular period within the ancient world. Still, by the 1960s even the more reputable scholars from the Albright School were studying the texts from archaeological sites at Mari, Nuzi, Alalakh and Ugarit to find all sorts of remarkable parallels that 'proved' the biblical text to be historically reliable.

From the Egyptian New Kingdom there came other texts which described the general conditions of the times and the ethnic groups who lived in Palestine and Egypt during the Late Bronze period (1500–1300 BCE). These texts seemed to form a body of writing from which a correlation between Egypt and Palestine could be constructed and with which the Ancestor period, the sojourn in Egypt and the Exodus could be synchronised.

These New Kingdom texts included Papyrus Anastasi 1, the account of an Egyptian officer who crossed the Palestinian highlands. It demonstrates clearly how unsafe travel was in the highlands, with virtually no Egyptian control and the traveller ever subject to attack by nomads. More important still was the discovery of 350 cuneiform letters in the ruins of Tell Amarna, the capital of the 'heretic' pharaoh, Akhenaten. These reports to the Pharaoh concerning the deteriorating conditions in Palestine made frequent reference to a group in Palestine known as the *'apiru*. The *'apiru* were wanderers, semi-nomads with small herds of goats and flocks of sheep. They moved around the Fertile Crescent between Mesopotamia and Palestine. For those anxious to find correlations, people like those allied to the Albright School, this term *'apiru* was suspiciously like 'Hebrew' or *heber* since, in Semitic languages, the vowels were easily changed and it was the consonants that counted, although *p* and *b* were often transposed. Therefore, *'-p-r* and *h-b-r* could have been the same word.

However, the most telling text was on the Merneptah stele, a victory column recounting all the victories in the Asian area of the nineteenth dynasty pharaoh, Merneptah, who reigned 1212–1202 BCE. The stele would have been erected about 1207 BCE. It contains the earliest known reference to the word 'Israel' outside the biblical texts. The relevant section reads:

> The Princes are prostrate, saying 'Peace!'
> Not one raises his head among the Nine Bows.
> Desolate is Tehenu: Hatti is pacified;
> Plundered is Canaan with every evil;
> Carried off is Ashkelon; seized upon is Gezer;
> Yanoam is made as that which does not exist;
> Israel is laid waste, his seed is not.[2]

It was the last line that grabbed attention. The hieroglyphic determinant for 'Israel' indicates that the text is referring to a people and not a territorial state. This was the crowning proof for the Albright School. Israel had arrived in Palestine somewhere before 1200 BCE but had not by then completely settled. Hence the manner in which the name of 'Israel' was written on the stele indicated an unsettled people.

Another significant clue was found in the hieroglyphic text on the walls of Medinet Habu, the funerary temple of the female pharaoh, Hatshepsut. Dated from about 1175 BCE, it recounted the fierce battle of the pharaoh Rameses III against the 'Sea Peoples'. The Sea Peoples included a group

2. The text is in JB Pritchard (1969), *Ancient Near Eastern Texts Relating to the Old Testament*, Princeton University Press: Princeton , 376–378.

called the *paleset* and that name seemed to correspond to the Philistines, the enemy of Israel who figured so prominently in the biblical texts of the book of Judges. Goliath had been a Philistine leader, brought low by David. The *paleset* or Philistines must have settled in Palestine some time after the Israelites and the two groups then came into conflict.

What could be made from these snippets of information? If there had been *'apiru* or Hebrews and an 'Israel' in Palestine from about 1207 BCE, and if the Philistines had been present in Egypt from about 1175 BCE, then this evidence pointed to the fact that the conquest of Canaan by the Hebrews, otherwise known as the Israelites, however it may have taken place, would need to be dated sometime after 1200 BCE. Once this date for the conquest had been confidently established, then other dates gleaned from the biblical text could be organised around it.

Thus, having determined what they considered to be a reliable and historically accurate time-line, the biblical historians saw their task as filling it in with a plausible sequence of events. While the events related in the biblical texts regarding the Ancestors and the Exodus from Egypt raised difficulties, the conquest of Palestine as described in the texts seemed at first to offer a more coherent historical outline. But, there was one blatant problem: the Bible contained two discrepant versions of the conquest of Palestine.

Jericho and the Conquest

The first of these is described in the book of Joshua—a united and coherent conquest of the land of Canaan (see figure 5). According to this story, the tribes under Joshua crossed the Jordan and mounted a central campaign. They besieged Jericho and took it. This was the pivotal victory, with the walls tumbling down when Joshua ordered the sacred trumpets to be sounded. The Israelite army then attacked 'Ai and Gibeon, and their forces moved into the hill country around Jerusalem. However they did not take Jerusalem. Instead, they marched swiftly to the south and took the cities of Makkedah, Libnah, Lachish, Eglon, Hebron and Debir. Finally they turned north and destroyed the city of Hazor which was called 'the head of all those kingdoms'.

However, there is another version of the story in Judges 1. This story recounts a series of individual and isolated battles with cities that included Jerusalem, Hebron and Debir. The book of Judges gives the distinct impression that Israelites, Philistines and Canaanites lived side by side throughout the period of the 'conquest' and recounts the frequent crises resulting from the tensions between them. These crises were met by the twelve 'Judges', interim leaders who organised an Israelite military force, although never a fully united one.

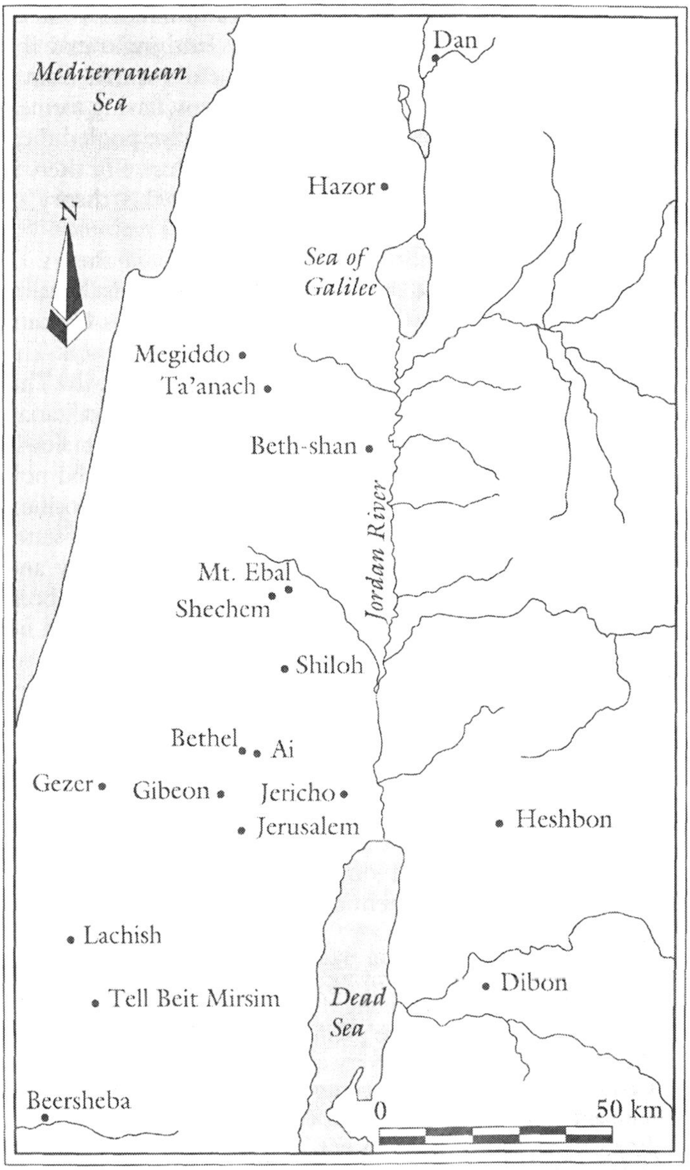

Figure 5: Sites in Canaan referred to in the texts regarding Settlement.

How could the two biblical stories plus the archaeological data be reconciled into one fluent historical account? That was the dominant aim of the Albright School. Before that could be tackled, however, there was one further festering problem: the archaeology of Jericho.

Jericho is to the north of Jerusalem and two kilometres outside the present-day town, which is mentioned in the Christian Scriptures as 'Jericho'. What remained was a huge mound or *tell* (which is simply the Arabic word for 'mound'), known as Tell es-Sultan. Since the last century this great *tell* had been a veritable honey-pot, drawing archaeologists to it. It seemed obvious that this desolate mound must cover the ancient Jericho of earlier biblical times.

No story in the Bible was as dramatic as that describing the walls of Jericho tumbling down; none it seemed could be so easily verified. The biblical narrative recounts how Joshua led the army of Israel across the Jordan river and confronted the armed might of the city of Jericho. On six successive days Joshua and the Israelite priests led a procession around the walls. On the seventh day they marched around the city seven times and then the priests blew the sacred trumpets. The walls of Jericho collapsed. Beneath the *tell* there must still lay those very walls which Joshua had dismantled. They just needed to be dug up.

In 1867 the Palestine Exploration Fund, set up earlier by the British Government, despatched a team to the *tell* at Jericho. The expedition was unsuccessful. It found some pottery but little else. Archaeology was then in its infancy. Later, in 1908–1911 an Austro-German team returned to the *tell*. They caused excitement when they found two lines of wall surrounding the *tell* ruins. But in those days dates could only be assigned if there were inscriptions or coins in the dig that actually recorded a date. There were none such. Joshua's Jericho was retaining its secret.

In 1930, John Garstang, an eminent British archaeologist, went back to Jericho. Under the auspices of the British School of Archaeology, based in Jerusalem, he dug through the *tell* and came upon the two lines of wall. By this stage archaeologists (following the lead of Flinders Petrie in Egypt) had learned to date by means of pottery. Pottery goes through fashions which can be dated just as we can date old photos by the hats, cars, even hair styles of those whose pictures have been taken. Archaeologists can date ruins by pottery styles found in the ruins. Garstang dated the outer wall to about 1400 BCE and announced to the world that he had found the wall destroyed by Joshua. Indeed the wall showed signs of violent destruction and there was even evidence of a fire that had affected it in parts.

To many practising Christians, Garstang's find was the cause of deep consolation, even jubilation. Here was tangible proof that one of the most spectacular events of the Bible, the collapse of the walls of Jericho as Joshua's army sounded the trumpets, was true. If this was true, then the rest surely must be true. But for many biblical historians Garstang's discovery brought only perplexity. His date of 1400 BCE was far too early!

As we have seen, working for many years on other data, biblical historians had been trying to identify a firm date for the Exodus of the people of Israel out of Egypt. Most scholars, mainly on the basis of the Stele of Merneptah and other archaeological digs, opted for a date just after 1250 BCE which would allow the People of Israel to arrive, after forty years of wandering, in Canaan in time to be recorded on Merneptah's stele in 1207 BCE. But here was Garstang saying that the destruction of Jericho, the first battle of the campaign to take the land, would have already taken place in 1400 BCE! It was some 200 years before they wanted it.

The years after Garstang concluded his digging at Tell es-Sultan saw many attempts to reconcile his date with other evidence. There was disarray among the scholars and some consternation among those few Christian believers who realised what was happening. So, in 1952 the British School of Archaeology decided to re-do Garstang's work. They asked Kathleen (later Dame Kathleen) Kenyon to go back to the *tell* and duplicate the previous work. Garstang had not of course destroyed the *tell*. He had cut through it at certain points and interpreted the layers as he went down. Kenyon did the same but at other places in the *tell*.

From the onset her findings were nothing less than sensational. Jericho, she discovered, was the oldest city known upon earth. Its origins could be placed well before 8000 BCE when a Stone Age people had moved into the area, attracted by the spring and the fertile land. They had built, close to the spring, a religious shrine. Perhaps a thousand years later another group had built a city on a more monumental scale. They constructed houses with mudbricks shaped like vienna loaves of bread and used mud for mortar.

They protected their city with a wall three metres thick. Within that wall Kenyon found a stone tower, nine metres high and eight and a half metres in diameter. The tower incorporated an inner staircase. Here was a fully functional city, with advanced technology and sophisticated defences, some four thousand years before the Egyptians united around the Nile or the Sumerians flourished in Mesopotamia. As a start, ancient history needed to be rewritten.

Kenyon then documented how a number of peoples had successively lived in Jericho, building and rebuilding over the millennia and changing the layout of the city.

But a greater surprise was to follow. Kenyon discovered that Garstang had erred over 'Joshua's wall'. The wall he had uncovered had actually collapsed before 2000 BCE, not in 1400 BCE. In fact that line of wall had been damaged severely or been thrown down some seventeen times in all and another new wall had been built around 1900 BCE by a new group who occupied the site. They only survived there for a relatively short period before, in 1580 BCE or so, the Egyptian army had attacked Jericho. The walls were again destroyed at that time—and never rebuilt.

Shock waves went through the world of biblical scholarship. There had been no walls of Jericho, therefore, since around 1580 BCE? In fact, there were only scattered remnants found at the *tell*—a juglet and an open-air oven—to record any occupation at all since that date. It looked as if, at any time the Israelites might conceivably have come into the land after the Exodus, the city of Jericho had already been a ruin. It would have been a *tell* when the Israelites arrived.

Kathleen Kenyon was profoundly embarrassed by her results. She had been sent to solve a problem; she had provoked a worse one. I met her in 1965 in Jerusalem. She was a formidable lady, most self-assured. I heard her deliver her official report at the Palestine Archaeological Museum (later known as the Rockefeller Museum) in Jerusalem, explaining the results of her years of excavation. Certainly, she stated, there was no Joshua wall and no signs of occupation from the period when Joshua would have been expected to have taken the city. Why? Because wind and rain had eroded away the walls and the city of that time. I do not think she ever really believed her own story.

Some scholars in desperation did clutch at the erosion theory. Others sought new explanations: perhaps the Exodus had taken place before 1580 BCE; perhaps Kenyon was mistaken, just as she claimed Garstang had been; or perhaps Tell es-Sultan never was Jericho in the first place.

It was in Robert North's class in Rome that I first heard of the Albright School and of these real problems with the archaeology of Jericho and their impact on the question of the Exodus out of Egypt. The anomalies with the 'normal science' that I had first learned in Australia were growing. But, North also offered us two 'models' in currency to solve the problem of the Exodus and still retain confidence that the Bible recounted basic history.

The 'conquest model'

The most popular of the models to explain how the Exodus event could be reconciled with the archaeology of Jericho came to be known as the 'conquest model'. It had been the commonly held model and it was driven further by the Albright School.

The conquest model is based on a literal reading of the biblical tradition and assumes that no people would have invented such a disreputable account of their origins. The most respected spokesperson for this model was Albright himself who, as explained above, accepted the biblical texts as ready-made history, even if it was incomplete. He supplemented and embellished that history by means of the material derived from ancient Near Eastern literature and archaeology.

Putting such sources together, Albright identified the Israelite ancestors in Canaan during the Ancestral period as the *'apiru* or Hebrews of the Amarna Letters. These Hebrews, he claimed, later descended into Egypt during the Hyksos period. These Hyksos were identified by the third century BCE Egyptian priest and historian, Manetho as newcomers who gained control of upper Egypt during a period of weakness. In his *Aegyptiaca*, a valuable history of ancient Egypt, he writes:

> . . . unexpectedly, from the regions of the East, invaders of an obscure race *(asemoi)* marched in confidence of victory against our land. By main force they easily overpowered the rulers of the land, they then burned our cities ruthlessly, razed to the ground the temples of the gods, and treated all the natives with a cruel hostility, massacring some and leading into slavery the wives and children of others. Finally, they appointed as king one of their number whose name was Salitis. He had his seat at Memphis, levying tribute from Upper and Lower Egypt and always leaving garrisons behind in the most advantageous positions. Above all, he fortified the district to the east, foreseeing that the Assyrians, as they grew stronger, would one day covet and attack his kingdom.
>
> In the Saite nome he founded a city very favourably situated on the east of the Bubastite branch of the Nile, and called Auaris after an ancient religious tradition. This place he rebuilt and fortified with massive walls, planting there a garrison of as many as 240,000 heavy-armed men to guard his frontier.

> Here he would come in summertime, partly to serve out rations and pay his troops, partly to train them carefully in manoeuvres and so strike terror into foreign tribes.
>
> (Manetho, *Aegyptiaca frag 42: 1.75-79.2)*

The Hyksos were called *asemoi* by Manetho in this text. Usually translated as 'obscure' or 'unknown', this clue sent modern historians looking for some group that would have been 'unknown' to the Egyptians.

But this was a first of many errors in the Albright reconstruction. The Egyptian term which Manetho was translating by *asemoi* should have been translated by 'vile' or 'ignoble'. It was a common epithet used by Egyptians to describe any outside group. There was in addition a second error. The name 'Hyksos' was interpreted by historians as a tribal name. It should have been recognised as a garbled Greek version of the generic Egyptian term for 'rulers of foreign lands'. Hence, there never were any people called the Hyksos and they were not obscure or unknown. Whoever they were and by whatever name they were called, they were well known to the Egyptians.

We have the personal names of some of these 'Hyksos' people from Egyptian inscriptions. They are Semitic names and it seems certain that we are dealing with a group who had come from Palestine and overran Egypt at a time when it was weak. The pharaoh who led the counterattack against them, Kamose, described them as coming from the 'land of the Asiatics' and having a Syrian leader. There is no great mystery about them.

It can be presumed that at some time when Egypt was at a low ebb in world power and when the Palestinian population was in uncustomary ascendancy, at least some part of Egypt was conquered by this Semitic group. They moved from a base in the northern delta region to the valley and took Memphis. It would have been a matter of considerable embarrassment for later Egyptians to have recorded this occupation. The 'Hyksos' were expelled from Egypt and forced to return back to the Palestinian region.

Returning to the conquest model, we hear that the Israelites, having settled into the Delta area during the Hyksos period, were persecuted by the dynastic Egyptians who had regained control. They were forced to construct the store cities of the pharaohs and to become slaves. This was the time when Moses became their leader. Under Moses they were led out of Egypt in the Exodus. They travelled through the Sinai peninsula and met their God, YHWH. Eventually, they reached the land of Canaan. Moses died and was succeeded by Joshua.

Under Joshua, they first of all took Jericho (despite the problems with the archaeology). Then they attacked 'Ai, which was a ruined *tell*, where defenders from nearby Shechem had positioned themselves. (In this way, Albright offset the argument that archaeology clearly identified 'Ai as a *tell*.) The Israelites then conquered the whole of Canaan, divided the land among the twelve tribes, occupied the cities and rebuilt them.

This new settlement would have had to leave some traces. The archaeological evidence, the theory claims, shows that in the central Palestinian area there was a period of gradual and complex transition from Late Bronze Age culture (1550–1200) to the Iron 1 Age culture (1200–900).

This vital claim is also open to contention. Certainly, the local Canaanite culture underwent some change, but there is no evidence of a conquest or a concerted revolt by the local inhabitants, only sporadic instances here and there of destructive violence. This cultural situation can be explained by the fact that, from the thirteenth to the twelfth centuries BCE, the traditional centres of power in the Fertile Crescent, Anatolia and around the Mediterranean had lost their control. Consequently, Canaanite groups that previously had been politically restrained were able to assert themselves without pressure. It could be expected that groups, profiting from the lull in control, would have developed new cultural forms. There is no need to postulate the arrival of a new population.

There was a personal agenda behind this conquest model. Albright, ever the conservative Christian, wanted to refute those earlier evolutionary theories, particularly Wellhausen's, that had maintained Israelite religion, having originally worshipped a number of gods, had only progressively come to believe in a single God. For Albright, the original Mosaic tradition was already firmly monotheistic and this constituted what was special about it. The major strands that made up the Torah - J, E, D and P - all gave similar witness to the story of Moses; there could be no historical doubt about it. The historical Moses had been the first person to believe in One God, and this cemented his place in the Israelite tradition.

Why was this so important to Albright? For him as a Christian, the monotheism of Israel was already leading to Christian monotheism with its belief in the Trinity.

However, Robert North also told us about another model, one proposed in more recent times by the German scholar, Martin Noth. In the Roman classroom, this was the first time I had heard of Noth. Later, he would also be influential in my thinking.

The 'peaceful infiltration model'

Martin Noth had proposed a second model known as the 'peaceful infiltration model'. It was based on his literary theory which he had developed with another and older German scholar, Albrecht Alt. They were both skeptical regarding the historical reliability of the biblical narratives and doubted whether archaeology could be reconciled with these literary traditions.

They claimed that biblical stories, such as the taking of Jericho and 'Ai, were aetiological legends, meant to explain the existence of substantial ruins found by Israelites at some stage in central Palestine. These ruins were attributed by the settled Israelites to the destruction wrought by an invasion of their 'Ancestors'. There would have been an appropriate religious ritual that accompanied a tale of victory and destruction for the sake of succeeding generations. In time the ritual infiltrated the story. Hence, the circling of Jericho's walls by invading Israelites, as described in Joshua 6, would have originally been a ritual circumambulation in celebration of the presumed victory of the Ancestors. This ritual action would have later been read back into the story of the event: the Ancestors had circled the city before its immediate destruction.

Alt and Noth made use of the Amarna letters from the period of Akhenaten, and their correlation with the biblical texts, to show that the area settled by the Israelites in the central hill area was never heavily occupied in the Late Bronze age. The Israelites did not threaten and certainly did not displace the previous Canaanite population. They had arrived as small groups of peaceful pastoral nomads in the process of settling down to an agricultural way of life. They came at various times from a number of areas and settled in different places. They were completely different to the Canaanites. They looked to a 'God of the Father or Ancestor', a tribal god, as their spiritual leader. The typical Israelite apodictic commandments, with their insistence on 'Thou shalt not . . . ', were unique to them.

In contrast to the Israelites, the Canaanites had their own gods, such as 'El and Ba'al, and their own distinctive agricultural laws. The 'taking of the land' was a gradual and peaceful settlement by originally unrelated tribal groups who formed an entity called 'Israel'. Noth was insistent that this entity had taken the form of an amphictyony, a confederation of twelve tribes, a social unit previously known in ancient Greece and other places.

This second model required three postulates: Canaanite city states which had possession of the land prior to the arrival of the nomads; an amphictyony formed around a central shrine; and nomads in search of a place to settle.

At a later date the Israelites were said, according to Alt and Noth, to have expanded their territorial gains with raids on neighbouring Canaanites, but these were sporadic and disorganised. In the process of coming into contact with the agriculturally based Canaanites, the Israelites adopted some of their practices and subsequently developed their uniquely Israelite way of life.

By this stage my mind in Rome was in top gear. As far as the general approach to the Hebrew Scriptures was concerned there had been no further revolution since the early days under Jerome. However, I was very much engaged in filling in the gaps and extending the boundaries. I turned at times to literary methods, at other times to the Albright School and at still other times to Martin Noth's theory. In doing so, I became aware of more and more anomalies.

The conquest of Canaan seemed to be such a pivotal event in any history of Israel and yet here there were doubts about how it actually took place and indeed, if there was no Jericho at that time and no change in the cultural setting, whether it had historically taken place. I was also more and more aware that the biblical text was a very human affair, admirable but constructed like any great literature. It no longer read like a historical text in any sense of the word. Yet, here was I maintaining that Christian thought and Christian practice was built on history. Where was the evidence for that history?

I was becoming aware that, as a student of biblical texts, I was drifting intellectually further and further from mainstream Catholicism. Also, the anomalies with my methodology were multiplying. I felt that I was extending the limits of the first revolution to breaking point. There were deep problems with the historical-critical approach. I was most unsure what would come next.

Note

The Albright School had a prolific output in the 1960s. Their leader, W. F Albright, summed up much of his thinking in a handy book, *The Biblical Period. From Abraham to Ezra*, New York and Evanston, 1963. John Bright's major work was *The History of Israel*, London, first published in 1960 while GE Wright wrote *Biblical Archaeology* second edition, Philadelphia and London first published in 1961.

On the other side of the fence, Martin Noth wrote *A History of Israel* Westminster: Philadelphia, 1950.

Chapter 8
STUDYING THE CHRISTIAN SCRIPTURES: ROME

In the alternate semester at the Biblical Institute, a Belgian Jesuit, Ignace de la Potterie (also now deceased), taught us a course on the passion narrative in John's gospel, the story of Jesus' suffering and death in chapters 18 and 19. Again, the stress was on the literary structure of the text and reclaiming a true history. The first paradigm was being pushed to its boundaries. Even if De la Potterie himself believed that the text reflected historical realities, and I am sure that he did as he was more conservative than Moran, I could see that such was not a necessary conclusion. The text lived its own life and I was becoming more and more convinced that there was little that could be called history in all of it.

John's Passion Story

De la Potterie showed us, for example, how the section in John's gospel concerning the condemnation of Jesus by Pilate had been constructed. De la Potterie's own thought had been stimulated by some earlier scholars, but in the main he put his results down to his own doggedness in examining the Greek text. He once confessed that he had spent an entire Sunday reading the Greek text of John to see how often a certain grammatical sequence of words occurred. It seemed to me that this use of time would be well worth the effort. The Belgian analysed the scene of Jesus appearing before Pilate. The secret was to recognise the writer's use of the two Greek verbs: *eiselthein*, 'to go in' and *exelthein*, 'to go out'.

> Pilate ***went out*** to them (the Jewish authorities) and said, 'What accusation do you bring against this man? They an-

swered, 'If this man were not a criminal, we would not have handed him over to you.' Pilate said to them, 'Take him yourselves and judge him according to your law.' The Jews replied, 'We are not permitted to put anyone to death.' (This was to fulfil what Jesus had said when he indicated the kind of death he was to die.)

Then Pilate ***went in*** the headquarters again, summoned Jesus, and asked him, 'Are you the King of the Jews?' Jesus answered, 'Do you ask this on your own, or did others tell you about me?' Pilate replied, 'I am not a Jew, am I? Your own nation and the chief priests have handed you over to me. What have you done?' Jesus answered, 'My kingdom is not from this world. If my kingdom were from this world, my followers would be fighting to keep me from being handed over to the Jews. But as it is, my kingdom is not from here.' Pilate asked him, 'So you are a king?' Jesus answered, 'You say that I am a king. For this I was born, and for this I came into the world, to testify to the truth. Everyone who belongs to the truth listens to my voice.' Pilate asked him, 'What is truth?'

After he had said this, he ***went out*** to the Jews again and told them, 'I find no case against him. But you have a custom that I release someone for you at the Passover. Do you want me to release for you the King of the Jews?' They shouted in reply, 'Not this man, but Barabbas!' Now Barabbas was a bandit.

Then Pilate took Jesus and had him flogged. And the soldiers wove a crown of thorns and put it on his head, and they dressed him in a purple robe. They kept coming up to him, saying, 'Hail, King of the Jews!' and striking him on the face.

Pilate ***went out*** again and said to them, 'Look, I am bringing him out to you to let you know that I find no case against him.' So Jesus came out, wearing the crown of thorns and the purple robe. Pilate said to them, 'Here is the man!' When the chief priests and the police saw him, they shouted, 'Crucify him! Crucify him!' Pilate said to them, 'Take him yourselves and crucify him.' The Jews answered him, 'We have a law, and

> according to that law he ought to die because he has claimed to be the Son of God.
>
> Now when Pilate heard this, he was more afraid than ever.
>
> He ***went in*** to his headquarters again and asked Jesus, 'Where are you from?' But Jesus gave him no answer. Pilate therefore said to him, 'Do you refuse to speak to me? Do you not know that I have power to release you, and power to crucify you?' Jesus answered him, 'You would have no power over me unless it had been given you from above; therefore the one who handed me over to you is guilty of a greater sin.' From then on Pilate tried to release him, but the Jews cried out, 'If you release this man, you are no friend of the emperor. Everyone who claims to be a king sets himself against the emperor.'
>
> When Pilate heard these words, he ***brought out*** Jesus and seated him on the judge's bench at a place called Lithostratos or in Hebrew Gabbatha. Now it was the day of Preparation for the Passover; and it was about noon. He said to the Jews, 'Here is your King!' They cried out, 'Away with him! Away with him! Crucify him!' Pilate asked them, 'Shall I crucify your King!' The chief priests answered, 'We have no king but the emperor.' Then he handed him over to them to be crucified.

De la Potterie played his trump card with us. He had the text with these verbs highlighted. With a certain unwonted enthusiasm he asked: had we noticed that Pilate goes out of the praetorium twice without going back inside? Why? Because the verbs mark off another chiasm and, of course, the chiasm usually has a centre. The centre was surrounded by the two 'going outs'.

Hence, the structure was as follows with corresponding scenes containing related material:

Scene 1: Pilate goes out The Jews demand Jesus' death	**Scene 7**: Pilate brings Jesus out The Jews demand Jesus' death
Scene 2: Pilate goes in Jesus declares that he the King of Truth	**Scene 6**: Pilate goes in Jesus discusses Pilate's power
Scene 3: Pilate goes out He declares Jesus to be innocent	**Scene 5**: Pilate goes out He declares Jesus to be innocent

Scene 4:
Jesus is scourged and crowned with thorns

The isolated scene, Scene 4, is unexpectedly the important one. In this scene Jesus is enthroned on Pilate's own judgement seat (despite the fact that most translations maintain that Pilate seated *himself* on the judgement seat) and, forced to wear in ignominy the royal insignia of crown of thorns and purple robe, he is presented as the King of Israel to the people by the Roman authority. This demonstration of kingship, even if performed in such an ironic way by the soldiers, was the key to understanding what the trial was about.

I found this literary work to be very persuasive, even exhilarating. I also realised that the text carried an important message, even if that same text was not necessarily historically accurate. How could the minute details of action and speech in the trial before Pilate have been accurately recorded? Could anyone be certain that this was historically how the trial had been carried out? Further, would an historical Jesus have been seated by Pilate on his own official curial seat? Most unlikely. But, then, did it matter?

At different points in interpreting the text we did similar literary gymnastics. The Christian gospels were very clever, human documents.

The Biblical Commission speaks

In 1964, while I was still engrossed in my studies in Rome, the Biblical Commission issued an *Instruction on the Historical Truth of the Gospels.* Up to this point the Biblical Commission had been, particularly as regards the Christian Scriptures, very conservative. This document, on the contrary, began with praise for the work of biblical scholars, quoting the admonition of Pius XII in the 1943 encyclical, *Divino Afflante Spiritu,* that they should be treated with charity. It stated further that the biblical scholar should

> diligently employ the new exegetical aids, above all those which the historical method, taken in its widest sense, offers to him—a method which carefully investigates sources and defines their nature and value, and makes use of such helps as textual criticism, literary criticism and the study of languages.

The most important section of the new document, however, outlined the three stages through which the written gospel materials had developed: the actual events of the life of Jesus, the traditions handed on in the early church and thirdly the gospel writers who put those traditions into order and wrote them down. This was neither more nor less what Bultmann and the Formcritics had proposed decades earlier.

The document, when dealing with the first stage, pointed out that the disciples, well equipped to be witnesses of what Jesus said and did, understood his activities as 'deeds performed or designed that men (*sic*) might believe in Christ through them'. It also stated that Jesus' teaching would have followed 'the modes of reasoning and exposition which were in vogue at the time'. At the second stage the apostles would have 'interpreted his words and deeds according to the needs of their listeners' which indicated, of course, that oral transmission had affected the actual form of the traditions.

After so many years the importance of the preliterary stage of the gospel tradition, the basic premise of Formcriticism, had been recognised by the Vatican authorities with some cautious safeguards. The document claimed that the evangelists, at the third stage of gospel formation, from the many things that had come down to them from Jesus

> selected some things, reduced others to a synthesis, and still others they explicated, keeping in mind the situation of the churches.

The Catholic biblical constituency could not believe that it was hearing correctly. This was all in line, more or less, with the modern methods in vogue, even if it was coming a little late. There was overt rejoicing in the corridors of the Pontifical Biblical Institute. They had been vindicated. They were no longer under siege.

This was the end of my two years in Rome. I seemed to have extended the boundaries of the study of both the Hebrew and the Christian Scriptures to breaking point. At the same time, there had been more anomalies than I could count in my study of biblical texts and I had reached a new watershed.

By this time I was highly sceptical that the biblical text contained any sort of rigid historical framework. Certainly the first chapters of Genesis dealing with the Creation, Adam and Eve, Cain and Abel, the Flood and the Tower of Babel were, in my opinion at that time, highly symbolic statements. They were stories that transmitted religious truths; they were not events that had ever occurred. They provided the primaeval history that explained the human condition and the human situation against which any understanding of the People of Israel had to take place. In a technical use of the term, they were myths.

My studies in Deuteronomy had led me to see that, while there was an admirable literary structure in the Hebrew text, there was no reason to think that this was an historical document. I was willing to concede that the Ancestor stories about Abraham, Isaac and Jacob contained kernels of historical veracity but the texts had been elaborated and reworked so as to form a transition from the earlier primaeval history to the formation of Israel. They were legendary stories, not history.

I had arrived in Rome believing that real biblical history began with the Ancestors. After all, they had created and formed the People of Israel. Now I doubted the historicity of the Ancestors, of Abraham, Isaac and Jacob and their female counterparts; I could not see that the evidence could substantiate them being historical figures. However, while I was puzzled by the archaeology surrounding the Exodus out of Egypt and Jericho, I still believed that this was the first substantial historical event in the story of ancient Israel. In fact, I saw it as imperative that the Exodus be acknowledged in some way as an historical event.

Likewise, I was more than ever sceptical about the historicity of the gospels. Having drilled down into the grammatical and linguistic structure of the original texts, I was enamoured of the gospels' literary character and the cleverness with which they had been constructed. However, I more clearly saw that there were irreconcilable discrepancies between them. I was not confident that a history of Jesus could be written without many gaps.

With both the Hebrew Scriptures and the Christian Scriptures I was experiencing disquiet. I was no longer simply deepening the knowledge I had acquired in Australia. I was becoming more and more sceptical of the historical basis for both the Hebrew and the Christian Scriptures. In some ways it was a frightening position to maintain. As yet, despite the anomalies, I was still within the 'normal science' of the historical-critical methodology to which Jerome had introduced us.

At the same time I now recognised that there was a guild of biblical scholarship. It was tightly knit and the requirements for linguistic excellence were part of its initiation procedures. We guild members would protect each other in our searching; at least, I hoped we would. We would also be understanding towards the older members of the priestly caste who might find the liberal views of their juniors somewhat annoying.

The exhausting exams, written and oral, required by the Pontifical Biblical Institute were over by May 1965 and I had passed and obtained a Baccalaureate in Sacred Scripture, a Bachelor's degree, the first year of a Licentiate or Master's degree. Both Moran, regarded as an ogre in an oral exam, and De la Potterie had personally commended me on my application and knowledge. At that time there were two ways forward for completing the Licentiate in Scripture.

Forward Planning

The first option was to do a second year at the Biblical Institute. That was the easiest and most straightforward procedure. The other was to enrol to take exams before the Pontifical Biblical Commission in eighteen months time. The Commission has already been mentioned as supervising all biblical matters for the Vatican and, among its other functions, it was also an examining body. It provided an extensive syllabus for the Baccalaureate and another for the Licentiate in Scripture. While the Commission had no teaching role, it could bestow degrees up to the doctorate on students who passed its exams.

By deciding to take the examinations provided by the Biblical Commission I would be free to spend a year at the École Biblique et Archéologique Française. This was the French Biblical and Archaeological School situated in what was then the Jordanian sector of Jerusalem.[1] As mentioned earlier, it had been founded towards the end of the nineteenth century by the progressive scholar, Lagrange, as a place where Roman Catholic clergy could do advanced work in Biblical Studies. It ran courses in languages associated with biblical studies (Hebrew, Greek, Aramaic, Syriac as well as Assyrian, Egyptian, Ugaritic), courses on the interpretation of the Bible as well as Biblical History and Near Eastern Archaeology. It also required its students to complete a *mémoire* or minor thesis under supervision on a biblical topic as part of their study program. My intention was to do the École's quite separate course and, simultaneously, to prepare for the second year of the degree before the Commission. Jerome Crowe had done this before me.

I must admit that there were a number of people who warned me against this plan. They saw the whole thing as fraught with difficulty, and much more arduous than simply completing the two years at the Biblical Institute. However, I had learned by this stage that such warnings about difficulty and even impossibility only spurred me on to do what seemed to be the more dangerous and adventurous thing. The main reason for the warnings against my plan was that the Licentiate syllabus for the Biblical Commission exam in Rome was immense. There were no classes only exams, but you needed to master by your own devices an enormous content.

The exams were as demanding as any ever devised. There would be a first written exam on Biblical History that covered the entire history behind the periods during which the Old and New Testaments had been written. It required in-depth knowledge and the ability to write for three hours in Latin on any one of sixteen topics covering the Ancestor period to the Acts of the Apostles.

A second written exam covered, in the first place, eight general topics on large swathes of biblical background such as the Jewish sects at the time of Jesus or the physical geography of Palestine and, in the second place, a general introduction to all the books of the Bible in both Hebrew Scriptures and Christian Scriptures. In the actual exam one would need to know enough to write for three hours, for example, on the topography of Jerusalem or the book of Isaiah or the epistle to the Hebrews.

1. When a ceasefire was concluded between the new State of Israel and the Arab countries attacking it, the borders were drawn at the ceasefire lines. In Jerusalem, the ceasefire line split the city into two. The Old City and East Jerusalem remained as part of the Hashemite Kingdom of Jordan. West Jerusalem became part of the State of Israel. The École Biblique was situated in East Jerusalem and hence was in Jordan.

After these two exams there followed the big one: a six hour paper on the interpretation of one small passage selected from three possibilities nominated by the examiners from anywhere in the four gospels or the Acts of the Apostles. This meant that the candidate would need to know the four gospels and Acts in great detail. Candidates could take into the exam the Greek text of the New Testament, the Hebrew/Aramaic of the Old Testament, a book of parallels between Matthew/Mark/Luke in Greek, a copy of the Latin Vulgate and a concordance of the words used in the Greek New Testament.

When these three exams had been completed there was a week's gap while they were assessed by experts from the Commission. After that, candidates had to visit privately the Secretary-General of the Commission who would tell them if they were invited to the oral exam. Being invited meant you had passed the written exams.

There was no way you could skimp on the preparation. Any one of the myriad topics could be posed in either the written or an oral examination. Even with the preparation for writing on the gospels/Acts it would be difficult to cut corners. I saw the obvious advantages, such as covering all of basic biblical scholarship in one almighty effort, but also the obvious disadvantages and risk in taking on this daunting task. My decision nevertheless was that I would travel to Jerusalem to study for a year and thereafter take the Pontifical Biblical Commission exams six months later.

I spent the summer in Nantes on the coast of Bretagne in an isolated French monastery where no-one spoke English. Part of my plan was to revive my spoken French in preparation for the study in Jerusalem.

During this time I spent long hours considering where I had reached at this point. I was besieged by the anomalies in the interpretation of the Bible as in any way an historical document. The first revolution was not producing any satisfaction. I felt that I had lost my moorings and that my life in a religious setting had very little meaning.

Note

At a later date, Ignace de la Potterie published his studies on John (on which he did his doctoral dissertation) in *The Hour of Jesus: the Passion and Resurrection of Jesus according to John*, Alba House: New York in 1989.

An English translation of the *Instruction on the Historical Truth of the Gospels* can be found in *Catholic Biblical Quarterly* 26 (1964), pp 305–312.

PART 3: THE SECOND REVOLUTION

Chapter 9
STUDYING THE HEBREW SCRIPTURES: JERUSALEM

I set off for Jerusalem with the idea that I could eventually resolve my doubts about the historical-critical method and that I could become more expert in its paradigm. There must be an answer to the anomalies.

So, in August 1965 I took a train from Rome to Brindisi and, on the next day, embarked on a ship to Beirut with several days stopover in Alexandria. I had only a vague idea of how I was going to get from Beirut to Jerusalem at a time when the Arab-Israeli conflict was still simmering.

By chance, on board the ship, were several other students en route to Jerusalem. Four of us decided to travel together. Two of them were Franciscans and we left the boat together and travelled to a Franciscan monastery in the suburbs of Beirut for the night. The monastery organised a taxi to Damascus for the next day, where we stayed a further night in another Franciscan monastery and picked up a second taxi. The next afternoon, after crossing the Jordanian border, we reached Jerusalem in an exhausted state, after having spent two days of sweltering heat and swirling dust in non-air-conditioned taxis.

The others went to a Franciscan postgraduate house of studies. I made my way to the École Biblique where by chance I was warmly welcomed by Marie-Émile Boismard. I had known his name as a great biblical scholar for so many years and, humble man that he was, he helped me carry my bags to my room.

The École Biblique

So began nearly eighteen months of an idyllic existence. I spent a year doing the regular course and writing my mémoire, and then spent another six months making final preparations for my final exams. I did virtually nothing in that period but study. The day after my arrival, I explained to the Director of the École Biblique, Pierre Benoit (another of my biblical scholar-heroes), what my plans were relative to the Biblical Commission and we charted a program that would fit in with that. I would do language courses in Hebrew and Syriac. I would also do courses in Archaeology, Biblical History, Topography of Jerusalem and various aspects of biblical exegesis. The course included several archaeological tours with a professor in attendance and experts on site: around Jordan, to Egypt and to Turkey.

I knew that my preparations for the Commission exam, still some eighteen months off, had to begin forthwith. I bought folders for each of the many sections of the exams and put materials that I had already covered over the years into sequence. Most of my luggage had been filled with papers and notes. Then I began to gather information on the other topics that still needed attention. In particular, I began an in-depth study of the gospels and Acts of the Apostles following the order of their chapters.

One of the large sections of work for the Commission exam pertained to Biblical History—from the Ancestors' period through to the end of the Acts of the Apostles. I knew that it would be important to decide from the start on a theoretical stance. Despite the reservations that Robert North had raised, I was still a fairly confirmed, if wavering, follower of the Albright School. This led me to take the biblical text and read it in the light of archaeological discoveries. I was still convinced that 'history' as regards ancient Israel must have begun with the Exodus out of Egypt. I simply needed proof.

A major commitment at the École Biblique was to archaeology. I was enrolled in two courses with Roland de Vaux. Besides being an active archaeologist, he was also the Editor-in-chief of the Dead Sea Scrolls. One course was Near Eastern Archaeology and the other was Biblical History. They both fitted in well with the upcoming Biblical Commission examination. The archaeological course, besides lectures, required attendance once a week, out of opening hours, at the Palestinian Archaeological Museum. De Vaux was the Director of the museum and he would allow us to handle and examine carefully various artifacts and, in his inimitable style, he made archaeology come to life.

So, in a little Arab world far from the hustle and bustle of modern civilisation and seemingly cut off from the mainstream ecclesiastical world I devoted myself to work. But in my mind the seeds of a second revolution were being planted.

Archaeology

Archaeology became more and more a fascination. There was the formal course at the École Biblique, but there was much small talk as well, particularly with De Vaux. While De Vaux was a representative of Biblical Archaeology, he was in fact on the edges of that tradition. He was respected by secular archaeologists and seen as one of them. In Jerusalem we were surrounded by secular archaeologists, mostly drawn by the historically fertile ground that lies under modern Jerusalem.

Secular archaeology, when it is applied to sites that have a biblical reference, does not intend to provide evidence for the factual confirmation of the Bible; it does not assume that it can provide a 'why'; it presumes that its task is to provide a 'when' and a 'how' and a 'what took place'. While it is not by any means ideologically neutral, it has a bias different from Biblical Archaeology.

Soon, archaeology caused me to reconsider where my thought was going. I was still puzzled about the Exodus out of Egypt and the results of the dig at Jericho. Early in our course we were taken to the Jericho *tell*. In those days we had full access and could climb over the mound, examining the ruins that had not been covered over. Kenyon was still in Jerusalem, on her subsequent dig in that city, and a familiar figure at meetings and seminars. I was still trying to hold more or less to the Albright hypothesis that Jericho had been destroyed by the Israelites (at some indefinite time) in their incursion into the land. While the archaeological record might be open to some debate, that fact of Israelite destruction still remained for me the vital historical point. But the anomalies were growing inexorably.

I gathered the anomalies together as part of my exam preparation. In the first place, it was by then known that the store cities, which the book of Exodus says the Israelites were forced to construct, were not called by the names of Pithom and Rameses until long after the time of Rameses.

Coming down to details, in Joshua 12 there is a list of thirty-one cities conquered by the Israelites. However, the Joshua narrative describes only four that are explicitly taken by them: Jericho, 'Ai, Hebron and Hazor. The archaeological evidence suggested that Jericho was destroyed towards the end of the Middle Bronze period (2000–1500), while 'Ai was destroyed during the Early Bronze period (3200–2000). Both were unoccupied during the Late Bronze period (1550–1200). Hebron was occupied during the Late Bronze period into Iron 1 period (1200–900), but there is no evidence of any destruction. The only archaeological evidence for a destruction in the Late Bronze period relates to Hazor, but there is no means of identifying the destructive force as Israel.

Those sites that were destroyed in the transition from Late Bronze to Iron I can all be explained by the invasion of the Sea Peoples, a coalition of tribal peoples probably from the Greek region. Sites such as Kadesh Barnea, Heshbon and Gibeon were originally settled only in the Iron I period.

In short, there was no archaeological evidence to support the conquest model. In fact, as has been said previously, recent archaeology has stressed the continuity of culture from the Late Bronze to the Iron I periods, not its discontinuity.

Further, there were real problems in identifying any unified Exodus from Egypt. If we take the Exodus as the central affirmation of the biblical creed, there is no mention of anything comparable to it in extant Egyptian records. The answer generally given is that the Exodus was a minor event given the vast scale of Egyptian history. However, Numbers 1:46 states that the Israelites who came out of Egypt reached 'six hundred and three thousand, five hundred and fifty' males, giving a total population including women and children of about 2.5 million. We can estimate that during the New Kingdom the approximate population of Egypt would have been around 3 to 4.5 million. If the story was to be taken as anything like literal fact, the loss of much more than half the population would surely have left some resonance in Egyptian historical annals and in the archaeological record.

Gradually, during my time at the École Biblique, I was losing more and more confidence in the Albright School. Talking to fellow students who were longer established in biblical studies, I learned more about Martin Noth, he of the 'peaceful infiltration' model for the Exodus and Conquest. He had not begun with the biblical text as Albright had. He began with archaeological discoveries. I was persuaded to have a closer look at his revolutionary theory.

Martin Noth worked with both written documents and oral traditions. His aim was to reconstruct the origin and development of the traditions that formed the Biblical narratives. As Noth was primarily an historian, he wanted to clarify the literary development of the Hebrew Scriptures so that he could write a reliable historical account of the beginnings of Israel.

He claimed that each of the early traditions was linked to a particular sacred place. Gradually these local traditions had been brought together to form five major themes: the Patriarchs, the Exodus, the Sinai event, Wanderings in the desert, Conquest of the land. Each had begun as an item of oral tradition. Moses was the 'editorial bracket' which held the five of them together.

Within the early confederation of twelve tribes, the so-called amphictony, these themes took on a written form. As tribal representatives met for common worship they would recite an account of their supposed common past, and the result was a first formulation of the Israelite tradition. In his opinion, this might have been either an oral or a written source. He assigned the siglum G (for *Grundschrift* or 'basic writing') to it for convenience.

Noth saw the Priestly narrative or P as the base story into which the J and E traditions had been inserted to give it richness. He was attempting to develop a grand scheme by which he could explain how traditions had originated in early social or cultic settings of the Israelite tribes, prior to the tribes being amalgamated into a kingdom under the great king, David. He also wanted to show the way in which individual and originally separate traditions coalesced into the narrative stories of the Hebrew Scriptures. This latter descriptive method became known as *Überlieferungsgeschichte* or Tradition History.

Tradition History searches for the process of vertical transmission of memories and traditions from one generation to the next. As a method, it has managed to change the emphasis from the time when the documents were written to the time when the oral traditions that lay behind the documents began. Starting with the existing written text, the method traces a line of development back to oral tradition. Tradition historians try to recover the earliest pre-literary stage of a text.

I began to read Noth's works, especially *A History of Israel,* voraciously and to compare his findings with those of the Albright School. This stressed for me the need for further research in secular archaeology. I needed desperately to establish a link between the literary traditions and the solid archaeological scholarship related to the Near East. Was there a correlation between traditions and archaeological record?

At a reception for some visiting German scholars at the École Biblique, I actually met Martin Noth and was struck by his demeanour as we formally shook hands with Teutonic formality. He was the archetypical German Professor and I was most impressed by his quiet and unassuming manner. His theory now became my centre of attention.

But there was to be a third model to explain the Exodus, which I was to hear from its author.

The 'peasants' revolt model'

One day at the École Biblique a notice was posted announcing that there would be a series of seminars to be delivered at the American Schools of Oriental Research, which was close by, by two visiting American scholars. The two scholars were George Mendenhall and James M. Robinson, one of the scholars in the forefront of the Second Search. I will return to Robinson later as he was to have his own impact on me. But, in the first place, I was delighted to have contact with George Mendenhall.

He was an historian but he had come under the influence of the Albright School and he had published some interesting articles on the founding of ancient Israel. I avidly attended his rather rambling seminars, with perhaps ten others sitting around a large table at the American Schools building.

Mendenhall had devised a third model for the Exodus, eventually dubbed the 'peasants' revolt model'. This theory identified the Hebrew people with the *'apiru* of the Amarna letters as others had done. However, Mendenhall had been one of the first scholars to claim that the *'apiru* were not an ethnic group but a social class. He claimed that *'apiru* names, mentioned in those texts from the fourteenth century BCE, were similar to Hebrew names, and that the lifestyles of the *'apiru*, living on the outskirts of settled society, were similar to those of the Biblical Hebrews. The historical Hebrews were therefore identified as outcasts from the dominant society, who had become revolutionaries.

The crux of the theory was that Israel did not originate as an ethnic group, separate from the Canaanites. The Israelites were sedentary Canaanite farmers, not infiltrating shepherds as Alt and Noth had claimed. They were a downtrodden Canaanite underclass, dominated by other Canaanites who had control of a string of city-states. This brutal, oppressive and dysfunctional social system, which was found throughout Palestine and Syria, demanded crippling taxes and forced labour from its subject peoples. The underclass eventually revolted against the overlords, and the result was the establishment of an 'Israel' when they prevailed.

The impetus for the revolt would have come from Yahwism, the religion related to the god YHWH, which centred on a covenant offered by the god to his underprivileged people. This ideology of being specially chosen gave the suffering peasants the initiative to rise up against the Canaanite kings. It also explained the emphasis Israel placed on its self-identification as an insignificant and marginal people. The Exodus out of

Egypt was a symbolic account of the revolt of the oppressed against their oppressors on Canaanite soil.

However, as with the previous two models, there were problems with this one too. In the first place, the Amarna Letters do not describe substantial Canaanite 'city-states' as required by the model. Instead, the texts indicate that the Canaanite cities of the period had drastically reduced populations; they were little more than villages. In one text, forty *'apiru* are described as being able to take one of these city-states. In other words, nomads could take control of a large settled area without substantial resources. Consequently, the Canaanite heads of these villages could only with considerable exaggeration be called 'kings'.

There is, therefore, no evidence for Mendenhall's 'network of interlocking Canaanite city-states', which could deprive an underclass group of its freedom, the essential element in the model. Furthermore, Mendenhall was not able to produce any evidence in the archaeological record that related to a widespread 'peasants' revolt'.

While at first I was fascinated by Mendenhall's proposition, I eventually came to reject it.

In short, I had found that none of the three models—the conquest, the peaceful infiltration or the peasants' revolt—was able to be sustained. I suffered a severe setback at this point. In the first place, I had been hoping (both for my own satisfaction and also for the purposes of the examination before the Biblical Commission) to construct a history of ancient Israel that was based on a harmonious blending of biblical texts and archaeology. But this required some sort of correlation between the texts and historical events. All along, I was convinced that if the date of the Exodus out of Egypt could be settled, then other events could be related to it as a pivotal point. But now it seemed that even this pivotal event, on which so much historically and thematically depended, was doubtful.

I realised that, for the Biblical Commission examination, I would have to write a factual history about which I had serious reservations. I could hardly write for three hours and then conclude that I did not think there was any point to the question that I had just answered.

As far as my studies of the Hebrew Scriptures were concerned I had travelled from naïve acceptance of the text as historical, through a first revolution in which I believed that I could harmonise text and archaeological findings to form a 'history' that was only partly literal. But now I was confronted by a growing number of anomalies. The onset of 'real historical events' had slipped from the Adam and Eve era, to the Ancestors, to the Exodus and now I was faced with a factual history that might only have commenced with the Israelite kingdom of David and Solomon.

With a sinking heart I realised that I had crossed a threshold. I was disenchanted with the first revolution. The anomalies were overwhelming. There was not even a modicum of history that could sustain the origins of ancient Israel or Judaism. There might not even have been an Exodus out of Egypt! Whatever faith might be based on it was not history. The Hebrew Scriptures were wonderful literature. But that was precisely what they were.

My study of the Christian Scriptures was likewise reaching a point of no return.

Note

The material in this chapter refers to the work of Roland de Vaux (1961) in *Ancient Israel*, McGraw-Hill, New York, and George Mendenhall (1973), in *The Tenth Generation. The Origins of the Biblical Tradition*, Johns Hopkins University Press: Baltimore and London.

Chapter 10
STUDYING THE CHRISTIAN SCRIPTURES: JERUSALEM

In my study of the Christian Scriptures at the École Biblique, the most impressive lecturer was Marie-Émile Boismard, who had insisted on carrying my bags on the day of my arrival. He ran a seminar on a Saturday afternoon on the Synoptic Problem, the question as to which of Matthew, Mark or Luke was the original text. There was only a small group of us involved, but he put in an enormous amount of preparatory labour and demanded a similar response from us. We were trying to work out the sequence of the three synoptic gospel writers. However, Boismard did not think that we had the original texts of any of Matthew, Mark or Luke.

The Synoptic Problem

He introduced us to UrMarkus, an original form of the Markan gospel, which had subsequently been expanded and changed. Then, there was Aramaic Matthew, an earlier form of Matthew written in Aramaic and then translated into Greek with additions and amendments. He even prodded me to try and translate part of the Greek text of Matthew back into Aramaic and see what I made of it. There was also a Proto-Luke, written earlier than the Lukan gospel known today.

Sometimes, Boismard pointed out, gospel texts had been quoted by some of the early Christian writers and they were not exactly the same as those in the texts that had come down later. Perhaps the writer had been citing from memory and had only given an approximation of a text; perhaps the writer's source was faulty. But perhaps again the text had been cited from an earlier form of the gospel. In order to prepare us for the seminar, Boismard would roneo-copy all the possible versions of a text.

For the most part they were in Greek, but at times we were dealing with Latin and even Syriac texts. We were required to play with the texts, to see if we could work out what the oldest form might have been, where changes might have been introduced and provide explanations for the changes. It was very painstaking work but very rewarding. Importantly, he brought along a few bottles of Jordanian beer each week to assist the thought processes.

Boismard encouraged us to find patterns in the text, such as inclusions and chiasms. In particular he pushed us to find additions to the text that might mask an original literary device and show that an editor's hand had been at work.

I spent inordinate hours on this task. For one thing, I was deeply interested and for another I realised that this was precisely the sort of skill I needed if I was going to be able to write for six hours in a Biblical Commission examination on a short gospel text in Greek.

The constant playing with texts was making me more aware of the tenuous historical substratum of the gospel texts. One hot Jerusalem afternoon, I set myself the task of working out how the texts about the Last Supper in Matthew, Mark, Luke and Paul's Letter to the Corinthians could be put into some order. I had the Greek texts set out on a large table in front of me. There did not seem to be anything in them that was common. There was variety in the order of events, variety in the interpretation of events, even a difference of opinion as to when the meal had taken place. Which of them was the more original, the more historically likely? Suddenly, an idea came into my mind—perhaps there never had been a Last Supper! Perhaps someone in the early Christian period had invented the idea of a final meal between Jesus and his close disciples on the eve of his death. The invention would have served to explain the Christian meaning of Jesus' death. By the time of Paul, this construction could already been accepted as an actual event.

I recall sitting for a long time at my desk staring at the texts in front of me. That did explain most of the differences. Despite the summer heat, I felt a chill. It was not only this particular conclusion about the historicity of the Last Supper that bothered me, it was the realisation that, if the Last Supper could be put aside, I could hold virtually nothing in the Jesus story as historically sound and inviolable. Was this historical vacuum sufficient to base one's life on? Did an appreciation of the Bible as Literature give me a firm enough foundation for a life of poverty, chastity and obedience in the Catholic Church?

This disturbing personal moment had been accompanied by another event. I have mentioned the simultaneous arrival in Jerusalem of the two scholars, Mendenhall and Robinson. Mendenhall had contributed to my thinking, but at the same time Robinson was to play his part. There was a further announcement that Robinson too would be giving a series of seminars at the American Schools of Oriental Research.

Robinson was an American expert in the Christian Scriptures. He was renown as one of the founders of the New Search for the Historical Jesus. I had expected that Robinson would be speaking about that Search and I thought that this would give me further material to add to my dossier in preparation for the Commission examinations. So, I turned up to the research centre in east Jerusalem eager and ready to gain more insights into the Second Search.

Robinson made no mention of the Second Search.

The Gnostics

He announced that he had just returned from Cairo, where he had been party to a wondrous new discovery. He then began to talk about Gnostic texts that had been unearthed much earlier and only recently made public and about the Gnostic tradition in early Christian history. He insisted that this discovery would change the whole direction of studies in Christianity; I did not realise that it would also have a deep personal affect on me too.

What he reported was that there had been another fortuitous discovery in Egypt, comparable to the Dead Sea Scrolls, which added much fuel to historical speculation. In Greek Ptolemaic times, just before the Christian era, there had been a settlement called Chenoboskion, later known by the more recent name of Nag Hammadi (see figure 6). There, in 1945 two peasant farmers were bagging fertiliser from the numerous caves along a rugged cliff face when one of them, Muhammad 'Ali al-Samman, came upon a reddish earthenware jar. He feared there might be a *djinn* or evil spirit inside, as had Muhammad ed-Dhib at Qumran, but he still smashed it open with a mattock and found twelve codices. They were books of papyrus leaves with a Coptic text and each bound in leather-covered wooden boards. Coptic was the last stage of ancient Egyptian, the spoken language of Egyptians in the early Christian period, written mostly in Greek characters but with many loan words from Greek.

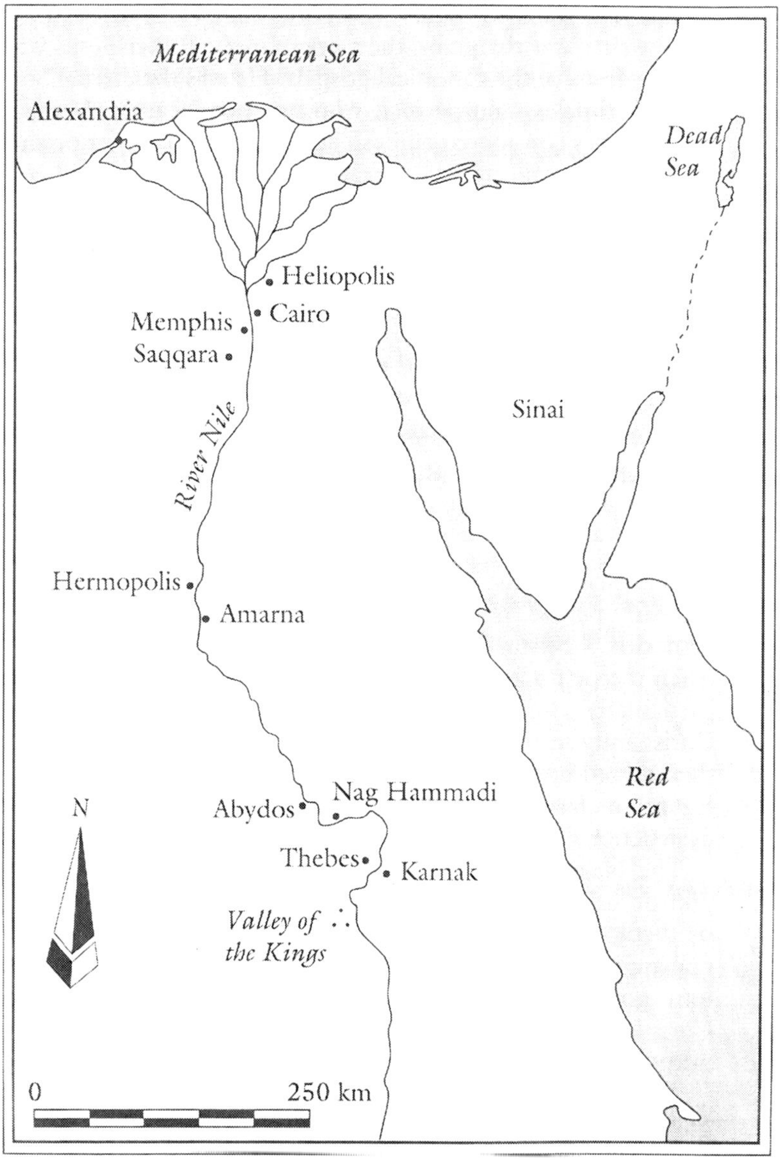

Figure 6: The location of Nag Hammadi

Because of the fact that the brothers were being investigated for a murder by which they had avenged their own father's death and because of protracted bureaucratic dealings and bargaining over the codices, the texts were not comprehensively studied until the 1960s. Altogether, 53 separate texts have been identified in the codices; six are duplicates. Most certainly some have been lost forever since Muhammad had confided that his mother used a number of the papyrus sheets as fire-starters.

The texts as they stand have been dated to about 350–400 CE (since the stuffing for the leather covers fortunately contained dated receipts), but they are copies of originals which could go back perhaps to the second century CE. This collection was probably deposited in the cave by monks from a nearby monastery of Saint Pachomius. The contents of the texts explain why they would have been hidden.

The contents show that most of the texts are clearly Gnostic. The Gnostics were a group of early Christians who were previously known to us only because they were viciously attacked in some early Christian writings. Their teachings stressed the need for *gnosis* or inner knowledge. They claimed that salvation was only possible through this secret knowledge which was reserved for the chosen few. Jesus, in their version of events, was one of a string of emanations from the Godhead who had come on earth to bestow that knowledge on the elect. However, their Jesus was not the Jesus of the canonical gospels. He was the eternal and divine Son of God, timeless and perfect, who was not incarnated since the Gnostics considered all flesh and matter to be inferior and evil. Both flesh and matter had been the result of the wayward actions of a truant emanation. Jesus had not died a real death and therefore had not undergone a physical resurrection.

The elect few or Gnostics, haters of the world and its attractions, were called to self-knowledge, and that knowledge led them to see this living, eternal Jesus within their inner selves, their own divine spark. They had come to realise their own divinity, comparable to the divinity of Jesus. The true Gnostic was the one who really understood this divine reality and thus found redemption even before death.

One of the early Gnostics, Theodotus, had written in the middle of the second century that the Gnostic understands

> . . . who we were and what we have become; where we were . . . whither we are hastening; from what we are being released; what birth is and what is rebirth.[1]

Gnosticism must have been a fully fledged movement during the early period of Christianity, posing a threat to what we know today as orthodox

1. In Clement of Alexandria, *Excerpta ex Theodoto, 78.2*

Christianity. It was denounced as a heresy and when the orthodox bishops gained complete power in Egypt, particularly after the time of Constantine's acceptance of the Christian religion in the fourth century, Gnostics were purged and their sacred books burned. No doubt the books found by the Egyptian farmer in 1945 had been hidden because of such impending destruction.

The Nag Hammadi texts consist, first of all, of Christian Gnostic writings such as the Gospel of Truth. This is a book of theology, almost like an extended sermon, dealing with Gnostic teachings. It is not a gospel in the same literary sense as the four canonical gospels. There were also some selections from non-Christian authors including Plato. Of most interest for our purposes are the Gnostic Gospels of Philip and Thomas.

The Gospel of Philip is a rather rambling discourse on the Gnostic rituals (baptism, anointing, eucharist and a ceremony called *apolotrosis* or redemption are mentioned) in the course of which some sayings of Jesus are recorded. For example it recounts a rivalry between Jesus' disciples and Mary Magdalene (the papyrus was damaged and there are some gaps for which reconstructions are offered in the text below):

> . . . the companion of the (Savior is) Mary Magdalene. (But Christ loved) her more than (all) the disciples and used to kiss her (often) on her (mouth). The rest of (the disciples were offended by it . . .). They said to him, 'Why do you love her more than all of us?' The Savior answered and said to them, 'Why do I not love you as (I love) her?'

While this text has been used in popular writings to prove that Jesus was intimate with Mary Magdalene and may have married her, its interpretation must take into account the Gnostic thought world. In that Gnostic scenario, Jesus is not human. He may have had the appearance of humanity, but he was essentially divine. There could be no question of a marriage between Jesus and anyone. The kiss refers to Mary Magdalene reaching the peak experience of divine illumination. She had attained full knowledge and, as a fully fledged Gnostic, she and the divine Jesus have become one. Therefore, the sacred kiss seals this sacred moment of mystical consummation.

There are a few scholars who consider that some of the Jesus-sayings in the Gospel of Philip may have preserved an early form of the Jesus tradition, but that is far from a universally held position.

Gospel of Thomas

More Jesus-scholars have shown interest in another Nag Hammadi text, the *Gospel of Thomas*. It is a collection of 114 sayings of Jesus. Only incidentally are any narrative details about Jesus given in the text. After the discovery at Nag Hammadi it was realised that three papyrus fragments found early in the twentieth century at Oxyrhynchus in Egypt had also contained some sayings from the *Gospel of Thomas* but they were written in Greek. Since the Coptic texts of the *Gospel of Thomas* are not a straight translation of the Greek of the Oxyrhynchus fragments, there must have been different versions of the original Greek sayings in circulation.

In the *Gospel of Thomas*, Jesus gives authority to Thomas to interpret his teaching, much as, in the synoptic gospels, Peter is given authority after being questioned concerning the messiahship of Jesus:

> Jesus said to his disciples, 'Compare me to someone and tell me whom I am like.'
> Simon Peter said to him, 'You are like a righteous angel.'
> Matthew said to him, 'You are like a wise philosopher.'
> Thomas said to him, 'Master, my mouth is wholly incapable of saying whom you are like.'
> Jesus said, 'I am not your master. Because you have drunk, you have become intoxicated from the bubbling spring which I have measured out.'
> And he took him and withdrew and told him three things.
> When Thomas returned to his companions, they asked him, 'What did Jesus say to you?'
> Thomas said to them, 'If I tell you one of the things which he told me, you will pick up stones and throw them at me; a fire will come out of the stones and burn you up.'

The sayings include pronouncement stories, parables, beatitudes, proverbs and 'I'-sayings. Among them there are 79 which are parallel to sayings in the gospels.

There is debate as to whether the *Gospel of Thomas* is really a Gnostic text or whether it was an orthodox Christian text used by Gnostics. It would seem that some of its sayings are clearly Gnostic in outlook, indicating as they do that Christians are saved by the revelation and teaching of Jesus, that the human soul should be very strictly demarcated from its worthless body and that the world is to be spurned. The Gnostic tendency to downplay the position of women is prevalent. It is said that women need to be transformed into men before they can be saved, since they are so closely caught up in the reproductive process.

> Simon Peter said to them, 'Let Mary leave us, for women are not worthy of life.'
> Jesus said, 'I myself shall lead her in order to make her male, so that she too may become a living spirit resembling you males. For every woman who will make herself male will enter the kingdom of heaven.'

Despite the fact that it is Gnostic, it is possible that some of the sayings in the *Gospel of Thomas* are closer to the oral traditions of early Christianity than the four gospels.

An example where some scholars prefer Thomas as more original in comparison to a canonical gospel would be the parable of the pearl:

GOSPEL OF THOMAS 76	GOSPEL OF MATTHEW 13:45-56
Jesus said, 'The kingdom of the father is like a merchant who had a consignment of merchandise and who discovered a pearl. The merchant was shrewd. He sold the merchandise and bought the pearl alone for himself.	'Again, the kingdom of heaven is like a merchant in search of fine pearls; on finding one pearl of great value, he went and sold all that he had and bought it.'

Some claim that the Thomas version is more internally consistent and makes more sense than the Matthew version. This is sufficient reason for them to consider the Thomas form of the saying more authentic, its wording closer to what would have been used by the historical Jesus.

To sum up: where had the writings come from, prior to their being hidden in the terracotta container? They were the remainder of a religious library, probably hidden in the fourth century CE by Coptic monks who had espoused Gnosticism, when Gnosticism was savagely rejected by mainstream Christianity.

These texts revealed that many Coptic Christians had constructed a very different Jesus to the one portrayed in the canonical gospels of Matthew, Mark, Luke and John. If, as some scholars were to maintain, the

Jesus-sayings and Jesus events in the Gnostic gospels could be shown to predate the canonical gospels, then these Gnostic texts could be accepted as independent historical witnesses to an historical Jesus.

The *Gospel of Thomas* and the *Gospel of Philip* are capable of three lines of interpretation. They might be considered i) the earliest existing form of the Jesus tradition or ii) a Jesus tradition that is contemporary with the canonical gospels or iii) a later Jesus tradition which is dependent on the canonical gospels. Again their usefulness will depend on which of these three possibilities is accepted.

At this stage, while living in Jerusalem, I had access to a version of the *Gospel of Thomas* in a Latin translation. However, I dutifully compared verse after verse with the four canonical gospels. While I was doubtful that any of the Thomas sayings could have been earlier versions of any of the canonical gospel sayings, I was intrigued by what Nag Hammadi was revealing about Gnostic communities.

If it were true that there were well established and widespread Gnostic communities in Egypt and perhaps elsewhere, why were they so invisible in the historical record? Perhaps such Gnostic communities had been the earliest form of Christianity? If so, then the later presentations of a life of Jesus in the canonical gospels were even less reliable.

I was becoming less and less satisfied with the official reconstruction of either ancient Israel or the early Christian church. If there was no Exodus out of Egypt, no Last Supper, alternative versions of Jesus such as the Gnostics put forward, what was there for a Christian to stand upon? I was being more and more caught up in the second revolution: the Bible is Literature, no more and no less.

The final exams

In a state of intellectual turmoil, I completed my preparations for the Biblical Commission examinations. When classes at the École Biblique finished in May 1966 and I had submitted a memoire on texts in the Synoptic gospels dealing with the Greek term *paidion* or 'little child' (supervised by Benoit), I would work seven days a week and sometimes spent up to fifteen hours per day at private study. Even as I shaved, the wall of my room was covered with lists of dates related to Near Eastern history, lists of kings' reigns, lists of facts, lists of all sorts. While I was confident that I could cope with anything that the examinations might throw up, I was not nearly so confident that I really knew any longer what the Bible was all about.

Talking once to Benoit about my preparations for these examinations before the Biblical Commission and the difficulties I was having in knowing how much to admit to my doubts, Benoit with a sly smile said: 'There's no need to tell the Commission everything you know.'

In November I left Jerusalem to return to Rome. I had drawn certain lines in the sand. I was enamoured with the literary prowess of both the Hebrew and Christian Scriptures. I had drilled deeply into both and they had revealed to me a sophisticated literary structure. But, I was not at all certain about the historical foundations of that writing.

While I felt that I knew and admired Ancient Israel, the People of YHWH, and knew a lot about the background against which they had developed, I was very unsure of the actual events that had taken place, particularly during the earlier part of their history.

Likewise with the gospels, the historical underpinnings had collapsed. I had begun by putting aside such events as the Ascension of Jesus and Pentecost as historical, and questioning the Resurrection. Then there was the Last Supper episode. However, I went further and, acknowledging the differences in chronology between the Synoptics and John, I became less and less certain that any historical sequence was possible. Each gospel had its own internal logic; no gospel had an historically reliable sequence. The gospels revealed what the early Christians considered important teachings; they did not reveal what had actually happened in the life of Jesus.

I travelled back to Rome by air, on a very cheap flight provided by Jordan's national airline. Once a week, one of its small Caravelle planes travelled from Jerusalem to Amman to Beirut to Rome to Paris and finally to London. Then it returned a day or two later in the opposite direction. I travelled as far as Rome and set myself up once more in Sts. John and Paul to prepare to face the examiners at the Biblical Commission.

At the end of November I sat, during the course of one week, for the three written exams, two of three hours and one of six, in a tranquil room hidden from the noise of Rome within the gardens of Vatican City. There were only seven of us taking the examinations and on each examination day an ancient member of the Commission would open an envelope and read out the topic for the examination. I first wrote for three hours on the historical background to the Ancestor period—that being the topic read from the envelope. I certainly took Benoit's advice and did not reveal all that I really thought.

Then, two days later, with another envelope being opened, I wrote for three hours on Paul's letter to the Galatians. Finally, on a Friday, I wrote for six hours on the parable of the lost coin in Luke's gospel. There had been three choices, two being parables from Matthew and the other a text from the Acts of the Apostles. The choice was one from the three and these three were unexpected; the Commission had never set a parable before and a similar text from the Acts had been asked the previous year. Each of the exams had to be written in Latin. For the final exam, I did not stop writing for five hours thirty-five minutes. Then I checked what I had done during the final twenty-five minutes. I was seeing black spots before my eyes.

A week later I had to visit the Secretary-General of the Biblical Commission, at that time a dour Dutchman called Bernard Wambacq. He informed me that I had passed and that I was invited to attend an oral examination. This took place several days later, with six Consultors of the Biblical Commission presiding behind a huge cedar desk in a very ornate Vatican room.

For an hour they questioned me in Latin concerning items on the syllabus. I discussed the notion of biblical inspiration and quoted, in Latin, long texts from Papal encyclicals; I listed for them all the names and dates of the Persian kings of the dynasty with which ancient Israel had been embroiled (I could luckily still see the lists of all regal reigns on my wall in Jerusalem); I resolved for them historical problems in the period of the restoration after the Exile, presumably to their satisfaction. Soon after I had been dismissed, one of them, Petrus Duncker came out and told me that I had passed. My relief must have been obvious.

A few days after the examinations I flew on the same small Jordanian plane to Paris and on to London where eventually I boarded a boat for a free passage to Australia as a migrant chaplain. I arrived back in Australia in January, 1967.

The night before I left Rome I met with two of my friends from the École Biblique, who were returning to the United States, to have a final meal. The mood was sombre. We were all returning home with a new viewpoint on biblical studies. The Bible was not historical in any sense. Any history that was there was fortuitous. Faith was not built on historical texts. History did not matter. A second revolution had taken place. One of them tried to persuade me to change my plans and to go back to America with them. My new ideas on biblical studies, he said, would never allow me to survive in Australia. I was more sanguine.

The world was changing; the Catholic Church was changing as could be seen by the hope generated by the Second Vatican Council. I had no doubt that I would be able to overcome any opposition that I might find in Australia and work within a new paradigm.

I was quite wrong about that.

Note

The Gnostic texts, as found in this chapter, are in JM Robinson (1978), *The Nag Hammadi Library in English*, HarperSanFrancisco: San Francisco.

For an introduction to the Gnostic writings and thought a good start can be made with some of the works of Elaine Pagels (1979), *The Gnostic Gospels,* Weidenfeld and Nicholson: London, *Adam, Eve and the Serpent* (1988), Weidenfeld and Nicholson: London and *The Origin of Satan* (1995), Random House: New York.

Chapter 11
RETURN TO AUSTRALIA

Between my return to Australia in 1967 and mid-1972 I taught Biblical Studies, Hebrew and Greek to seminarians studying for the Catholic priesthood in Melbourne. I also taught Old Testament Studies to an amalgam of Christian denominations at the United Faculty of Theology, attached to the University of Melbourne.

It was the heady days after the Vatican Council. Many of us were sure that we were on the cusp of a new era when new ideas would come into vogue.

My mind was more and more looking to the Bible as Literature as a result of my experiences in Jerusalem. I was interested in the history underlying both the Hebrew Scriptures and the Greek Scriptures but only as an historian, not as a believer and interpreter. I actually taught students how to extract this fractured history although I was clear in my own mind that history was not the basis for the interpretation of the text or for Christian faith.

The Scriptures were symbolic statements that presented in a number of literary forms. Sometimes they may state historical fact. Whether that history was reliable was another argument and, from my point of view, it did not matter.

I soon realised that I was entrenched in the second revolution, from the historical-critical method to the Bible as Literature, and was now working in the 'normal science' of this second revolution.

Soon I was able to give a name to the version of the new paradigm in which I was more and more involved—Rhetorical Criticism. I now saw that the work I had done under De la Potterie, Moran and Boismard could be continued, without any need to refer to historicity. The text was the important thing. History was a diversion as far as interpretation was concerned.

However, I realised that this line of interpretation was dangerous; the official Church could not take it in. I could not reveal my full scepticism regarding the historical basis of either Ancient Israel or Jesus. I continued to follow my interests in the biblical texts. At first, I used Rhetorical Criticism to search for structures and meanings in the texts. I had never denied the fact that I admired their subtlety and structure. I was sure that there was a vibrant story underlying the Hebrew Scriptures that had been constructed by astute writers and I admired that story for its persuasive quality; I also admired the gospel texts as astute pieces of literature as well as examining the epistolary structures of the various Christian letters and the strange Book of Revelation. I simply no longer saw any relevance in proving it all to be historically reliable.

Rhetorical Criticism

Rhetorical Criticism had come into vogue after an American, James Muilenburg, had given the presidential address to the Society of Biblical Literature in 1968. Before this it had certainly existed, but without a name. In this address Muilenburg demonstrated that Form Criticism had limitations when applied to the Hebrew Scriptures. He turned his attention to poetic forms, to strategies of style and other literary devices which were intended to attract the reader's attention and to get a text's message across. Following this watershed paper, the focus of many biblical scholars began to move away from diachronic interests (such as when and where a document might have been written, its connection to historical events and how it might have been amended over time) to synchronic interests (how the present text is structured here and now and how does it get its message across)?

Rhetorical Criticism overlooks the historical development of the stories and concentrates on their final form. It determines just how the biblical texts work as persuasive documents, identifying literary stratagems that gently coerce the reader to accept their argument. I discovered that the concentration on the chiasm, on which I had done a lot of work in the past, had actually become part of the developing methodology of Rhetorical Criticism.

I saw this methodology as a way forward for studying the Hebrew Scriptures. For example, I could now see more clearly that the Torah, the story of Israel's formation, was based on a persuasive line of argument:

Suffering in Egypt *leads to* the Exodus out of Egypt and this *leads to* Land and Life.

This theme had been filled in by traditional stories, which might have come from a number of sources, historical and otherwise, and these stories answered certain dominant questions related to the principal theme:

Why was there evil and suffering in the world?

> This question was answered by the Sin stories: Adam and Eve, Cain and Abel, The Flood generation, the Tower of Babel. Based on Mesopotamian mythology, they provided a cumulative image of human incompetence and the need for some external intervention.

Where had the chosen people of Israel come from and how had they ended up in Egypt?

> This second question was answered by the stories of the Ancestors: Abraham, Isaac, Jacob and Joseph to whose group should be attached the female Ancestors. I saw that there were a number of alternative stories, that the genealogical links between the Ancestors as father/son were artificial. Specifically, there had been a number of Abraham stories, Isaac stories and Jacob or Israel stories. The Joseph story had been a novella that had then been manipulated to provide the link with Egypt. None of these stories were in any sense historical, even if they perchance retained some small elements of historical reminiscence.

> Essentially these Ancestor stories told of a people who had come from afar, by divine command, to settle in the Land and to find Life.

What happened during the Exodus?

> The Exodus Generation traditions were a mixture of story and law. The Moses story, telling of a great leader taking the People from Egypt to the land of Canaan, was an alternative to the Abraham stories of another great leader taking the People from Mesopotamia to the land of Canaan. The actual story of a great journey through the desert was a construct. It did not relate historical events. It stood side by side with the great journey-stories, such as the voyage of Odysseus to return home and Aeneas to reach Italy.

How had the People of Israel achieved their ideals of Land and Life?

> The Conquest of Canaan stories contained two alternatives: a unified tribal movement through the land of Canaan or a series of incursions at different times and places. The alternatives had been allowed to stand side by side. Neither was necessarily historical; there was no archaeological evidence for the arrival of a new population. The important point was not how the acquisition had been historically achieved, simply the point that the People did achieve a Land and new life.

The story of a 'People of Israel' who had come from Ur of the Chaldees and settled in the land of Canaan, going down to Egypt because of famine, and then, under the guidance of the god YHWH, been led into the promised land and conquered it was a vibrant religious story.

The earlier nagging question had been: was this story in any sense at all an historical one? The new question was: did it really matter whether it was historical or not? The answer was No and the final question was: What was this piece of literature trying to say and argue?

Rhetorical Criticism was being boldly applied to the gospels as well. Generally, the established conclusions of earlier scholars were accepted. Mark was still regarded as the original gospel, although it was widely admitted that even Mark had been considerably reworked by the early Christian groups. But there was ever greater interest being shown in Q. More and more, Q was seen as less a miscellany of Jesus-sayings and more as a complex but coherent composition, often referred to as the 'Sayings

Gospel', that scholars endeavoured to situate in a credible socio-historical context.

My interest in Rhetorical Criticism drew me to analyse the written gospels further. I found complex literary stratagems in them. For example, I was convinced that I could break the entirety of Mark's gospel down into a cleverly devised structure. It consisted of a Prologue and three parts similarly constructed and all related. Reading a complete text of Mark by following the structure meant that the meaning of the text became clearer.

Again and again, I would be asked: but did these events really happen? I had no idea. From my immersion in the second revolution I was now sure that the basis for Christian belief was not history but cultural tradition and literature. Even if there had not been an Israel or a Jesus, this literature was the basis for living. I wanted to push the second paradigm to its limits.

What follows is the way I (certainly drawing on the research of others at times) analysed the literary content of Mark:

Prologue

John the Baptist: the one who announces Jesus' coming
Jesus is baptised as the Messiah
Jesus begins a battle with Satan

1 Mark shows from stories and sayings that Jesus is the Messiah

This contains three subdivisions, each of which is similarly structured:

Summary of Jesus' teachings
Call, proclamation and mission of The Twelve
Jesus reveals himself as Messiah: he teaches, heals, debates
Unbelief and failure to understand

Cure of a blind man

The first disciples confess: 'You are the Messiah!'

2 Mark shows what following a Messiah really entails

This contains three subdivisions, each of which is similarly structured:

Prediction of suffering and death
Incomprehension on the part of the disciples
Instruction by Jesus

Cure of a blind man

The first disciples decide to follow the Messiah to Jerusalem

3 Mark describes the death and resurrection of the Messiah

This was an extremely clever structure. Presuming that the reader only had the gospel of Mark to follow, then the line of persuasion took hold of that reader and led him or her to an inevitable conclusion: Jesus was the Messiah who had died and who had triumphed over his death.

One example of how the text was embedded in the overall structure was in the second section where Jesus has twice revealed himself to be the Messiah but has been met with incomprehension. His final revelation of himself as the Messiah takes the form of two feeding stories. Both stories have similar general contexts:

6:30-7:37	**8:1-26**
Feeding of 5000	Feeding of 4000
Crossing of the sea	Crossing of the sea
Dispute with Pharisees	Dispute with Pharisees
Conversation about bread	Conversation about bread
A healing	A healing

The stories are very similar, with local variations. When we examine the actual feeding stories there is also remarkable similarity:

Both take place in a desert (6:32 and 8:4)
The central question is the same: how many loaves have you? (6:38 and 8:4)
Jesus' actions over the bread are similar (6:41 and 8:6)

We find the answer to this duplication in the conversation that Jesus conducts with his disciples after the second feeding story (8:17-21), a conversation which also provokes their final response, one of misunderstanding and failure to perceive the messiahship of Jesus. We can lay out the conversation in dialogue form to make its point clearer:

> **JESUS:** *Why are you talking about having no bread? Do you still not perceive or understand? Are your hearts hardened? Do you have ears, and fail to hear? And do you not remember? When I broke the five loaves for the five thousand, how many baskets (kophinoi) full of broken pieces did you collect?*
>
> **DISCIPLES:** *Twelve*
>
> **JESUS:** *And the seven for the four thousand, how many baskets (spyreis) full of broken pieces did you collect?*
>
> **DISCIPLES:** *Seven.*
>
> **JESUS:** *Do you not yet understand?*

What can be deduced? First, the numbers are clearly very important. Secondly, each of the two stories involves a different type of basket. In the first a *kophinos* was used, a distinctively Jewish basket, while in the second story a *spyris* was used, a common fish basket.

Gradually the elements fall into place. Two sets of numbers and two types of basket are involved:

5000 people	4000 people
5 loaves	7 loaves
12 baskets (*kophinoi*)	7 baskets (*spyreis*)

The first set of 5 and 12 are Jewish numbers. There were five books in the Torah of Moses and there were twelve tribes of Israel. The second set of 4 and 7 are universal numbers: the world was considered to be divided into four quarters and seven was the perfect number, the number of completion. Mark's audience would have understood the message, cryptic though it might have been. The first feeding story refers to the Jews and the second to the entire world. This interpretation is made clearer by the distinction of the baskets, Jewish and common.

Reference to the desert, to the feeding of a multitude in the desert, to the dividing up of the people into groups of hundreds and fifties all point to the Exodus story. There were Jews expecting that at the end of times the messiah would feed his people during a new Exodus just as Moses had provided food in the first Exodus. This new Exodus would mark the end of time. The idea of a final meal in which God lavished his people with good food at the end of time was common:

> On this mountain the LORD of hosts will make for all peoples
> a feast of rich food, a feast of well-aged wines,
> of rich food filled with marrow, of well-aged wines strained clear.
> And he will destroy on this mountain
> the shroud that is cast over all peoples,
> the sheet that is spread over all nations. Isaiah 25:6-7

Mark dramatically shows that this has been fulfilled: Jesus was the new Moses for the Jews (the five thousand) and he was also the new Moses for the gentiles or 'peoples' (the four thousand).

There is another dimension to this very rich and complex twin story. The bread is accompanied by fish. Among the early Christians the fish was a secret symbol

The Greek word for fish (*ichthus*) spelled out the first letters of the basic statement of Christian faith: Jesus (*i*) Christ (*ch*) of-God (*th*) Son (*u*) and Saviour (*s*). It also became the symbol of the eucharist in the early church. The eating of the sacramental bread was a proclamation of Christian faith, the ritual moment when the presence of Jesus was overwhelmingly experienced. The language used to describe the distribution of the bread and fish in these two accounts is typically eucharistic. It is as if Christian deacons were handing out the eucharist.

The story therefore has three levels. On the level of the Markan narrative Jesus reveals for a third and last time by his feeding activity that he is the new Moses, come to gather his people together and to lead them to the final salvation. On a second level the meal is the meal of the last time which was awaited by the prophets of Israel. On a third level the meal is an anticipation of the Christian eucharist, the core-ritual in which Jesus' saving presence is available to Christians.

The valiant group of disciples in the story are typically human. That is Mark's constant point. He is not trying to downgrade them nor is he trying to make them superhuman. They have followed Jesus; they are overawed; they are attracted to him. They see what he does, hear what he preaches; they are given inside information. Mark depicts them as obtuse, because that is the way of humans. They participate in the two feedings, the final messianic activity, but they still fail to understand the significance of the numbers. They have not yet come to faith. Mark wants his readers to know that faith does not come by human endeavour. That is the core of the next story, the cure of a blind man.

The cure of the blind man is not simply one story from the catalogue of miracle stories, detailing the conquest of the power of evil. This is a special narrative, a unique miracle story. The blind man is cured in two stages; no other miracle story requires two attempts. In the first stage the blind man sees something vaguely:

> I can see people, but they look like trees, walking.

His vision is indistinct and mistaken. Then Jesus lays his hands on him and he sees everything with clarity. The two stages of healing have a vital purpose in Mark's narrative.

The blind man epitomises the first group of disciples. He could also be any disciple of any time. The most that can be expected of a person who comes or, as in the case of this blind man, is brought by others, to Jesus is that the person will understand Jesus vaguely, imperfectly. There must come a point of inexplicable enlightenment. That is the moment of faith.

Mark's gospel has reached its climax. According to his storyline, Jesus had exorcised evil spirits, healed the sick, debated with those in the throes of ignorance, explained the parables. These are the works of a Messiah. People were trying to understand him. He asks for their response. Their response is the equivalent of the imperfect vision of the blind man who saw people as trees. He is told that some people interpret him as John the Baptist raised from the dead, as Elijah who was expected to return to earth, as the Prophet who would precede the messiah. They are vague, imperfect, mistaken responses to what had been perceived.

Jesus now turns to the chosen group of disciples and asks the most telling question in Mark's gospel:

> 'But who do you say that I am?'

Peter gives the group's solemn response when he says: 'You are the Messiah.' He expresses simply but adequately the faith-response of the group. Like the blind man, cured in the second stage, the group see things clearly.

The site of this pivotal cure is identified as Caesarea Philippi. It is not meant to be an exact geographical location, although such a city was known at the time. This coming-to-faith of the first group is symbolic of the coming-to-faith of all Christians. For every Christian there is a time of misapprehension, uncertainty, indecision. For every Christian there should be a coming-to-faith that is a deep experience, not explicable on the grounds of logic and rationality. Every committed Christian has a Caesarea Philippi.

The group of disciples who had been called in the midst of their everyday occupations, been formed into a 'Twelve' of a renewed Israel, then sent on a mission to continue the messianic task of Jesus, have finally come to faith and they accompany him on The Way. This is no ordinary journey; it will lead to Jerusalem, the centre of the world, the place where history is to come to its high point with the death and resurrection of the Messiah. Before they can confront this last stage another blind man is cured. The repeated cure of a blind man is one of the rhetorical devices included in the Markan story.

Mark's gospel leaves the reader confronting the crucified Jesus and the claims that death was not final for him. I suspect that the latter part of the gospel, now lost, would have contained the cure of a third blind man.

This was extremely clever writing. Once the structure was determined and the line of persuasion followed then it fell into place. As I had done for Mark, I did the same for the gospels of Matthew, Luke-Acts (which are two volumes of the one work) and John. I was now convinced that none of these was historical. The gospel of Mark, with its literary structure, had been taken over by Matthew and Luke who had their own agendas.

The gospel of John was entirely separate. No doubt they had all drawn on a common reservoir of traditions about what Jesus had said and what Jesus had done. But they were not what we would call history. Attempts to reconcile the chronology of the Synoptics and John were doomed to failure. The only way to study the Bible was as a self-sufficient literature that may or may not have had any relationship to history. This was the normal science of the second revolution.

Vatican II in Australia

As I calmly performed this work in Rhetorical Criticism I was struck by the positive atmosphere of the post-Vatican II church and I was hopeful. Towards the end of the Vatican Council in 1965 a new document, called *The Dogmatic Constitution on Divine Revelation,* had appeared to replace the one removed by John XXIII years earlier. It assimilated the spirit and even some of the wording of the Biblical Commission's Instruction of 1964. The document left unsolved the long standing controversy between Rome and the Protestants over the sources of revelation, whether God's revelation to humanity derived from two separate sources (the Bible and Tradition) or whether it derived from one source (the Bible). The compromise is interesting:

> Hence there exists a close connection and communication between sacred tradition and sacred Scripture. For both of them, flowing from the same divine well-spring, in a certain way merge into a unity and tend toward the same end.

In other words, revelation comes from the Bible-as-interpreted-by-Tradition! At this stage in the latter 1960s, Roman Catholic scholars had to some extent caught up with their Protestant confreres in biblical research. The historical-critical method was appreciated and was made use of openly by those scholars and seemingly with the blessing of authority. Even though I was past historical criticism, these were, I considered, all hopeful signs for the future. At least the first revolution was being considered.

However, this Vatican II documentation and the new developments it heralded still had to be absorbed by the Catholic authorities and, more importantly, handed on to the masses. Just when it seemed that some progress was being made, Paul VI in 1968, manipulated by Vatican bureaucrats, published his encyclical *Humanae Vitae* forbidding artificial birth control. It was a rehash of outdated theological thinking, based on the Natural Law thesis, and demonstrated that, despite the brave words of Vatican II, there had not been any real progress in Church thinking. The encyclical was published despite the fact that a special Commission set up by the Pope to advise him had sent to him a majority report stating that the Church teaching on birth control must change. The Pope disregarded it.

Paul VI was met, to his consternation, by massive resistance and even ridicule from both lay Catholics and the world press. He never wrote another encyclical. As I heard the news report about the content of the encyclical on a 6pm broadcast on Australian radio I knew that my tenure in an ecclesiastical teaching position would be short-lived.

My elder brother, Michael (known then as Nicholas), who was also a Passionist priest and an academic in the field of Ethics, went public and published two articles in *The Australian* newspaper. In these articles, he wrote unambiguously that the Pope's encyclical was based on outmoded theology and flawed logic. His church faculties were immediately removed. He was no longer able to act as a priest or teach under Church auspices. He went to America and taught there for several years, after which he resigned from the priesthood.

I seriously intended to speak out. Both in Jerusalem and when in Rome for my exams, I had heard of the Commission set up in Rome to advise the Pope on the issue of contraception. With their advice ignored, with my brother silenced, I realised that there was no real future. Michael persuaded me to lay low. I could not say any more than what he had said, he claimed; better to stay within the institution and fight from there.

Over the next few weeks perhaps a dozen priests in Melbourne were so persuaded; one other went public and lost his priestly faculties too. I now think the strategy was wrong. We should all have spoken up and all had our faculties removed. There would not be another opportunity for further fighting for the cause.

At this point, I must claim that my teaching, whether to the Australian seminarians or to lay audiences, had always been restrained and judicious. I was always mindful of Pierre Benoit's admonition that it was not necessary to tell them all that I was thinking. I did not set out to destroy commitments or to belabour beloved and entrenched beliefs with which I might have disagreed. However, I considered it my duty as an educator to challenge people, to provide them with a new way of thinking and to lead them towards what I was thinking, if that is what they wanted. But I think I did it gently and with consideration.

The result, on the part of the Australian Church hierarchy, was my persecution and rejection. From the time of the publication of *Humanae Vitae* I became a marked person. I was regarded with suspicion and I eventually found out that my public writing and public speaking was being monitored and reported back to the authorities.

In 1970 I was brought before a hearing organised by Archbishop (later Cardinal) James Knox. The charge, laid by a priest who was shocked by the advances in biblical scholarship, was that my teaching on the topic of revelation (how does God communicate with Christians?) was suspect. This was a cover for attacking my ideas more generally on biblical interpretation. There was a protracted hearing over some six weeks and I was only invited to the final session. I intended announcing my departure from the priesthood that very night. Unexpectedly, at least from my vantage point, I was acquitted, only because Knox and the authorities did not have enough evidence to convict me. I knew it would only be time before they did. At a later date I would write to Archbishop Knox and admit that I had been guilty as charged that night.

Exhausted by the intrigues, the subterfuges, the constant need for vigilance and the fact that I saw no sense in changing people who did not want to be changed, in early 1972 I voluntarily resigned from the Catholic priesthood and moved back to secular life at the age of 35, with very little money, no job and no permanent roof over my head.

Note

I endeavoured to sum up my ideas on Rhetorical Criticism in an article published in 1985: 'Changing Fashions in Biblical Interpretation', *Australian Biblical Review* XXXIII, pp15-30.

PART 4: THE THIRD REVOLUTION

Chapter 12
STUDYING RELIGION AND RELIGIONS

University of Melbourne

I decided to return to university as that had been the context where I felt most safe. At the University of Melbourne I had an acquaintance, a former priest and Jesuit, Greg Dening. He had not long before become the Professor of History at Melbourne. I discussed my situation and told him that I wanted to move out of the mainstream of biblical studies, cluttered as I saw it with ecclesiastical potholes, into the discourse of a secular university. What did he think of my starting again in Anthropology?

Greg dismissed my plan. I had spent too much of my life, he explained, in one academic field to let it all go. He suggested that I move sideways into ancient history, but history supported by anthropology. That combination was his own specialisation. Through Greg, I enrolled in a Masters degree, to be supervised by an Oxford trained historian and archaeologist Bill Cullicen (who stimulated my interest in objective history writing), and Greg and others arranged for me to become a tutor in the Classics Department. I applied for and received a Commonwealth Scholarship, enough to provide for my living expenses. Greg directed my reading in anthropology and I became involved with the classical texts in the area as well as modern anthropological thinkers.

I now had time to read books such as EE Evans-Pritchard's study of *Nuer Religion* (1956) and his earlier book *The Divine Kingship of the Shilluk of the Nilotic Sudan* (1948). For the first time, I became aware of the broader structure of religion, of what religion did for a people. The answers that Evans-Pritchard received from his Nuer respondents threw light on my own ideas of Judaism and Christianity as religious systems. I became engrossed in other tomes such as Raymond Firth's *Human Types* (1956),

SH Hooke's *Myth, Ritual and Kingship* (1958) and I struggled through Claude Levi-Stauss' *Structural Anthropology* (1963). I began seriously to rethink my ideas on religion, its origins, its structure and its manifestations within human societies and cultures.

I graduated to the works of Henri Frankfort *Kingship and the Gods* (1948), *The Birth of Civilisation* (1950) and his collection *Before Philosophy* (1949). From a rather narrow study of ancient Judaism and Christianity, I became more and more interested in religion generally and the Middle Eastern religions generally. More importantly perhaps, I became engrossed in the study of human culture and the way that the human mind develops and affects human behaviour and human society. I now asked the question: where does religion fit into human life both individually and socially?

I did not know it at the time but all of this was providing the basis for a third revolution. I still needed to work through the 'normal science' that had resulted from the second revolution but I was beginning to see things afresh.

Towards the end of my time at Melbourne University I had found Max Black's *Models and Metaphors* (1962) enlightening and then, even more so, Ian Barbour's *Myths, Models and Paradigms* (1974). They enabled me to begin elaborating the description of a new cultural world where my study of the Hebrew Scriptures and the Christian Scriptures took on a new meaning and even made sense.

But the real breakthrough was the discovery of the works of two scholars: Clifford Geertz, *The Interpretation of Cultures* (1973) and Thomas Kuhn *The Structure of Scientific Revolutions* (1969/1972). As I read them, I knew that I could not think as I had previously. Geertz explained to me how I could gain a purchase on what religion in general was about and how it operated in human societies while, as I have mentioned in the Introduction, I adapted Kuhn to explain how change took place in the study of religion and religions.

I found this university setting a great relief following the politics of ecclesiastical life. After two years at Melbourne University, making use of some of the new thinking that was exciting my brain, I submitted an MA thesis on the social structures of ancient Israel and the relationship of those structures to its religious development. This combined the anthropology to which I had been exposed and the history that I had been struggling with for so long; the thesis did not presume that any religious authority had the slightest control over my thinking. It was accepted with first class honours.

After completing the Masters degree, I obtained a position as Lecturer in History and Religion Studies in South Australia in a College of Advanced Education that would at a later date become part of the new University of South Australia. I had married in 1973 and we had a son in 1976 and a daughter in 1979 (three events that have been joyous beyond description and which still envelop my personal life). Slowly, I would advance through the academic ranks as Lecturer, Senior Lecturer, Associate Professor and Professor of Religion and Education. The scope of my study moved more and more into the broader field of the study of religion and religions.

Soon after I moved to Adelaide I made contact with some educational academics at the University of Adelaide and, through them, I came under the mentorship of JJ (George) Smolicz who would become the Professor of Education at Adelaide. I had initially mentioned to him that I was interested in Kuhn and applying his thinking to religion. George was also interested in Kuhn and in applying his theory to the social sciences rather than the natural sciences. For George and myself to work together was an obvious match and I began a doctorate under his supervision. I now wanted to identify specifically religious forms of knowledge and how these forms of knowledge influenced religious thought, the structure of religious communities and also the directions of the study of religion. The thesis carried on from the Masters.

George was Polish by birth and dedicated to his Polish ethnicity. He introduced me to the works of Polish sociologists and I read with great benefit Jerzy Szacki on the concept of human tradition and more particularly the methodology devised by Florian Znaniecki in *The Method of Sociology* (1968) to unravel the inner structures and workings of human groups. George and I wrote a journal article incorporating this new thinking into the literary study of the Bible.

I worked steadily in the History and Religion Studies Department at the College, where I was responsible for Religion Studies but participated in the History discipline. I needed to become much more *au fait* with Islamic history and writings, Buddhist history and writings and so on. I began to study more of Anthropology of Religion, Philosophy of Religion, Sociology of Religion. I lectured in Roman and Greek History as well as Ancient Near Eastern History.

All of this opened my eyes to a new world of thought. I saw religion, whether in the past or in the present, from an entirely new vantage point. Judaism and Christianity were instances of the plurality of religion across space and time. The study of their Scriptures needed to be seen from this vantage point. A third revolution had taken place in my thinking. It was based primarily on an anthropological approach to religion and religions. I will now try to summarise the foundations of this new world of thought.

The summary deals with culture, religion, human thinking and models of thinking and the effect of all of these on religious individuals and communities. It owes much to the authors I cited earlier, although the way it is put together has been my own endeavour.

Everyday Culture

Culture is a human creation. It is not something static; it develops and adapts, just as the human group, within which it has its being, develops and adapts to a changing physical environment. The development and adaptation of a culture and the development and adaptation of its attendant human group are not separate issues.

Without human beings there could be no culture; development and adaptation of culture and humans must happen synchronically. Some anthropologists would even claim that without culture there would be no human beings; the very notion of being human requires being programmed by culture. While animals, to a large extent, have their behavioural patterns predetermined by their genetic code, the behaviour of human beings is regulated genetically to a far less extent. The cat is born with sharpened instincts. It is programmed not only to suckle but to hunt. It does not learn how to communicate; it is programmed to produce a distinctive set of sounds, each of which has a specific meaning.

Humans have a need to make meaning of those events in which they are involved and they do so by means of a system of symbols, a culture. They need to bring order into a maze of events and observations; culture enables them to achieve order. What other animals achieve through instinct, humans largely achieve through culture.

Does this vital human culture exist in reality or only in the human mind? It would seem that there is a tendency for humans to situate culture 'out there', in what they would define as reality. It is natural, accordingly, for people to consider their own particular culture to be the 'true' culture, to think that their way of living is really real; it comes as a shock for them to realise that there are other humans who regard their own cultures equally as valid.

What does culture, understood in this way, offer to the human being? The human individual has a need for order. To make sense of the universe, self and others, the individual within the group requires a direction, a purpose, a sense of meaning. All cultural activity takes place in the context of the construction of a cultural 'world' of meanings. These constructed worlds achieve viability because they are supported by a group which, by its general acceptance, gives plausibility to such constructed worlds. The supportive group commits itself to its 'world' and defines its own roles and identities vis-à-vis it. Culture is a meaning-seeking procedure.

Culture, every culture, offers this advantage to its adherents. In order to find meaning and direction, individuals and groups must accept and then adapt themselves to this cultural heritage of a constructed world. When the group has achieved meaning and direction, it acts to retain its cultural heritage with the same tenacity as an individual displays in maintaining personal, physical life. Hence there is always an element of adherence and continuity in culture, together with a capacity to adapt and change.

European culture, Chinese culture, Aboriginal Australian culture are similar but different. Which is best? None is better or best.

Religion and Religious Pluralism

How can what has been said about culture be applied advantageously to religion? Like culture, religion is a meaning-seeking activity and presents itself as a organised system of symbols. The symbols of religion can be catalogued mainly under the subsets of myth and ritual, but they also include beliefs, objects, natural phenomena, clothing and so forth. It is a particular type of culture, a very important one.

Religion, seen as religious culture, must be appreciated in its vital role of attaining a unique form of order, 'ultimate order' or 'ultimacy'.

What we have been discussing about culture to this point could be called 'secular culture' which provides its adherents with everyday order, with the ability to get through the day. Secular culture allows human beings to find order amid a chaos of common human experience, to explain historical events, to solve problems of identity. However, there are certain points in life where disorder can reassert itself. Were I to find myself overwhelmed with the mysteries of the universe, with severe and continued suffering that seems to have no cause, with the problem of evil (why do innocent children suffer? why are innocent people killed by earthquakes and floods?), I would find that the world has lost its order and that I do not know where I am going any longer. Should there be the remotest indication that a secular culture is unable to cope with such experiences then severe anxiety results for the affected individual.

At this point, where secular or everyday culture is not coping, there is an urgent need for religious culture. A 'religious culture' could include the living world religions (Christianity, Buddhism etc.), indigenous religions (the Aboriginal Australian religions etc), syncretistic religion (mixes of different religions), and philosophical systems such as Marxism, Humanism, Existentialism and so on. It could also include personal religious systems where the individual might be a Humanist but practises Buddhist meditation and is attracted to the ritual of High Anglicanism.

No matter which of the above religious cultural systems might be used, the religious person interprets what is happening in the world in terms of ultimacy, of ultimate order. It would seem that all humans have an inborn capacity to do this; which system they adopt will depend on their own life circumstances, whereby they come across a religion and activate the capacity. This would happen to all human persons who have reached a level of discretion and are not mentally handicapped to a significant degree. Most people therefore can be designated as 'religious persons', although the 'religion' of some of them might not necessarily be recognised as a conventional religion. Many would probably not appreciate being called 'religious'.

Although the two might be separable in theory, secular culture and religious culture are not distinct in real terms. Each affects the other and each is interconnected with the other. The symbols of ultimate order and direction are shaped in a specific way within a particular secular culture. Alternatively, once it has been constructed, a religious culture then deeply affects the secular culture by its particular cultural logic.

I understand ultimacy, the state of ultimate order and meaning that goes beyond everyday order, to be defined in a religious culture by symbolic means. Thus, the religious culture of Buddhism is mainly defined by the figure of the Buddha, by the *dharma* or the collected teachings of the Buddha and the *sangha* or the community of Buddhists. These combine to introduce the symbol of *nirvana* or the state of perfect enlightenment. For the Buddhist, this is ultimacy.

Beyond the symbol, does this ultimacy really exist? The symbol of ultimacy is formed within a cultural setting. *Nirvana* and the other symbols exist within real historical Buddhist communities in Thailand or elsewhere. The symbols do seem to be real but they are no more real than other important cultural symbols.

Sometimes the religious cultural system maintains that humans and ultimacy are far distant from each other, even though there is a bridge between the two. Usually, in this case, the main symbol of ultimacy is personal. Thus we get a personal god or many gods such as Zeus, Allah or YHWH. If, on the other hand there is an intimate closeness between the focus and the human group, then the symbol of ultimacy is often impersonal. An example would be *brahman*, the Hindu symbol of infinite being that encroaches on an individual's personal space and yet extends forever.

Religious cultural activity is about bridging the gulf or activating the intimate closeness between the individual and ultimate order and meaning by means of a focus. The focus is always symbolic. The Qur'an is a symbolic focus for Muslims; Jesus is the focus for Christians. In some religions there are alternative focuses.

Once again, as was the case with secular cultures, the distinction needs to be drawn between ultimacy in itself, 'out there', and the focus as humanly symbolised by a particular religious group. Ultimacy in itself is ultimate order and harmony. It is very real to those who see it via their focus, but that reality cannot be proved to others who are outside the religious cultural system. In other words, a symbol of ultimacy such as Allah is unique and can only be understood or critiqued within the context of the religious culture of Islam. The outsider can make use of the Qur'an and appreciate the Allah symbol, but this requires enormous sensitivity. The same is true of understanding one of The Dreaming symbols in Aboriginal Australian religions or *nirvana* in Buddhism.

Religious cultures, therefore, are different from each other because they have different symbolic focuses on different symbols of ultimacy. While there will always be family resemblances between them, religious traditions remain, each of them, unique and very difficult for outsiders to understand.

Religious Experience

We need now to analyse a religious culture in broader detail. The central feature of any religion would not be its sacred text (if it should be a literate society) nor its ethical system nor its doctrinal teaching, but its religious experience. Religious experience is a deep reaction that is aroused when a person or group make contact by means of a focus with the symbol of ultimacy.

At this point I take an example that is outside Judaism and Christianity. A specific religious experience is central, for example, to Islam. Its sacred story (which may or may not be based on history) recounts that at a certain moment Muhammad, while deep in meditation on a hill outside Mecca, was confronted by his own perception of a focus on ultimacy, which he identified as *al 'ilah*, 'The God' or Allah. For him, *al 'ilah* became a new symbol of ultimacy. In direct fusion, he underwent the deepest experience of *islam*, submission and awareness of human frailty in the presence of ultimacy.

He thereby achieved ultimate order in his life. At the same time he was relieved of a deep sense of alienation that had burdened him up to that moment. This complex reaction of submission and fulfilment was the typical Islamic experience, an experience that subsequently the Islamic religion offers to all its adherents. Muhammad's religion is the religion of *islam* or 'submission' and its adherents are *muslims* or 'people submitted' to Allah.

In further ecstatic experiences Muhammad is said (with or without historical accuracy is immaterial) to have acquired the means to focus on Allah—the written book of the Qur'an. This book was available for others to use as a focus to attain the experience that Muhammad had attained directly.

Every other religion could discourse similarly on its typical religious experience. Judaism has its core experience of chosenness; Christianity has its core experience of *agape*, unconditional love; Buddhism has its core experience of enlightenment.

But how is the transition made from the unique religious experience of an individual founder to the religious experiences of subsequent followers of this founder? When the founder dies, what remains?

It is religious myth and ritual that normally activate the specific religious experience for subsequent adherents by drawing them into the focus, and this experience brings ultimate meaning and direction into the adherents' lives. Myth and ritual become the essential carriers of the focus, recreating the initial experience of the founder. We will deal with them separately.

Myth and Ritual

Myth or sacred story is the dominant discourse of religion. All religious traditions have a fund of such stories. Sacred stories are not necessarily historical stories; in fact, historicity is of no consequence. Myth is a metaphor that conveys the most profound spiritual truth, a truth not communicable by everyday language. It communicates the essential features of a religious culture in story form. But myth does more than recount. It re-creates the original 'world' of the 'time of the beginnings', the primeval world, in which the way of life of a human group, the fund of its common understandings and its principal values were established.

This world cannot now be directly accessed by humans in historical time and space; it certainly cannot be accessed by the methods of history or science. Myth is a symbol that explains the religious charter for how things should be, for what needs to be done and what needs to be avoided. What was said and done in the 'time of the beginnings', as the myth relates it, effects and affects the way of life of the religious group here and now.

Myth guides the group as to how life should be led, informs the group as to how outside reality came to be the way it is, and it warns the group of the threats that could disturb the order of things. Myths are like public dreams; like all dreams, they link the conscious to the unconscious.

Myths convey information to the group about the cosmos' link with ultimacy ('creation' or beginning stories), about alienation from ultimacy (stories about a primordial fall, an initial distancing of the group from ultimacy), about the possibility of the group's own reinstated link with ultimacy (for example, the Exodus myth or the Jesus myth or sacred stories of other founders), about the possibility of final reconciliation with ultimacy or final distancing from it (eschatological myths).

Myth, understood in this way, is organically connected with sacred ritual. Ritual is sacred drama, a dramatic social portrayal. A core ritual is the symbolic re-enactment of the past event, when contact was initially made between a founder or founding group and the sacred world. But ritual, like myth, can only be understood when it is acknowledged to be essentially and inextricably connected with religious experience.

Myth and ritual create the ambient of the focus by which the symbol of ultimacy is contacted by a human community.

I could now understand that the celebration of the Jewish Passover is the dramatic, ritual portrayal of the Exodus out of Egypt. It is the story or myth of Passover in dramatic form. The ritual of Passover brings the past Exodus event into the present for the believing group. It is as if a particular group of Jews, gathered in the home on the festival of Passover, becomes part of the original Passover people and personally experiences the saving, guiding, comforting presence of its God, YHWH by means of a Moses who leads, guides and fulfils his people. That Exodus-experience was considered to be the founding experience of Judaism, and celebrating Passover brings the experience of the past event into the present. Other Jewish rituals find their relevance by reason of their relationship to the Passover *seder*. Whether there ever was an historical Exodus is immaterial to this discussion.

Likewise for Christians, I could see that the celebration of the Eucharist is the dramatic, ritualistic re-enactment of the death and resurrection of Jesus. Jesus as the new Moses had passed, according to the proclamation of the early Christians, from this suffering life to eternal life, a return to life with the Father. His was a once-and-for-all 'return', establishing a mode of future human contact with ultimacy. The symbolic ritual of the Eucharist lies at the foundation of Christianity. Jesus was the first to make the New Exodus journey. Those Christians who ritually eat the bread and drink the wine in the prescribed manner share the event with him in anticipation of the final reality. The Moses-focus and the Jesus-focus are not static, they are dynamic. Other Christian and Jewish rituals derive their relevance and meaning from their core ritual. Asking the question whether these events were historically verifiable has no relevance.

Myth, with its accompanying ritual, activates the specific focus of a religion and inducts the religious adherents into the religious experience proper to that religion; in turn, this experience provides ultimate meaning and gives ultimate direction to the participants.

We can say that a particular religion devolves from the experience generated by the religious cultural discourse inherent within a set of myths and the cultural action of its core rituals. This is the myth-making activity proper to religion. In point of fact there are many religions, and individuals are free, at least potentially, to select between them or combine aspects of them at will. I will now concentrate on the notion of religious experience, and on the predictability of the choices whereby individuals tend to choose a religious discourse along predetermined lines.

Mediation

Religious experience is, as has been seen, the profound human reaction that results when humans overcome their fear in confrontation with the unknown and the ever-changing universe and find ultimate meaning. Humans have a capacity to bridge the gulf between themselves and this ultimacy. When the bridging has at least been initiated to an individual's satisfaction in symbolic form, the experience is profound. This is mediation.

Why is the choice of a religious culture to achieve this end, from a wide possible range, so predictable that individuals often end up adhering to one or other of the world religions or a religious surrogate such as Marxism, Humanism or Existentialism? Individualised religions, constructed by particular humans for their own advantage, are rare. They are difficult to construct and they take initiative and deep insight. The answer is that a ready-made religious culture not only presents the individual with the possibility for ultimate order, it also imposes on that person an obligation to choose it. The person is told by the religious culture itself: this is the true religion for us. And so Greeks usually take on Greek Orthodox Christianity, those born of Catholics become Roman Catholics, Indians become Hindu and so it goes on.

More often than not, a religious culture looks back to a 'founder'. Sometimes the 'founder' is still identifiable as a person, whether historical or not (such as a Jesus or a Buddha or a Muhammad), but at other times the founding event is represented only by the existing myth/ritual process (as in Aboriginal Australian religions); there is little difference since the founder-person takes on a mythical form anyway.

Let us go over once more the example of Islam and its founder, Muhammad. Muhammad (whether the historical figure or the Muhammad of Islamic religious discourse it does not matter) did not come from a neutral, non-religious background. The complex religious cultural discourse to which he had access would have included elements of Arab tribal religion, Judaism and Christianity. But Muhammad did not find religious satisfaction in this amalgam.

At a certain moment he underwent a profound religious experience. From an infinite possible number of choices to construct a new symbol on ultimacy, he constructed a new one, Allah, a symbol that was fashioned in some way from the religions around him. In doing so, he at once experienced the resolution of his own dissatisfaction. This resolution was accompanied by an internal reaction, a distinctive religious experience of submissiveness, of *islam*. While his personal situation was stabilised as a result, the question was left open as to whether his experience could be replicated for others. If not, then Muhammad's new, individual religious culture, personally satisfying as it undoubtedly was, would be spontaneously aborted. There would not have been an Islam. There needed to be a focus that others could utilise.

This element of replication is absolutely vital for the establishment of a religion. Can the founding experience have a successor? Can the mediation which the founder experiences be available for others? 'Founders' are like great artists. Most people occasionally have profound experiences of life, nature and human relationships. These experiences are usually deeply personal; they cannot be described and they cannot be compared to anything else. The artist is that gifted individual who is able to use a medium - words, paint, musical sound—to communicate such a profound, personal experience; the artist is able to use the medium to allow others to feel the same. Similarly, the religious 'founder' is the person who has undergone a personal religious mediation and is able to construct a mediatorial system, which can convey the original religious experience to others. The mediatorial system includes the focus on ultimacy.

That mediatorial system would consist primarily of the recitation of myth and the performance of an accompanying ritual. These construct the focus. Sometimes the memory of the founder disappears and the mediatorial system consists only of the myth and ritual process in oral form or in a text. At other times the founding individual remains indelibly identified with the mediatorial system.

The Mediatorial System

This mediatorial system is the organising framework for all religious phenomena. Its driving mechanism, the complex of myth and ritual which found the focus brings about a religious experience, considered to be the same as that experienced by the founder. The same myth-making mechanism establishes a social structure: the people who share the same experience are not all equals, some are more important than others and some have more important roles in the group. The entire mediatorial system and the people associated with it are safeguarded by a code of ethical practice, by a catalogue of ordered beliefs or a creed and, in literate societies, by a canonical text.

Mythical descriptions of the original meeting between the founder and ultimacy may depict the founder as a Hero or King or even the First Person. There will also be descriptions on how successors are to be appointed to that founder. These could be later kings or prophets or priests or something else. The story will relate how the myth and ritual should be handed on and protected by a religious leadership. Thus, the religious structure will identify a symbol of the focus on ultimacy and a symbol of the community. There will also be a symbol of ultimacy itself.

We can now outline the main aspects of this mediatorial system. Mediation, linking a human group to an ultimate focus, is required to allay religious fear regarding the possibility of an experience of disorder in life. For example: the community of Israel (depicted as the people wandering through the desert) are represented by Moses their leader who meets YHWH (the symbol of ultimacy) on Mount Sinai. The Buddhist *sangha* or community are led by The Buddha who achieves Enlightenment and finds *nirvana* (the symbol of ultimacy).

In short, a religious group takes up a particular posture before a sacred symbol which it regards as its specific focus on ultimacy. In so doing, it aims to achieve mediation, contact with ultimacy, and so find the secret knowledge that will guide the group through the mysteries of life and the universe.

While most religions function in this way, by an indirect mediatorial system (going from Moses of the Exodus to YHWH or from the Qur'an received by Muhammad to Allah) there are some where the meeting is more direct. In some forms of Hinduism and Buddhism a direct relationship is formed between the community and ultimacy; at times mystical forms of Judaism and Christianity achieve the same. This is an immediate system where ultimacy is usually symbolised as impersonal, such as *brahman*, the great world soul.

Summary

In summary, religions are built on a founding 'event' that dictates the symbols that will enable later believers to undergo a similar religious experience to that discovered at the beginning of the religion. This is achieved by the recitation of myth and the performance of ritual. The past is thereby brought into the present.

However, the religious phenomena of myth, ritual and experience do not exist apart from a human group. They only exist because the religious group has accepted the authority of myth and ritual and then the experience structures the group. The group is obliged to hold to a list of beliefs and to acknowledge key symbols, and a certain code of ethics is imposed on the life of the group. In literate societies, aspects of the myth, ritual, beliefs, ethics are often consigned to writing and become sacred texts. This is where the study of the Hebrew Scriptures and the Christian Scriptures needs to be situated.

This was my new explanation for religion and religions, including the religions of Judaism and Christianity. The new paradigm also re-situated the sacred texts of the Christian Bible. For the moment the paradigm lay side by side with the work I was still doing on the texts of the Bible, trying to stretch to the full the normal science of the second revolution. I had long left behind the history of Israel and the history of Jesus. I was more interested in the texts and the structures within the texts.

This study became more and more directed by the third revolution. I was beginning to realise that all my thinking up to this point, buffeted as it was through two disturbing revolutions, had been built on the premise that Judaism and Christianity were privileged religious systems. I had been willing to admit that other religions were also valid. However, they were valid because they were essentially similar to Judaism and Christianity. Now, I was coming to the inevitable conclusion that Judaism and Christianity were no better or worse than other religious traditions.

This was a pluralist outlook. It would have repercussions for my thinking about religion and about sacred texts. It would have repercussions for my interpretation of the Hebrew Scriptures and the Christian Scriptures.

Postscript

At this point I will add a few final words on Jerome Crowe. Jerome had begun the revolutionary process not only for myself but for many others. He was a very cautious person and, in my evaluation, he never moved beyond the first revolution. This was true of many other scholars in the field. He was highly competent as an academic and he examined the normal science of that first revolution in great depth. He wrote well but within the parameters of the initial paradigm. Jerome eventually came to the University of South Australia and took charge of a special course in Catholic Studies (set up for students who proposed to teach in Catholic schools). We remained close friends. What he taught was comparable to what he had taught us some fifty years previously. This is not a criticism, simply a fact; he was an excellent scholar and competent teacher.

Jerome died suddenly in August 1996 and I deeply mourned his passing.

Note

I will give references to some of the books which, as noted in this chapter, have affected me deeply:

Barbour, Ian (1974), *Myths, Models and Paradigms,* Harper and Row: New York.

Black, Max (1962), *Models and Metaphors: Studies in Method*, Cornell University Press: Ithaca

Geertz, Clifford (1973), *The Interpretation of Cultures*, Basic Books: New York, which contains his essay defining religion as:

> (1) a system of symbols which acts to (2) establish powerful, pervasive, and long-lasting moods and motivations in men by (3) formulating conceptions of a general order of existence and (4) clothing these conceptions with such an aura of factuality that (5) the moods and motivations seem uniquely realistic.

Szacki, J (1969), 'Three concepts of tradition', *Polish Sociological Bulletin*, 2, pp 17-31

Znaniecki, F (1968), *The Method of Sociology*, new edition, Farrar and Rinehart: New York

Znaniecki, F (1940), *The Social Role of the Man of Knowledge*, Columbia University Press: New York

Znaniecki, F (1952), *Cultural Sciences: their Origin and Development*, University of Illinois Press: Urbana

A more formal treatment of my thinking on the structures within religion can be found in Crotty, R (1995), 'Towards Classifying Religious Phenomena', *Australian Religion Studies Review*, 8, pp 34-41.

Chapter 13
A DIVERSION:
BACK TO HISTORY

There was to be a diversion in my intellectual endeavours. The very history that I had put aside in interpreting Biblical texts beaconed to me again, but in a quite different context.

I was now a tertiary educator involved with both history students and students of religion in a secular institution. By the 1980s there were new developments relating to history taking place that I needed to take into consideration in my university role. I continued to teach Greek and Roman History and Ancient Near Eastern History as well as Religion Studies. I would have to consider the possibility of a history of Ancient Israel as well as Jesus and early Christianity but from a completely secular viewpoint. To some extent I put aside the interpretation of texts to take into account the historical claims that were being readily made not only by international scholars but in the world press.

History and the Hebrew Scriptures

It was this search for history, first of all with regards to Israel in the Ancient Near East, that sustained my continued interest in archaeology. In 1981 I went to Jerusalem again and took courses in archaeology at the Hebrew University and met up with some Israeli archaeologists. Some of the Israeli academics with whom I made contact were sincere believers in the historicity of ancient Israel as depicted in the biblical text. There was a strong motive, not always religious, for these Israelis, whose forebears had taken over much of former Palestine, to believe that the land had previously belonged to their Ancestors.

I did not share their need to prove the rightful establishment of the modern State of Israel. I found other Israeli academics as highly sceptical as myself as regards the religious basis for modern occupation. Any confidence that the story of Israel as contained in the biblical text could be substantially sustained as historical had almost disappeared.

I was, of course, still certain that the links that Albright, Noth and Mendenhall and others had fashioned between the biblical story and archaeology were unsustainable. There were certainly overlaps between what was in the pages of the Hebrew Scriptures and what archaeologists had discovered over time. For example, I could still point to the following:

- The Merneptah Stele from 1209 BCE which contained the first mention of an 'Israel'
- Shalmaneser III's inscription from about 853 BCE in which one of the kings of the northern kingdom, 'Ahab the Israelite', was mentioned
- An inscription on black basalt, probably from around 835 BCE, written in Aramaic relating an invasion of the north by an unnamed Aramean king and boasting of killing '(Ahaz)iahu son of (Jehoram kin)g of the House of David'.
- The Black Obelisk from about 825 BCE which had a reference to the king 'Jehu, son of Omri' (together with an image of Jehu)
- The inscription of Mesha, king of Moab from about 840 BCE which referred to 'Omri', one of the very powerful northern kings
- The inscription of Adad-nirari III from about 803 BCE which mentioned 'The land of Omri'
- Tiglath-pileser III's (743-732 BCE) document that contained a reference to 'Menahem of Samaria'
- Sargon II's (721-705 BCE) document referring to him as defeating the city of 'Samaria' and 'the whole house of Omri'

However, these were indications at the most that there had been some group called 'Israel' in the north of Palestine and that this people called Israel had kings called Ahab, Jehu, Omri and Menahem in their capital Samaria and there had been some instances of succession. But there was no proof for anything like the extended stories concerning the events and characters that were described in the Bible. There was also the sole reference to the southern kingdom and the 'House of David' (and there are scholars who debate that 'David' is in the text) that did not at all substantiate a widespread kingdom of David and Solomon.

The scrappy evidence of these non-biblical texts could not offset the fact that there was no archaeological evidence for an Exodus, none for the extensive united kingdom of David and Solomon (even if there was the enigmatic passing reference to a House of David), none for a split between Judah in the south and Israel in the north, none for the interwoven succession of kings in the northern and southern kingdoms. Where had the story in the Hebrew Scriptures come from?

My time at the Hebrew University only confirmed my deep scepticism about the Bible and history. Any of my previous reconstructions of ancient Israel were completely in limbo. While I continued to be interested in the ancient history of the Near East and its religions, I could not see that it had any direct impact on the study of the Hebrew Scriptures. They lived their own life and had their own messages. They were part of the sacred story of one religion among many. They had nothing to do with history.

History and the Christian Scriptures

In the field of the Christian Scriptures there were even more historical novelties in the public domain. I became deeply involved in this study. I will categorise the new developments as follows:

- an attempt, particularly by the so-called Jesus Seminar, to determine which of the gospel sayings were the actual words of Jesus,
- new developments in the study of the Dead Sea Scrolls,
- an evaluation of the Gnostic texts from Nag Hammadi,
- new information from archaeology that threw light on the history of Palestine in the Greek and Roman periods,
- new information on Galilee in the first century BCE and the first century CE.

The Jesus Seminar

I will take the first of these new developments because it involved some of the people that I had made contact with overseas. In the world of scholarship there was a new focus on the historical authenticity of the sayings of Jesus. Stimulated by the possibilities of advances in literary methodology, more certain dating of gospel texts and the Q hypothesis, the 'Jesus Seminar', a convocation of biblical scholars, was established in the United States in 1985. Up to 200 scholars have since then met twice a year to debate the authenticity of the sayings of Jesus, his *ipsissima verba*. What had he actually said?

The Jesus Seminar's discussion would range over the number of separate attestations of any saying attributed to Jesus in the gospels. If a particular saying occurred in Matthew and Luke, that counted as only one attestation, since both often copied from Mark or from Q. But if the saying occurred in Mark and John or Mark and Q that would be two attestations; if it also occurred in Thomas, that was three attestations. The more attestations, the more likely that the text would be considered authentic.

The level at which an attestation was found was also considered important. An attestation in Mark would be regarded as earlier (and therefore more likely to have been accurately recalled) than an attestation in Matthew, Luke or John. Debate continued as to whether an attestation in Thomas would have predated the canonical gospels. The Seminar also considered whether Jesus, given his Jewish background, the probability that his native language was Aramaic and the time and circumstances in which he lived, was more or less likely to have said such a thing.

After discussion the members of the Jesus Seminar would vote on a particular saying of Jesus: a red counter indicated that the voter thought that Jesus had actually said what was recorded in the gospel text; a pink counter meant that he probably would have said it; a grey counter that is was unlikely he had said it; a black counter meant that he definitely had not said it.

In the end, there were very few red votes, only some fifteen in total. But there were enough for many scholars to have a new confidence in what Jesus might have actually said. I was never convinced by this attempt to uncover the actual words of Jesus. Nor was I interested whether the words were those of Jesus or not

Next, I will turn to more recent Dead Sea Scroll research.

New developments in the study of the Dead Sea Scrolls

We have already seen that the first seven scrolls had been purchased by the State of Israel and housed in their purpose-built Shrine of the Book. After the cessation of the War of Independence other scrolls and fragments were obtained by scholars attached to the Palestine Archaeological Museum. The first editor-in-chief was Roland de Vaux. Huge numbers of fragments were laid out on tables to be joined together like parts of a jigsaw. Slowly, very slowly, these were being published and interpretations of the collection proliferated.

By the 1970s scholars interested in the study of early Christianity had taken up one or other of the three positions on the scrolls. A minority had seen them as the literature of proto-Christians, an Essene group who in some way transmogrified into the Christian church. For these scholars the characters mentioned in the texts of the sectarian scrolls invited further study: the Teacher of Righteousness, the Wicked Priest. Earlier, Edmund Wilson had hinted that Jesus was the Teacher of Righteousness or at least similar to the Teacher. This defied the common dating of the scrolls which mentioned the Teacher of Righteousness in the second century BCE.

Robert Eisenman, on the other hand, identified James, the brother of Jesus, as the Teacher of Righteousness and Paul as the Wicked Priest. In Australia, controversy would rage for a decade or more after Barbara Thiering claimed that Jesus was the Wicked Priest of the scrolls. Both redated the relevant scrolls. These identifications had always made observant Christians uneasy since they challenged the uniqueness of Christianity as a world religion and seemed to downplay the role of Jesus as the founder of Christianity.

Other scholars recognised in the scrolls the literature of a Jewish group from whom some of the early Christian disciples, for example John the Baptist, had come. Perhaps John the Baptist had been the Teacher of Righteousness. Consequently, this group held that the early Christians would have modelled themselves on the Qumran sect as far as aspects of community organisation, administration and cult were concerned.

A much larger group maintained that the scrolls belonged to a Jewish sect, or perhaps a number of sects, which flourished at the same time as early Christianity, although there was no direct contact between the two groups. The scrolls gave these scholars fortuitous access to the Jewish background of Jesus and the gospels, the Palestinian Jewish matrix of the Second Temple period. These scholars recognised real parallels in religious language and religious ideas and similar use of proof-texts among the Qumran community and the early Christians. They presumed that these commonalities were to be found among most branches of first century Judaism and were to be expected.

Most of these scholars were from a Christian background, even if they were not particularly demonstrative as far as their faith was concerned.

Mention must be made of a group also involved at the cutting edge of scrolls research who were Israeli or at least of Jewish background. From the time of Eleazar Sukenik, the professor who had bought some of the first scrolls, they had had access to the seven scrolls in the Israeli Shrine of the Book and these scrolls were regarded as precious relics testifying to the miracle of Israel's national rebirth.

While, for Christian or non-Jewish scholars, the sectarian scrolls have provided invaluable background against which to explain the evolution of Christianity from an earlier phase of Judaism, for many Jews they are the tangible proof that their ancestors had actually lived in the land and fought for its integrity. For these people, the presumed community behind these sectarian scrolls was not composed of pacifist proto-Christian Jews; they were Jews who had anticipated the bloody struggle of 1948 and after. They were presumed to have died in battle at Qumran fighting the Romans, having first hid the scrolls, in order that a later generation in 1948 might succeed.

Consciously or unconsciously modern Israelis have evoked the mythic images of the Bible to give a beleaguered people the energy to survive in a hostile Arab environment. Israeli archaeology, searching as it does for evidence of Jewish roots, arouses fierce public interest; it has become almost a secular religion in itself. Qumran fulfilled such a mythic image - a pious Jewish minority, upholding traditional values, had been accosted and destroyed by a belligerent world power and yet they managed to hand on the sacred scroll relics to another generation. The scrolls could be compared to the relics of the 'true cross' that have been treasured by Christians over the centuries.

This Israeli group had a need to publish and to publish quickly, to put their scrolls into the public domain, and to claim that all scrolls, including those under the control of the editorial board, were theirs. They were Jewish scrolls, not Christian. Hershel Shanks, the rather fiery editor of *Biblical Archaeologist,* wrote:

> I believe that under international law these editors are trustees, fiduciaries. The real beneficiaries of this trust are all the people, whose heritage is illuminated by these precious texts—not an elite group of scholars or even a single country, culture or religion.[1]

1. *New York Times,* September 7, 1991.

Both the Israelis and the other groups had reason to claim that the scrolls were theirs. The Israelis claimed that the scrolls had belonged to their forebears; those entrusted with the scrolls collected at the Palestine Archaeological Museum claimed that their institutions had paid good money for the scrolls or had actually discovered them. Each had a different reason for esteeming the find. Each had a different timetable in mind for publication. It was inevitable that confrontation would be followed by recrimination and accusation.

In 1967 the Six Day War ended with the Israelis in control of East Jerusalem, the Jordanian sector, and they took military possession of it. Israel did not immediately interfere with the administration of the Palestine Archaeological Museum, soon renamed as the Rockefeller Museum, or the control of the scrolls. De Vaux had been succeeded by his confrere and my onetime mentor, Pierre Benoit, as editor-in-chief. On the death of Benoit in 1987 the position of editor-in-chief passed to John Strugnell who had been on the board of editors since he was a young man. At this point the board of editors still did not have any Jewish representatives since, for one thing, there had been no way a Jew could have had access to a meeting in East Jerusalem. In 1988 Amir Drori, an ex-army general, was made director of the Israel Antiquities Authority. He set up a committee to represent Israeli and Jewish interests regarding the scrolls.

But matters were coming to a head. There had been a concordance to the scrolls commissioned by the editors since the 1960s. This listed each word used in the texts and documented where it occurred, the column, line and adjacent words. In 1988 Strugnell decided to publish thirty copies of the concordance for the use of scholars engaged in translation and editing. In 1990, after having obtained one of the copies and using a clever computer program, two American Jewish scholars at Hebrew Union College in Cincinnati, reconstructed texts from the concordance. The news made front page of prestigious American newspapers.

Events were soon to make this ingenious advance redundant. The Huntington Library in California had obtained a set of negatives of the scrolls from the deceased estate of an Elizabeth Bechtel, who had founded the Ancient Biblical Manuscript Center in Claremont, California. The photos had been taken in Jerusalem in 1961 in case any disaster overtook the original scrolls. One copy of the photos, under strict agreement concerning no access, was lodged in the Claremont Center; Elizabeth Bechtel held a duplicate copy given to her because of her financial support. She bequeathed them to the Huntington Library when she died in 1987. In

1990 a new director of the Huntington Library decided scholars could have access to these photos of the scrolls.

By this stage the editorial board in Jerusalem was in chaos. To complicate matters further in 1990 Emmanuel Tov, a highly respected Israeli scholar, was made co-editor of the board of editors side by side with John Strugnell by the Israel Antiquities Authority. Strugnell reacted violently to Tov's appointment, which he claimed was an attempt by the Israeli academic establishment to gain kudos for the research done by the original board. He gave an interview to an Israeli journalist from the leading newspaper *Ha'aretz* in which he made anti-Israeli and anti-Jewish statements which were interpreted as anti-Semitic. This interview was reprinted in the *New York Times* of 12 December, 1990. Of Judaism he was reported to have said, 'It's a horrible religion. It's a Christian heresy'.

Understandably, a furore followed. He was dismissed as editor-in-chief, although he still remained on the board of editors. Tov became sole editor-in-chief.

In 1991 Tov called a meeting in Jerusalem of those who had photos of the scrolls. This group included the Ancient Biblical Manuscript Center, the Huntington Library, the Hebrew Union College and the Centre for Postgraduate Hebrew Studies at Oxford University (later called the Oxford Centre for Hebrew and Jewish Studies). The Israelis had given this Centre at Oxford a complete set of the photos and it had been delegated to head a new editing team. The meeting in Jerusalem was cancelled when the Huntington Library refused to attend.

In November 1991 the Biblical Archaeology Society obtained a copy of the photographs from a still undisclosed source and published them in two volumes containing 1787 plates. There could no longer be argument over access; any scholar could now peruse the photos. There was full access. Since that date the editing process was speeded up and the volumes came out at a regular rate during the 1990s and in the new millennium. The very last volume appeared in 2009.

What has been the outcome of the full publication? More recent thinking in the 1990s, due to both further consideration of the earlier archaeological reports from the 1950s and access to all scroll texts, have tended to question the two fundamental supports of the original consensus: first, that the scrolls belonged to one particular Jewish sectarian group and secondly, that the scrolls were organically connected with the excavated ruins.

We can consider the first of these supports: that the scrolls belonged to one particular sectarian Jewish group. The full publication of all the scroll texts in 1991 has shown that, while there were certainly parallels with Essene thought and practice, there were parallels with other groups within Second Temple Judaism. Theories have proliferated that identified the group as Sadducean, Pharisaic or Zealot rather than Essene.

The Sadducees were the conservative, upper class Jews attached to the Temple in Jerusalem in the period immediately prior to Christianity; the Pharisees were a lay group, dedicated to the reading of the sacred texts and to pious observance in the same historical period; the Zealots were the warrior Jews who saw no other way forward than by martial combat with the occupying forces of Rome. It is becoming increasingly difficult to identify any one group as the owner of the entire scroll complex. While Josephus refers specifically to three *haireses* or schools of thought—Pharisees, Sadducees and Essenes—and elsewhere he also mentions the Zealots and the Judaeo-Christians, that does not mean he has given a complete listing. There could well have been many more Jewish factions of whom we are simply uninformed. Certainly, the attribution of all the scrolls to the Essene sect is now highly questionable.

Other scholars have stressed the wide range of teaching and practice reflected in the texts, wide enough to satisfy them that we are dealing not with the collected library of any one group but a *geniza* or storehouse for the discarded texts of many different groups. They see the Qumran texts as the remains of libraries belonging to those groups.

Neither is the second support, the organic connection between scrolls and the archaeological site, any longer taken as proven. Pliny's statement quoted earlier (*'infra hos Engada'*) is not interpreted as meaning 'Below them is Engedi' or 'Engedi is to the south'. Rather, its more obvious meaning is: 'down below (the Essenes) is Engedi'. The geographical reference would have been to some Essene site in the mountain area above Engedi, not to the north where Qumran is situated. Pliny therefore would not have been making a reference to an Essene habitation at Qumran. Further, the function of the room identified as a scriptorium with desks and inkwells in the Qumran *tell*, a key piece of evidence in linking scrolls and the 'monastery', has been reassigned as, among other possibilities, a dining room or even a dyeing room and the 'desks' identified as tables or dyeing vats.

Hence there is less certainty now about the significance of the Qumran scrolls and the adjacent *tell* than at any time since the initial discoveries. The possibility of a direct link between early Christianity and the scrolls becomes less likely. Instead, we are left with the broad conclusion that the scrolls provide incomparable access to the matrix of Second Temple Judaism—neither more nor less. The scholar of early Christianity should be aware of their potential and aware of their limitations.

I did not believe there was any direct connection between the Christian groups of the first century and the groups responsible for the Qumran texts. The writings discovered in the eleven caves would have derived from many hands, written over many periods of time and reflected the mindset of a number of groups. The value of the corpus is that it is the most extensive and reliable entry point into the matrix of Second Temple Jewish thought that we possess. For my purposes that matrix is invaluable, but there is no identification of a 'Christian' group within the Dead Sea Scroll literature.

The third area of academic research involved assessing the importance of the Coptic texts that have already been described.

Evaluating the Nag Hammadi Codices

Where should the Nag Hammadi texts fit into gospel research? There were a variety of opinions: they were later than the canonical gospels; they were earlier than the canonical gospels. At this point, I should declare that I do not consider that the Gnostic gospels, and specifically Thomas, predate the canonical gospels.

For one thing, I think there is enough evidence that the Gospel of Thomas (as we now have it in Coptic) contains sayings that have parallels in Q. There are also parallels with Mark and John. This could still mean that the canonical gospels copied from an earlier Gospel of Thomas. However, there are parallels with Matthew who has reworked Mark. This does not seem to indicate that the entire Gospel of Thomas is earlier than the canonical gospels. Pushing further forward, we have no evidence that the Coptic Thomas, for example, was the direct translation of a pre-existing Greek text. While the Greek text from Oxyrhynchus shows that there were sayings of Jesus in circulation in Egypt at an earlier period, on which the Coptic Thomas must have drawn, there is no reason to suspect that a sayings-text comparable to the entire Coptic Thomas ever existed in Greek.

In fact, the extant version of Thomas shows that its text has been influenced by the canonical synoptic gospels. The following diagram would illustrate my stance.

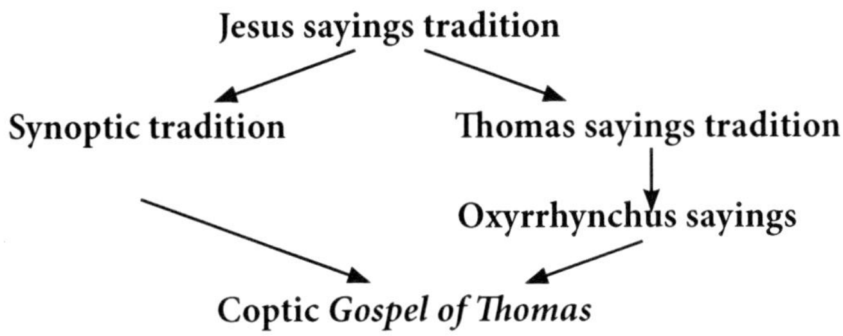

It follows that the Coptic *Gospel of Thomas* is later than and to some extent dependent on the synoptic tradition. I therefore do not consider that its Jesus sayings can be used to document an historical Jesus prior to the form that that Jesus takes in the synoptics or John.

However, as I have written above, what the discovery of the fifty-three codices at Nag Hammadi, plus the earlier ones discovered in other places, does demonstrate is that Christian Gnosticism was much more developed and widespread than previously thought. It was thought to have been a deviation from mainstream Christianity. Now it is more clearly seen to have been a competitor for the mainstream Christianity that eventually was decided by Constantine in the fourth century. That adoption by Constantine virtually put an end to further competition.

Finally, archaeological work continued and threw more light on Palestinian history. What follows gives some idea about the new discoveries and the rewriting of history around the time of Jesus.

The new archaeological discoveries

Beside the Qumran and Nag Hammadi discoveries there were other, intermittent archaeological finds. After 1967, when the modern state of Israel took over the West Bank area from the Hashemite Kingdom of Jordan, archaeology became a national Israeli pastime. In 1968, for example, the first skeletal remains of an identifiably crucified man called Jehochanan were discovered in a Jewish grave, northeast of Jerusalem. It demonstrated graphically the cruel method of execution used by the Roman colonisers on slaves and recalcitrant non-Roman subjects. There has also been the uncovering of an ossuary of a Caiaphas, perhaps the High Priest of the gospels, and the house of Peter in Capernaum.

Other archaeological work in Galilee has produced new and unexpected results. The city of Sepphoris just north of Nazareth has changed thinking about the youthful days of Jesus. On a broader level, Galilean archaeology has caused a rethinking of the economic structure and life style within the area. As the archaeological evidence has increased, the history of Galilee and Judaea in the time of Jesus has needed to be revised and considerably expanded. Those histories can now be situated in the wider context of Greek history from the latter part of the fourth century. This has thrown considerable light not only on the Christian period but the history of the Second Temple in Judaism and the time during which the Dead Sea Scrolls were written.

Now I realised that neither Christianity certainly, and probably Judaism too, could be properly understood apart from their situation in the Greek historical period. I saw the need to delve deeper into this period when first the Greeks were in control of Palestine and then were supplanted by the Romans.

I will first review Greek history and then Roman history up to this point.

New evaluation of Greek history in the East

In the latter part of the fourth century BCE, the political tide was turning against the Persian world empire. The Persians had tried in the fifth century to spread westwards and to control Greece. They failed, and Greece, which had never previously been a unified political unit, eventually found political cohesion under Alexander of Macedon. Although he was only twenty years old when his father, Philip II, was assassinated, he was able to gather Greek city-states together into a unified army of some 35,000 soldiers; Alexander then crossed Asia Minor towards the East.

He was victorious in the East. Egypt docilely accepted him without any resistance, acknowledging him to be a successor to the divine pharaohs, a god sent to deliver the Egyptian people from the Persian yoke. His armies swept into Persia and by 326 BCE they had reached the Indus valley.

Alexander unexpectedly died, possibly of fever, in 323 BCE at the age of 32. As no successor had been groomed, his generals carved up the vast empire between themselves. Egypt was ruled by Ptolemy, an unpretentious general who had been personally commissioned from peasant ranks by Alexander. Mesopotamia and Syria fell to another general, Seleucus. The Palestinian area was therefore positioned between the two capitals of Syrian Antioch in the north and Alexandria, the new Egyptian capital chosen by Alexander prior to his death. The Jewish people were caught up in these new historical developments.

The two successors in the Near East, Ptolemy and Seleucus, were political and military rivals but they both, in their own way, intended to promote Greek culture.

The external signs of Greek culture, or Hellenism, were to be seen throughout the far-flung Greek empire in town planning (featuring the *agora* or central market place, the stadium, the theatre, the gymnasium), the use of Greek language (even if it took the form of a local dialect known as *koine),* Greek dress, Greek customs and, perhaps the most vital manifestation of that culture, Greek religion. The Jews were overwhelmed by this cultural invasion. Greek names became the fashion among young Jews; the Greek drachma became the local currency; Greek language became the *lingua franca.* Greek religion became an attractive even if beguiling option for Jews.

Religion would in fact be the vital issue. Hellenism confronted Judaism in the area known as Yehud. This Aramaic term had been used by the Persians to describe the section of their foreign territory (or satrapy) that was a small province, smaller even than Judah had been in the late seventh century BCE. It consisted of Jerusalem and an area around it, perhaps only about twenty-five kilometres on all sides.

The intensity of that confrontation can be seen in two examples. From about 250 BCE, the Hebrew Scriptures became available in Greek in a version called the Septuagint. The languages of the people who had constructed the earlier texts were under challenge.[2] There were now Hebrew and Greek versions of the Scriptures side by side.

The second example involved the Greek gymnasium. The gymnasium was a major force in Hellenistic social life. It provided the venue for naked males in athletic training, exercising and bathing. The parade of male bodies was a social display and the elders inspected the congregated young men as to their eventual social promotion. Jews were conspicuous in the gymnasium because of their circumcision, the sacred sign that they belonged to the people of Israel. It also made them different. Some employed surgeons to perform the *epispasm,* a surgical reversal of circumcision, which was no doubt painful but allowed the Jewish male to compete for social and economic advancement on an equal status in the new, Hel-

2. Legend relates that Ptolemy II, the Greek king of Egypt, asked seventy-two Jews, six from each of the twelve tribes, to do the translation separately. In seventy-two days they produced seventy-two identical translations. The version is called the Septuagint from the Greek for 'seventy'.

lenised state. Once again Greek cultural mores were encroaching on the religious domain of Judaism.

Faced by an invasion of their religious and cultural sensitivities, the Jews in Egypt managed to adapt and cope under the Ptolemies. But the same was not true of the Jews in Palestine. At first, the Palestinian Jews had also been ruled by the Ptolemies, who exercised an open and relaxed form of authority. Certainly, there was no religious coercion. Many Jews therefore saw no contradiction in accepting Greek ways of living, speaking Greek and using Greek for their sacred writings, so long as they could continue to practise their Jewish religion freely. But the Ptolemaic rule of Palestine was not to last.

However, the Greek Ptolemies in Egypt and the Greek Seleucids based in Syria both coveted Palestine; control of the Mediterranean coastline would give undoubted political advantage. There were outbreaks of violence between the two powers. In 198 BCE Antiochus III of Syria defeated the Egyptian Ptolemy V at Panias in northern Palestine and the former Jewish territory passed into Antiochus' control. The Jews in Palestine were now subject to the Seleucids rather than the Ptolemies and a new historical era began.

Antiochus III managed to live peaceably with the Jews, but his successor, Antiochus IV, did not. The latter came to the throne in 175 BCE, and six years later took the title *Epiphanes* which was short for *theos epiphanes* or 'God Manifest' since he claimed to be a manifestation of the god Zeus. He allowed the worship of other gods in the lands under his control, but all peoples had to submit to Zeus, from whom Antiochus' authority was said to derive.

Palestinian Jews saw a grave problem with this imposed form of Hellenism. Greek religious culture was a seduction, a temptation that would inevitably water down Jewish religious adherence. It was this Jewish resistance which gave rise to the group known as the *Hasidim* or 'pious ones', whose identity is still somewhat enigmatic. They were strict adherents of the Torah, who resisted the inroads of Greek culture. It is at this point that the ferment aroused by hellenisation in the early second century brought about new Jewish sect formation (the beginnings of sects like Pharisees, Sadducees, Essenes). Resistance began as a reaction to a religious threat, but it would soon take a political turn.

Antiochus had invaded Egypt and aroused Roman suspicions. A Roman embassy was dispatched to Egypt which ordered him to withdraw. The story circulated that he asked the Roman general, Popilius Laenus, for time to consider his position. Popilius drew a circle in the dust around him and told him to make up his mind prior to leaving the circle. He did reconsider and withdraw, naturally, but with bad grace and from that time he was subject to sudden mood changes. His courtiers secretly called him *Epimanes* or 'The Mad One', a derogatory play on *Epiphanes.* Within his limited area of authority, he became far less moderate.

From the onset, Antiochus IV had aroused Jewish religious resentment by his flagrant attack on their fundamental tenet of monotheism. As time went on, he raised taxes to pay for his wars against the Ptolemies, just when the Jewish population was struggling to survive. The last straw was his offer to sell the position of the high priesthood of Jerusalem. A demeaning succession of events followed.

The incumbent high priest was Onias III, looked upon later as the epitome of all virtue. He was called Onias the Just by his fellow Jews. His brother Jason, who had enthusiastically accepted Greek cultural ways and promised to promote them, paid a bribe to Antiochus for the position of High Priest. However, there was still another contender called Menelaus, equally corrupt and Greek in manners, and he paid even more to outbid Jason. Menelaus received the post; Onias III was banished and later murdered.

The thwarted Jason, not to be outdone, led his own forces into Jerusalem and unseated Menelaus who then appealed to Antiochus, to whom he had outlaid the requisite bribe. Antiochus came to Jerusalem, reinstated Menelaus and took the opportunity to plunder the Temple. This marked the beginning of an anti-Jewish campaign on the part of the Greeks.

The Jewish religion was outlawed; boys were not allowed to be circumcised, Torah scrolls were to be burned. In 168 BCE Antiochus marched his troops once again into Jerusalem and set up an altar to Zeus in the Temple precinct. This altar is what the book of Daniel was to call 'the transgression/abomination that makes desolate'. On this altar he had a pig offered as a sacrifice to his Greek patron god, Zeus. No worse sacrilege could have been imagined since the pig was unclean according to the Law. Greek soldiers were detailed to march through Palestine to ensure that the anti-Jewish regulations were being upheld.

We do not have any strictly historical record for what was to happen next. From the apocryphal books of Maccabees (as close to historical writing as we have from Judaism) we have the story that a revolt against the Greeks began in Modein, a town north west of Jerusalem and the purported leader was a Jew called Mattathias. A guerrilla war broke out between the loyal Jews and the Greeks.

Mattathias died soon after but he was succeeded by his eldest son, Judas, known as 'Maccabeus'[3]. Father and son had begun a line that would become known as the Hasmoneans[4]. Within that Hasmonean house, Judas and his four brothers would be known as the Maccabees.

The Maccabee group had been joined by the Hasidim, the 'pious ones'. Filled with religious zeal, Judas and his growing group of discontented Jews managed to defeat rather dispirited Greek forces. They soon retook Jerusalem and demolished Antiochus' Greek altar and restored the Jewish ritual. This cleansing of the Temple was to be commemorated by the establishment of a feast called *Hanukkah* or Feast of Dedication. For the Hasmoneans, this victory was the pivotal moment of world history.

I now began to see that the Hasmoneans were at the very centre of Jewish history in the pre-Christian period. If any significant work had been done on the texts then this period would be one to require scrutiny.

New Evaluation of Roman History in the East

Indeed, the Greek power was on the decline in world affairs. After their demise in Palestine, the land came under Roman rule. This brings us even more proximately to the time of Christianity. The Roman general Pompey had arrived in 63 BCE and brought to an end any semblance of an independent Jewish state. Aware of the unique attitude of the Jews to the land, he made Hyrcanus, a member of the Hasmonean family, an ethnarch, a 'ruler of the people', rather than a vassal king. Hence from 63 until 40 BCE the lands of Judaea (as the area of Yehud around Jerusalem became known), Galilee, Eastern Idumaea and Jewish Trans-Jordan formed a state under Rome. There were civil and political disturbances.

Now a new and important figure entered the Judaean landscape. Herod was the son of Antipater, an Idumaean who had been forcibly converted to Judaism. Having sided with Julius Caesar, Antipater became prefect of Judaea and his son Herod became the governor of Galilee. In 40BCE, having won favour in Rome, Herod became 'King of Judaea', a post that he needed to enforce by arms. This took three years and in 37 he became a local king, a *rex socius*.

3. We are unsure what the sobriquet meant, possibly 'The Hammer'.
4. Probably because Mattathias' grandfather had been named Asamonaeus.

There was widespread social disruption, and the need for a new form of aristocracy became apparent. In an important move, Herod turned to the diaspora for the appointment of a new High Priest. Hananel of Babylonia and the priestly families in Egypt were recruited as a new priestly oligarchy. These High Priestly families remained in power after Herod, but appointments to this high office were virtually controlled by the Roman governor.

However, in 4 BCE, after the death of Herod, the people acknowledged one of their own as 'king' and asserted independence. It would seem that beneath the surface there was a simmering popular movement that needed only a trigger to turn violent.

Reading the texts of Josephus which deal with such uprisings, it becomes clear that the typical motive force behind them was the religious tradition of the Exodus story. There is a stress on gathering in the 'wilderness' and 'crossing the river'.

> Now it came to pass, while Fadus was procurator of Judea, that a certain magician, whose name was Theudas, persuaded a great part of the people to take their effects with them, and follow him to the river Jordan; for he told them he was a prophet, and that he would, by his own command, divide the river, and afford them an easy passage over it. (*Ant* 20: 5.1)

> There were such men as deceived and deluded the people under pretence of divine inspiration, but were for procuring innovations and changes of the government, and these prevailed with the multitude to act like madmen, and went before them into the wilderness, as pretending that God would there show them the signals of liberty. (*Wars* 2: 13. 4)

Josephus then tells of an 'Egyptian false prophet' who gathered a following in the 'wilderness' and led them against Jerusalem and the Romans. He is clearly connecting these uprisings to the original Exodus. They were messianic movements.

John the Baptist should be placed in this context. His offer of a baptism in the Jordan was of a piece with the other messianic movements mentioned in Josephus. His purpose was clearly to gather together a group who would be ready to form a new Israel. The Exodus motif is evident in the descriptions of his activity; just as the people under Moses had crossed the Sea of Reeds and Joshua had led the remnant of the Exodus group across the Jordan, so John devised a ritual crossing of the Jordan to initiate members into his group.

In Judaea, direct rule was discontinued in 6 CE when the Roman Coponius was made prefect. He ordered a census to determine how much tax could be requisitioned. This was the occasion for further widespread Jewish discontent and revolt. However, the High Priest Joazar who, like his immediate predecessors, had been appointed at the whim of the king, determined that taxation was within the domain of the civil ruler. This restored a semblance of stability at least in Judaea. In Judaea, there was a coalition of absentee emperor, Roman prefect, High Priest and the Sanhedrin (the Jewish privy council), all of which acted in unison to preserve imperial power and ensure the efficient collection of tribute for Rome.

There were periods of relative calm in Palestine generally until Pontius Pilate was appointed prefect of Judaea in 26 and continued in office until 36 CE. He affronted Jewish sensitivities and caused deep provocation. From Josephus we learn that Pilate allowed his soldiers to enter Jerusalem carrying their standards. This was not normal procedure in a Jewish city since the standards were regarded as symbols of the divine emperor and were accorded ritual honour. There was also the instance of Pilate using Temple monies to fund the building of an aqueduct into Jerusalem. Finally, there was an incident in which Roman soldiers publicly burned a Torah-scroll.

Josephus reports that there were unusually high levels of tension at the times of the festivals in Jerusalem, particularly Passover in the time of Archelaus. Archelaus was ethnarch from 4 BCE to 6 CE. At such times the Romans had to resort to military repression.

These were the outward symptoms of a serious social malaise in Palestine. They indicated an underlying structural problem. Rome had inherited a Greek economic system in Palestine. From Seleucid times a feudal type of economy had been set up as an infrastructure, intended to return wealth to the Greek ruling class. The system was based on intensive economic exploitation of the land. The Romans, upon taking control, had modified the system only in order to cater for their own requirements. They cultivated special centres, particularly the cities of the Decapolis, which depended like parasites on the rural lands around them for the generation of wealth. Romans acted as absentee landlords and acquired land by means of purchase, foreclosure on non-repayment of debts and even direct confiscation.

Tenant farmers throughout Palestine were subjected to a constant drain on their meagre resources: the *tributum soli* (a land tax), *tributum capitis* (a poll tax), a direct tribute to Rome together with special levies for public works, customs tolls and sales tax. There were, in addition, Temple taxes and other dues required from the religious authorities in Jerusalem. The Jewish population had to fulfil its contractual arrangements with its absentee landlords who had no interest in the economic survival of the local area. The absentee landlords did not even use their profits for the good of the local economy, but poured the surplus into lavish display and consumption, further injuring that economy. Enforced labour on Roman public works drained the labour force at the local farm level.

From this broad survey of a disintegrating Eastern society, Galilee needs to be extrapolated and considered especially, since it was there that the Jesus-movement had its origins.

New Evaluation of the history of Galilee

Galilee was agriculturally rich. It covered an area of approximately 2000 square kilometres, with a population of around 200,000 (see figure 7). In the first century CE however it was still expanding; the towns and villages were growing. Historical sources do not substantiate a picture of a homeless poor. They may have been poor, but they still had homes.

It was Roman policy to try and pacify their provincial areas, which it regarded as being inhabited by backward peoples. A central part of this policy was urbanisation, the setting up of substantial urban centres as symbols of Roman imperial culture. In the first twenty years of the rule of Herod Antipas, a period that covers the time of Jesus, there was considerable building in the capital of Galilee, Sepphoris, and the establishment of a separate royal city at Tiberias, dedicated to the emperor Tiberius. It became the new capital, displacing Sepphoris.

By the first century CE, the end result was a virtual army of rural Jews in Galilee, who felt the impact of social trauma in their daily lives. These people were also largely alienated from the Temple cult in Jerusalem and its aristocratic personnel. Such was the breeding ground for the spread of Jewish eschatological hopes.

The Jesus generation in Lower Galilee had therefore been brought up with the glorious memory of being incorporated into a Temple-state system by the Hasmoneans, being invaded by Pompey, being subjected to Herod and then ruled by Herod Antipas, his son, who wished to transform the area by means of his Romano-Hellenistic building program.

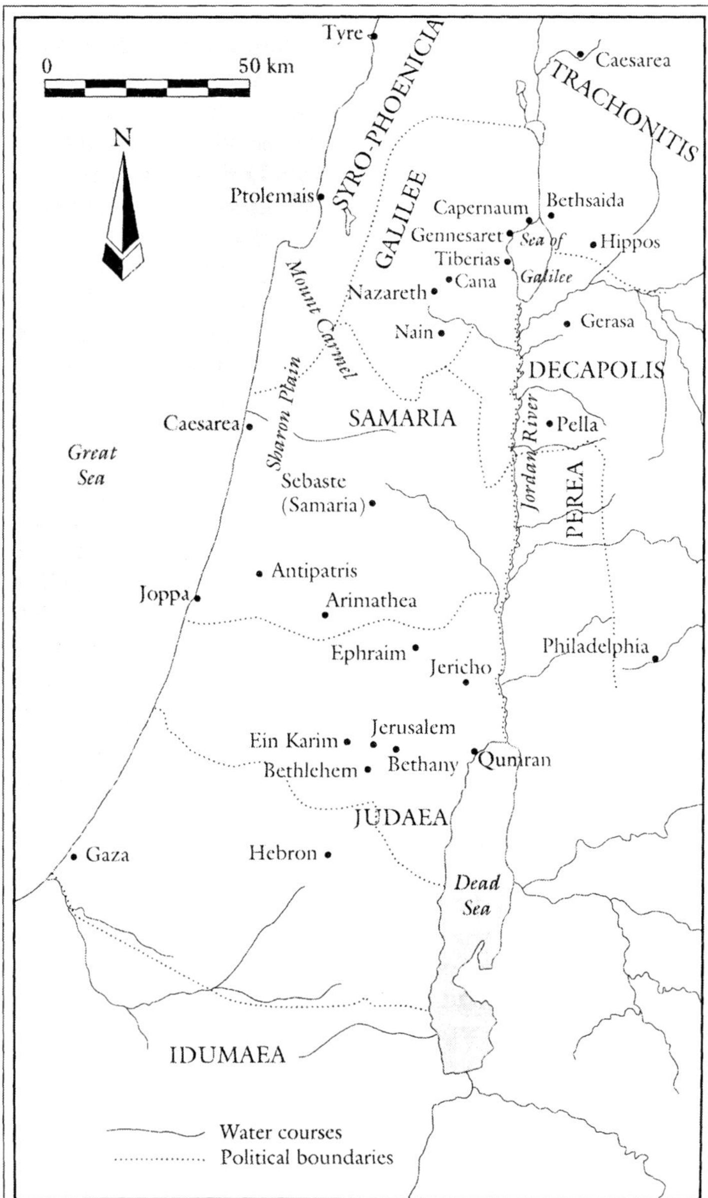

Figure 7: Palestine in the first century CE.

The Herodians, who represented Rome, were looked upon as the real enemy by that generation of Jews. Galilean loyalty to the Jerusalem Temple was offset by this disdain for the Herodian faction. We have specific instances of revolts and revolutionaries connected with Galilee. Ezekias a Galilean, known as the *archilestes* or 'chief revolutionary' by Josephus, was put down by the young Herod. Judas the Galilean and Zadok, a Pharisee, rose up after 6 CE against the census called by Caponius. In the final stand-off of Zealots against Romans in the Jerusalem siege of 70 CE, John son of Levi and the 'Galilean contingent' were described by Josephus as possessing 'mischievous ingenuity and audacity'.

This insurrectionist activity shows that the villages of Galilee did not passively accept the Romano-Hellenistic culture, which in many ways was a veneer. The villages were self-contained, having only casual contact (based on taxes and commerce) with the major cities such as Sepphoris and Tiberias.

While archaeology may demonstrate that the material culture was profoundly affected by Romano-Hellenism, Galilee remained stolidly Jewish in character. As against Judaea, which came under direct Roman rule during the first century, Galilee remained under the rule of Herodian kings. Consequently, there was little purpose in fomenting a widespread anti-Roman revolution. Galilee could not therefore be called a hotbed of Roman revolt. In a political sense, the area remained relatively calm until the war against Rome began in the 60s. But there was still room for new religious movements in the village context and these did happen.

We are able to see this in action in the recorded history of Galilee. Early in the common era, there was an uprising against the Romans which led to the destruction of Sepphoris, whose population would have been about 500. The revolt was put down by the Roman legate Varus who crucified the combatants in Sepphoris. The city was later rebuilt under Herod Antipas, but he also established the city of Tiberias as the new capital. The rebuilding of Sepphoris and the change of political focus to Tiberias would have broken up kinship and familial values. The stability of peasant life in Galilee would have undergone significant upheaval.

But it was the easy access that, as in the time of the Maccabees, became the temptation. What was clearly required was a program of local group revitalisation, in which the basic institutions of family, marriage and group relations would be renewed according to the tenets of Israelite tradition. In Galilee there was a ready-made program at hand in the living structure of the Israelite religion. This tradition had access to the symbolic figures of Moses and his successors, Elijah and Elisha. They were considered to have undertaken a renewal of the people of their own day and to offer the possibility of continuing renewal in the contemporary period.

However, these same Galilean Jews were also regarded by other Palestinian Jews as peasants, religiously unsophisticated. Living as a deprived people, marginalised, of ambiguous status, they tended to turn in their need to local 'saints', the *zaddikim* or Just Ones, since the population had no regular access to the Temple or the ritual life in Jerusalem. Local Just Ones in Galilee became focal points for resisting evil and injustice.

There is yet another related aspect of the religious amalgam in Galilean society—apocalypticism. Apocalypticism thrives amid the deprivation and anxiety of social dislocation and amid those difficulties associated with acculturation, common factors in a colonial takeover. Under such circumstances, time can be interpreted in a linear fashion, leading directly and imminently to an idealistic future. Apocalyptic thought defines a model leader, a mediator, who will parade those ideals that are required in the ideal future state. The *Parables of Enoch* (*1 Enoch* 37-71), a typically apocalyptic text, describe such an intermediary as the Son of Man, the Messiah, the Elect One, the Just One. They are synonyms, but the use of Just One is interesting. In *1 Enoch* 47 we read:

> The prayer of the just ones and the blood of the Just One will have ascended from the earth before the Lord of Spirits.

This is further evidence of the Jewish expectation of a coming Just One who would restore the fortunes of the people. For this dispossessed and alienated people it was the time of testing, the Temptation it was called, the struggle between the forces of good and the forces of evil at the beginning of the End of Times. The Jewish populace had been detached from their social moorings. They were economically poor and they saw themselves in conflict with the broader social structure.

Summary

I spent much time doing this historical work and published my results in a book, *The Jesus Question*, published by HarperCollinsReligious in Melbourne in 1996. In the book I related the research on the history of Israel and the research on the later topics to the search for an historical Jesus. I was not trying to prove the historicity of either the texts of ancient Israel or the gospel accounts. I had long given up both those projects. Instead, I was interested in seeing, from an historical vantage point, how such phenomena as ancient Israel and the Jesus movement, and their accompanying literatures, could have come into being.

Thus, I felt more confident that I could understand where an Israel had come from and how it intersected with the archaeological and historical materials. Linking the other data such as the full account of the Qumran library (providing the matrix from which Second Temple Judaism could be studied), the Gnostic writings from Nag Hammadi (which demonstrated how another version of 'Jesus' could be presented), the archaeological data and the reconstructed history of the Greek and Roman times, I was comfortable that I could finally understand the situation which would have given birth to the Jesus-movement and eventually to the writing of the gospels.

I now felt it was time to return to the study of texts.

Note

I append some references.

First, in the area of history and archaeology relative to new thinking concerning the Hebrew Scriptures see

Finkelstein, I and Silberman, N (2001), *The Bible Unearthed: Archaeology's New Vision of Ancient Israel and the Origin of its Sacred Texts*, The Free Press: New York and London

Marcus, A (2000), *Rewriting the Bible: How Archaeology is Reshaping the Middle East*, Little, Brown and Company: London

For information on the Jesus Seminar see

Funk, R et al (1993), *The Five Gospels*, Macmillan: New York.

On identifying Jesus with characters mentioned in the Dead Sea Scrolls see (with caution)

Eisenman, R (1997), *James the Brother of Jesus*, Faber and Faber: London and Thiering, B (1995), *Jesus the Man*, Doubleday: Sydney.

For information and bibliography on the Dead Sea Scrolls after the publication of all the major texts see

Davies, P, Brooke, G and Callaway, P (2002), *The Complete World of the Dead Sea Scrolls*, Thames and Hudson: London

A good overview of the later impact of the Gnostic writings can be found in

Meyer, M (2005), *The Gnostic Discoveries: The Impact of the Nag Hammadi Library*, HarperSanFrancisco: New York

A good coverage of the archaeological discoveries relative to the Christian Scriptures can be found in:

Crossan, JD and Reed, J (2001), *Excavating Jesus: Beneath the Stones, Behind the Texts*, HarperSanFrancisco: New York

In particular on Galilee see the interesting work done by Sean Freyne:

Freyne, S (2004), *Jesus, a Jewish Galilean. A New Reading of the Jesus Story,* T and T Clark International (Continuum): London and New York.

Freyne, S (2000), *Galilee and Gospel. Selected Essays,* JCB Mohr: Tübingen.

Chapter 14
'ISRAEL', JUDAISM AND THE HEBREW SCRIPTURES

Returning once more to the texts of the Hebrew Scriptures and the Christian Scriptures, I was aware that for me a third revolution had certainly taken place. Having studied much about religion in general and many religions other than ancient Judaism and Christianity, I saw too many anomalies in privileging the literatures of these two religions. Their writings needed to be seen as a phenomenon in the whole religious process.

The third revolution went beyond the parameters of the second revolution, which saw the Bible as Literature. It had begun with anthropology and had been advanced by the diversion into history that had allowed me to see things more clearly. This revolution had not only taken place in my thinking, but in the thinking of many others working in the same field. My interest in anthropology and in history (dissociated from proving the Bible to be 'right') had been replicated by many people in many places.

At this point I will tabulate the results that the third revolution, based on an anthropological approach, had on my thinking regarding the Hebrew Scriptures in the first instance.

A New Terminology

I have necessarily needed to adopt a new terminology to explain the effect of the new revolution and that terminology needs to be explained. Applying myself first to Israel, I now want to distinguish between a Literary Israel, an Historical Israel and a Biblical Israel.

There is a Literary Israel contained in the amalgam of texts and stories within the Hebrew Scripture. The Literary Israel has its own chronology, its own succession of events, its own characters, who successively appear from Adam to Ezra. There is also an Historical Israel, the sequence that can be reliably reconstructed from various historical documents (not the Bible!) and archaeology which defines an ancient entity called Israel. The Biblical Israel is constructed by inserting Historical Israel into Literary Israel (or sometimes, vice-versa)

We will begin with Historical Israel, not Literary Israel.

The Historical Israel

I was by now sure that there had actually been an Historical Israel, an entity of people, places and events that had actually impacted on the historical record, but I also was sure that it was largely beyond the skills of any modern historian to reconstruct it. For example, I had searched for the historical roots of the religion of YHWH. The religion of YHWH as refracted through the debris of archaeological remains appeared as a normal development from Canaanite religion. It was worked out on the soil of Canaan from the disintegrating and pre-existing cult of 'El and involved a complex process of social, economic, political as well as religious change.

In the Historical Israel there would have been a number of cults and a number of religious practices that would have been based on fertility and leadership in war. Among them would have been the cult of YHWH. YHWH was a revitalised 'El, who at first had a consort Asherah but later all mention of Asherah worship was removed. This sanitisation of YWHH as a celibate High God was another and much later step. YHWH would have had a history analogous to other ancient Near Eastern gods.

So, I now admitted that there had been an Historical Israel from the beginning of the Iron Age, around 1200. It may have been the name of a geographical area or it may have been applied to a particular group of people. Certainly, in the highlands to the north a kingdom called Israel developed and it was destroyed by the Assyrians in 722. It belongs to a wider Historical Israel and we can say little more about it than the features relating to kings and conquests that have been noted above in the list of inscriptions. No doubt the biblical writers had access to more resources than we do, but they had overlain these resources with so much of their own thinking that we cannot recover the historical data.

What then of Judah in the south, included in the term 'People of Israel'? We saw that there is one passing reference to the 'House of David' but nothing as regards a united kingdom in any inscriptions. That united kingdom, belonging to David and Solomon, of vast proportions exists only in Literary Israel. There is no evidence that the northern kingdom ever broke away from the south as the biblical text narrates. The evidence points to the fact that southern Judah did not even exist at the period that Israel did in the north. Archaeology in fact would tend to demonstrate that there was nothing like an administrative state in the southern area until the eighth century BCE. Somewhere after this time Jerusalem became the capital of this southern kingdom. It would last as a capital until the attacks by the Babylonians destroyed it in 586 BCE.

Literary Israel tells of the cream of the Judahite population being taken into Mesopotamia as exiles. There is no historical record of such specifics. It cannot be confirmed in Historical Israel. There are no historical records of the time spent by this extensive cohort in exile. Lists of who went, who returned and locations of where the exiles were lodged are found only in Literary Israel. We have the books of Ezra and Nehemiah, detailing the story of the return of the exiles to Jerusalem, but they are also part of the Literary Israel. They do not belong to Historical Israel.

We turn to the historical record. The answer would seem to be that most probably there had been indeed historical deportations of Judahites from Yehud into Mesopotamia. That was the method employed by the Babylonians in dealing with their subject nations in the Near East, and Mesopotamia would be the logical place for the deportations.

Of more importance is the 'return of the Exiles'. More recent archaeology has shown that, after resettlement, there was an increase in the population of Yehud by 25%, mostly in previously uninhabited regions distant from Jerusalem. Is this evidence of the 'return of the Exiles' as it is narrated in the texts of Literary Israel? That would raise new problems. Why would they have built new towns in previously uninhabited areas? Why would they not have simply returned to their ancestral homes?

That resettlement would seem to have been of a new population, not the population that had been originally deported; that was why the new arrivals built in previously uninhabited areas. This would also have been in line with Mesopotamian policy elsewhere in the Near East: transport people out of their homeland and transport a new population into that homeland. The new population lessened the possibility of rebellion, while at the same time the economic development of the rural areas required a new population to tend the land.

That is a truncated review of Historical Israel. It has gaps and shortcomings as an historical writing. Historians can do better, but this has little to do with Judaism. Where then did the biblical story of Literary Israel come from?

Literary Israel

Literary Israel is a narrative filled out with other literary materials. It consists of the story of Beginnings and Sin Stories (Adam and Eve, Cain and Abel, the Flood Generation, the Tower of Babel), followed by the stories of the Ancestors, the Exodus from Egypt, the Conquest of the land, the united kingships of David and Solomon, the divided kingdoms of Israel and Judah, the destruction of Jerusalem, the Exile and the Restoration.

It is important to maintain the clear distinction between this Literary Israel and Historical Israel. We have already seen that the 'Exile' in Historical Israel is a matter of contention. Was it really a matter of a significant part of the population being transported to Mesopotamia and then being allowed, after some decades, to return? The story contained in Literary Israel was adamant: it told of the Exile of the leading personages—the king, the royal family and courtiers, the administrative staff and the priestly caste.

If we can presume, on the contrary, that something like what happened in the latter stages of the Historical Israel occurred as described above, the foreign newcomers would have needed a social identity. They had not been locals.They would have found themselves side by side with locals who had never been dislocated by deportation; there would have been many people who had simply remained where they always had been. The newcomers needed, in some way, to see themselves not as perpetual outsiders but as linked to the existing population. They had been forced to come to Yehud and they would have brought with them their own sacred stories and their own god-cult.

First, let's look at the stories they might have imported. Possibly the bases for the stories of Adam and Eve, Cain and Abel, the Flood generation and the Tower of Babel were native to them. Scholars have always seen parallels between these stories and similar Mesopotamian myths and folklore. They would have also brought a particular god-cult, a High God tradition. Mesopotamia had been the place that spawned High Gods. There had been the High Gods, Sin and Marduk, that featured prominently in their texts. There was also the long tradition of the Good God, Ahura Mazda, who had long functioned in Zoroastrianism.

Now comes a leap in the logic in this historical reconstruction. I think it is justified. These newcomers who sought legitimacy in a new land provided the context that gave rise to Literary Israel. The stories of the Ancestors were constructed on a set of originally competing stories that told of an outsider group, called by a High God. The outsider group identified the High God with a local god, YHWH. YHWH was popular among the locals and was known under a number of regional titles such as El Shaddai (perhaps, 'God of the mountains'), El Elyon ('the Most High God'), El 'Olam ('the Eternal God'), El Ro'i ('the God who Sees'). He had a wife and was a fertility god similar in all ways to the Canaanite 'El and Ba'al except in name.

In these alternative and refurbished stories those living in the land and hostile to the newcomers' presence were identified as the 'Canaanites'. YHWH the High God ordered the newcomers to dispossess the Canaanites and to take over their land. The outsiders made themselves the chosen people of YHWH—they were 'Isaac'; they made the locals 'the Canaanites'. This was the foundation story adapted by Literary Israel. The present biblical stories of Abraham still contain the remnants of these original stories.

Another set of subsidiary stories told of another Ancestor, Moses, who also led his people from outside the land (this time it was Egypt, not Mesopotamia) to take over the land and dispossess the Canaanites. The Exodus and Conquest stories, featuring Moses and Joshua, were simply an alternative version of the Ancestor Stories of a victorious takeover of a new land by a chosen people under Abraham and his successive sons at the behest of its High God.

I had found a factual background history that would explain the construction of Literary Israel, but not a factual basis for the stories themselves, an Historical Israel. The explanation for the stories was in the history of this newcomer group who had arrived, perhaps quite unwillingly, in Yehud in the Persian period.

The newcomers would have been placed in a position of power by their Persian superiors. They would have been given orders to provide the land with economic security. For this reason the Temple of Jerusalem was rebuilt to be an administrative centre to be run by them. Most probably the first Temple, destroyed by the Babylonians in 586 BCE, had been a Canaanite temple dedicated to one or more of the Canaanite gods. YHWH may have been included among them. It may have been a YHWH temple, but not a High God YHWH. The newcomers rebuilt the Temple, now dedicated to the High God YHWH, and supplied it with a priesthood, taking on a supposed family lineage that dated back to the fiction of Moses' brother Aaron and a fictional genealogy from the High Priest Zadok who had served David in Literary Israel.

Of importance, within this new Temple setup, with its Mesopotamian features, was the scribal school, necessary to write down and record whatever was required for administration, for taxation, for rendering economic benefit to the Persian powers far away and for protecting the new social group that had taken control in Yehud.

The scribal school would have accumulated archives which it then manipulated. The scribes had their libraries in the Temple where they would have deposited a growing literature coming from the remnants that had survived the earlier destruction. Two things can be said about the way this literature was then manipulated by the scribes. In the first place, the new writing was not historical; it was not intended to be historical in our sense. Its purpose was not to record the past but to give social identity to a burgeoning group in power in the present. Secondly, this was not primarily religious literature, at least in our sense. It was a literature that created the tradition of a cultural heritage. The culture could be described as both religious and secular. In that society secular culture and religion were not as clearly distinguished as they are in more modern societies.

The newcomers were involved in real historical events. There was the real Persian policy of resettlement of newcomers for economic and agricultural redevelopment. There was a call for Persian military strengthening of the boundaries of Yehud. This was reflected in the mainly fictional account of the mission of Nehemiah, sent by the Persians to protect the fledging satrapy. Nehemiah was a literary figure representing the newcomers and their role in the land. There was the legal and constitutional restructuring of the satrapy, reflected in the even more fictional story of Ezra. Ezra stood for the newcomers again as they reconstructed society according to their socio-religious plan. It was the scribal school of the newcomers who slowly constructed their claim to the land and who constructed a glorious even if fictional past in the land.

These historical events of resettlement and military, economic and legal structuring of Yehud and its culture were the background for the initial gathering of the traditions of Literary Israel and the composition of the story. Literary Israel was in the process of being created by the scribal schools. The scribes collected and adapted in their Temple library the stories of return to the land under the guidance of a High God, of settlement, of development; they gathered typical wisdom proverbs, songs and law collections. The collection of stories, traditions, hymns, prophetic writings and wisdom writings became the heritage of the newcomers who now headed the locals of the land. It would be shared with the locals.

This was the beginning of Judaism, which at this point in time was not an exclusively religious entity. The newcomers constructed a cultural statement on their presumed origins in the land.[1]

Then, at a certain point, the many varied, and sometimes quite discrepant collections of literature were amalgamated. Choices were made between diverging stories and collections of materials. There was large scale editing and correlating between the materials. The trigger for doing this and for smoothing over the discrepancies was the arrival of Greek culture and its confrontation with the culture of Judaism as we have already seen happened.

This bulk of literary materials were then put in order. Eventually they would be given a chronology. But this was another step. We have already seen how scholars in the past endeavoured to extract an historical dateline from the chronological indicators in the biblical text. When we now turn to a study of biblical chronology it is not to substantiate history; it is to show how the stories and other literary materials came to be ordered with three main turning points: the Exodus, the building of the first temple and the building of the second temple.

A closer study of the chronology surrounding these turning points now leads us to the final piece in the jigsaw. By simply counting the figures given in the biblical text, the period from creation until the Exodus from Egypt is 2666 years. This is two-thirds of 4000 years, a period regarded as a world epoch in Jewish thought. The coincidence is obvious. This full cycle of 4000 years would end with the re-dedication of the Temple under Judas Maccabeus in 164 BCE.

Creation → 'Exodus': 2666 years
Creation → Re-dedication of Temple: 4000 years

The significant text in 1 Kings 6:1 (which earlier we saw fundamentalists mining and massaging for an historical chronology) records the turning-point of the building of the first Temple:

> In the four hundred and eightieth year after the Israelites came out of the land of Egypt, in the fourth year of Solomon's

1. Coincidentally, it was a similar venture to what has been done by modern Israelis, who came from many different geographical areas, and (with the help of a compliant archaeology) constructed a previous culture for themselves looking back to a biblical origin.

> reign over Israel, in the month of Ziv, which is the second month, he began to build the house of YHWH.

If the other dates given in the various books regarding the reigns of kings are followed, without allowance for co-regnums or other adjustments (as poor Pavlovsky at the Biblical Institute had spent his life doing), then the period from the fourth year of Solomon to the destruction of this first Temple is 430 years, precisely the time that the sojourn in Egypt lasted. Among priestly circles the period of the exile was calculated as fifty years, the time of sabbatical rest for the land, seven times seven followed by a jubilee year.

Hence the sum of 430 years plus the 50 years of the exile gives another 480 years, the period at which a start was made on the second temple, according to the text of Ezra.

> **'Exodus' → Building of First Temple: 480 years**
> **Building of First Temple → Building of Second Temple: 480 years**

Why 480? Probably it was the sum of 12 (the purported Israelite tribal basis) multiplied by the universal number of 40 (as Albright had guessed). However, we may never clearly understand the system on which the biblical dates have been based. It is sufficient to say that they were not intended to be historical reference points; they are symbolic numbers.

The authors are demonstrating that YHWH controls the events of Israel's history and that, despite all vicissitudes, these events have direction and purpose and move towards a final point. What is important for the authors of the texts is the representation of both sacred time and sacred place. Sacred time is inherent in the thread of purposeful activity, while sacred place is indicated by setting up the sanctuary in the wilderness and the subsequent establishment of the first and second Temples in the land of Canaan.

This is the synchronic framework. Where does it all reach its climax: in the Maccabean period with the rededication of the Temple that had been desecrated. The obvious conclusion is that it was the Hasmoneans in the second century BCE who took the materials constructed by the returnees and made this final chronological adjustment, portraying their own achievement in retaking Jerusalem as the culmination of sacred time and space. No other authority had the will or the opportunity to manipulate the earlier tradition in such a way.

Literary Israel then, the biblical stories as they have come down to us, are much later than what we have thought, at least in anything like the form we have them in. While they might depend on some nuggets of history and some ancient traditions and gathering of literary materials, the final version that we have would have begun around the fifth century BCE in the Persian period and have been finalised around the second century BCE in the Greek period. What scholars have identified as JEDP and other literary devices are, on the whole, not editorial works from the time of David, nor from the period of the so-called united and divided kingdoms but from many centuries later.

Biblical Israel

Finally, there is a Biblical Israel, a construct brought about by inserting Historical Israel (plus some questionable data that pretends to belong to Historical Israel) into Literary Israel. The opposite is also feasible and has been attempted. For example, Historical Israel is able to point to archaeological remains in Jerusalem dating back to the tenth century BCE. Biblical Israel would claim that these must be the remains of building projects completed under Solomon and can, from Literary Israel, even give names to royal buildings of that time. Biblical Israel uses archaeology and the Bible to give substance to the Ancestors, to date the Exodus, to identify the geographical locations of the battles waged by Judges, to chart the activities of kings of the North and South.

In fact there are many competing versions of this Biblical Israel. Albright, and Mendenhall later, had produced one (by inserting Historical Israel into Literary Israel), so had Noth (by inserting Literary Israel into Historical Israel) and a myriad number of other biblical commentators have had a try. Even I myself had been spending time attempting to do this with ever greater frustration. I now realised that the task was not only impossible but that the construction of a Biblical Israel was a nonsense and useless. There never was a Biblical Israel. There is no need for a Biblical Israel. It is a phantasm.

Conclusion

Consequently, it would seem to be a possible conclusion that Judaism as a religion only came into existence just prior to the Christian period. The writing of the Dead Sea Scrolls, biblical manuscripts and sectarian manuscripts, were part of this process of redeveloping the past. It is not just that the Dead Sea Scrolls are the oldest biblical manuscripts we have. They are at the very beginning of the writing of biblical manuscripts in their present form. But these texts came into existence to protect and explicate the deep experience that Judaism offered to its adherents.

Judaism therefore offers a way of life, one which can be described from the conglomeration of literature and which could be experienced by means of the sacred story of Literary Israel and its attendant ritual. This religion has provided fulfilment in its religious experience for many people in the past and continues to do so in the present. That experience is produced by involvement in sacred story and sacred ritual. These, in turn, are protected and verified by the Hebrew Scriptures. That is their purpose. There is no more to be said.

What now of Jesus and the Christian Scriptures?

Note

Much of my thinking on the Hebrew Scriptures in this chapter has been particularly affected by the work of Philip Davies and Thomas Thompson.

Davies, Philip (1992), *In Search of 'Ancient Israel'*, Sheffield Academic Press: London and New York

Davies, Philip (1998), *Scribes and Schools. The Canonisation of the Hebrew Scriptures*, Westminster John Knox Press: Louisville

Thompson, Thomas (2000), *The Bible in History. How writers create a past,* Pimlico: London

Davies makes use of the terminology: Historical Israel, Biblical Israel and Ancient Israel.

For more depth on the refurbishment of the Abraham and Isaac story see my article:

Crotty, R (2005), 'The Literary Structure of the Binding of Isaac in Genesis 22', *Australian Biblical Review,* 53, pp 31-41

Chapter 15
'JESUS', CHRISTIANITY AND THE CHRISTIAN SCRIPTURES

The third revolution affected my study of the Christian Scriptures in a profound way too. As was the case with the study of Israel, I need to introduce a new terminology which has been stimulated by the developments in studies in anthropology and the new advances in historical thinking in the study of the Christian Scriptures. The new terminology relates to a Historical Jesus, a Literary Jesus and a Biblical Jesus.

From the outset, I want to make it clear that there was certainly, in my opinion, an Historical Jesus, a person who took part in historical events in the early part of the first millennium CE. The Literary Jesus is the story of a Jesus as it is contained in the Christian Scriptures. The Biblical Jesus is the insertion of the Historical Jesus into the Literary Jesus or vice-versa. It has produced a hybrid that never existed and has no purpose.

We begin with the Historical Jesus.

The Historical Jesus

Indeed Jesus existed as an historical personage and we can be confident about some of the features of his biography. We can begin with the fact that Jesus was a Jew who lived primarily in Galilee and died by execution during the Second Temple period. Secular sources such as Josephus, Tacitus, Suetonius and Pliny document this minimal outline.

What these sources assure us, with as much reliability as anything in the historical record, is that there was a Jesus who was executed by crucifixion during the time of the Roman prefect Pontius Pilate, that is between 26 and 36 CE, and while Tiberius was emperor of Rome. However, scholars have endeavoured to produce a much more detailed Historical Jesus than that. The real problem in recent times has been that there are too many Historical Jesus-es.

The developments in the interpretation of the text of the Christian Scriptures, the new thinking on the Dead Sea Scrolls and the Nag Hammadi texts and the revived interest in Palestinian history, all covered in a previous chapter, gave rise by the mid-1980s to a Third Search for the Historical Jesus with significantly new portrayals of an Historical Jesus.

Jesus has been presented to us as an eschatological prophet (Sanders, 1985), a Hellenistic Cynic teacher (Mack, 1988), a subversive wisdom teacher (Borg, 1987), a social prophet (Horsley, 1987), an eschatological prophet of the present and coming Kingdom (Meier, 1994), a Mediterranean Jewish peasant (Crossan, 1991), an egalitarian prophet of Wisdom (Schussler Fiorenza, 1994). In addition, but with less backing from peer academics, we saw earlier that he has been depicted as the 'Wicked Priest' spoken of in the Dead Sea Scrolls (Thiering, 1992).

What methods have the Third Searchers used to come to such conclusions? They have used, in the first place, the new literary analyses of the gospels, often dating the Nag Hammadi gospels early, in order to refind the *verba ipsissima* of Jesus. The Jesus Seminar scholars have been very much involved in this. They have also used the revised history and archaeology of the Palestinian area, particularly Galilee, to fill in the context in which an Historical Jesus lived. However, less and less are the Dead Sea Scrolls or their archaeological context seen as significant by those engaged in the Third Search. More importantly, the Third Search has introduced new interdisciplinary models and perspectives, such as those taken from social anthropology, social history, sociology and feminist studies.

While the First and Second Searches for an Historical Jesus were, in the main, supported by university Departments of Theology and Christian Seminaries, the Third Search has relied more on the support of secular Departments of Religion Studies, where the study of religion as a human phenomenon is carried out by interdisciplinary methods. Any religious truth claims tend to be bracketed out of the equation in these Departments. Jesus' miracles, for example, are studied by the same methods and within the same parameters as the miracles reported by other religious groups, ancient or modern. For many Third Searchers, there is no theological imperative to maintain the supernatural aspects of Jesus' activity or even his personal divinity.

The Third Searchers have claimed significant success. Thus, EP Sanders can write:

> The dominant view today seems to be that we can know pretty well what Jesus was out to accomplish, that we can know a lot about what he said and that these two things make sense within the world of first century Judaism.[1]

If we look at the work of John Dominic Crossan (1991), a stalwart Third Searcher and a co-convenor of the Jesus Seminar, we find that he relies for the elements of his historical Jesus on what can be recovered from a methodological 'triad'. The triad consists, first of all, of the Jesus-sayings which are neatly stratified into four levels, by analogy with an archaeological *tell*, from the time of the written gospels back to the Jesus period: level 1, 30–60 CE (eg Q, Thomas, early Paul, miracles collection); level 2, 60–80 CE (eg Mark, Matthew and Luke); level 3, 80–120 CE (eg John); level 4, 120–150 CE (sayings quoted in early Christian writers). Jesus-sayings with multiple attestations and belonging to an early stratum are more likely to be authentic; those with only one attestation or belonging to later strata are usually relegated to later constructions made by the early Christians.

The second element in the triad is cultural and social anthropology and the third is Greco-Roman history.

To give a concrete example, Crossan is able to use reputable anthropological studies to describe scientifically the multiple manifestations of trance among oppressed human groups. One such manifestation is demon possession. Next, he relies on modern studies in Greco-Roman history to demonstrate that Galileans, in the later Second Temple period, were under stringent colonial oppression by Rome, an oppressed state that could be expected to give rise to manifestations of trance.

Into this theoretical construct, he introduces those Jesus-sayings and Jesus-events concerning exorcism which can be reliably situated in the actual Jesus period on the basis of attestation and stratification. He then feels confident that he has contextualised a complex of sayings and actions related to Jesus' exorcism activity within its relevant historico-cultural setting, and that this can function as one solid building block in his historical reconstruction of an historical Jesus.

The end result of many such exercises in historical block-building is an historical Jesus, cast by Crossan as a Mediterranean Jewish peasant with an alternative social vision.

1. *Jesus and Judaism* (1985), SCM: London, p 2.

At this point a new factor needs to be addressed. Many—but not all—of the Third Searchers and some of the Jesus Seminar Fellows are Christian adherents, admittedly with varying degrees of commitment. Is there a difference when a committed Christian works on a history of Jesus? Again, Crossan, for example, makes it patently clear that he is working as an historian. He explicitly distinguishes his work from that of a Christian theologian.

> There were always historians who said it (historical Jesus research) could not be done because of historical problems. There were always theologians who said it should not be done because of theological objections. And there were always scholars who said the former but meant the latter.[2]

Nevertheless, Crossan sees a close link between his historical work and the task of the Christian theologian. He would say that unless the Christian theologian has a reliable historical construct for Jesus (presumably Crossan's own construct would be preferable), any subsequent Christian theological statement is going to be warped.

The Third Search has certainly brought about a more critical questioning of biblical inspiration and inerrancy and a questioning of the historicity of the gospel texts. For some Historical Jesus researchers one or other of the reconstructions mentioned above might be satisfying. Other scholars think that the search has taken academe back to the nineteenth century.

I have always had my personal reservations about the Third Search.

I do not think it can produce the full blown biography that so many would claim. However, there are some items of information about the Historical Jesus that are interesting and vital to any reconstruction. First of all, it seems clear enough that the Historical Jesus would have come from a traditionalist Jewish setting. The names of his male siblings as recorded in the gospels—James, Joses, Simon and Judas—show a preference for the biblical names of the past. They are conservative Jewish names. We should not be looking at a revolutionary family for his origins.

Secondly, there is the consistent claim in biblical texts, as the tradition developed, that Jesus was of Davidic descent.[3] Whatever may have been

---

2. (1991) *The Historical Jesus: The Life of a Mediterranean Jewish Peasant*, HarperCollins: San Francisco, p xxvii.
3. The gospel of Matthew begins with the clear assertion:

   An account of the genealogy of Jesus the Messiah, the son of David, the son of the historicity of David himself, to account for this identification of Jesus there must have been a local tradition in Galilee that Jesus and his family had descended from David. This would have substantiated the claim that the family could produce a Davidic royal messiah.

The third item is the reference to Jesus being by occupation a *tekton,* a relatively unusual term which described someone in the broad category of a carpenter, a stonemason or a smithy. The term is used in Mark 6:3 ('Is this not the carpenter, *tekton*?') without any elaboration on its meaning.[4] Further, he was a *tekton* who came from Nazareth in Galilee. Most probably, this occupation indicated that his predecessors had been dispossessed of land and consequently he belonged to a lower social stratum in Galilee. From our knowledge about Galilee, it would seem that he certainly would have been well aware of economic hardship and social division.[5]

So we begin with an assumption: Jesus came from a traditional Jewish background, with the possibility of being recognised as a Jewish messiah in an impoverished and challenging social context. But what about any actual facts about his life? We have exhausted the secular historians of the time and their evidence is scanty. We can, with discretion and caution, look at the texts of the Literary Jesus and see what can be derived from them.

The Third Searchers make much of the reliability of one fact: his baptism by John the Baptist. This is treated with such embarrassed circumspection by the four evangelists that it could hardly have been an invention. By the time of John's gospel it is difficult to determine if Jesus was actually baptised by John at all. Further, there is mention of John's baptismal activity in Josephus and, in Acts, there is a clear statement that his

---

Abraham. (Matthew 1:1)

Luke's gospel traces his lineage back via David to Adam (Luke 3:23-38) while there is an equally strong claim to Davidic descent in the Pauline writings:

> . . . the gospel concerning his Son, who was descended from David according to the flesh . . . (Romans 1:3)
>
> Remember Jesus Christ, raised from the dead, a descendant of David—that is my gospel . . . (2 Timothy 2:8)

4. Justin Martyr at a later date remarked that Jesus 'made yokes and ploughs' (*Dialogue with Trypho* 88:8).
5. His parables which, even if they are not his actual words, at least reflect his followers' milieu, demonstrate an awareness of the plight of the poor and powerless such as the day-labourers and the labour market (Matt 26: 1-16), absentee landlords (Mark 12: 1-19) and the problem of debt (Matthew 18: 23-35).

baptismal ministry was continued in the diaspora by his followers even after his execution.

John was a charismatic prophetic type whose action of baptising in the waters of the Jordan, we saw above, was a ritual identifying those who were prepared to meet the coming messianic era. Specific mention is made of the fact that it began in Perea, the very area where Elijah had disappeared and Elijah was supposed to be the precursor of the Messiah. John's ritual baptism was an acting-out of the crossing of the Jordan by the first generation of Israelites, itself a replication of the crossing of the Sea of Reeds, and those who participated emerged from the river water and ritually entered a new promised land, a sacred space and sacred time. It seems that John gathered two types of followers: those who underwent the ritual and then returned home to await a further call and those who remained with John. These latter lived a life of ritual fasting and prayer with their leader, awaiting the arrival of the Messiah.

The emphasis on the baptism of Jesus by John seems to indicate that Jesus would have been the latter kind of follower, attached to John who was a prophet, foretelling the imminent closure of the present order of things. Jesus doubtless found a temporary niche in John's following but then they separated.

The indications in John's gospel are that John the Baptist subsequently went to Aenon near Salim, while Jesus went into Judaea. What is being described is a coordinated campaign to cover all of Israel by the master prophet and his apprentice-prophet. In the midst of this campaign some disciples transferred their allegiance from John to Jesus. This might be as close as we can get to an historical Jesus, the celibate prophet-leader who called followers to come to him in order to revitalise Galilean Judaism.

Jesus would have been initially stimulated by John's charismatic rhetoric, but his own calling was to take a different turn. At some point in time Jesus moved away from John. It would seem that this would have coincided with him being recognised as a Just One, *dikaios*, Jesus the Just. The title was repeated without comment in the Christian Scriptures.[6] This toehold can lead to some more historical reflection.

---

6. The Just One in Greek is *ho dikaios*. In Peter's speech in Acts we have:

    But you rejected the Holy and Just One (*ho dikaios*). (Acts 3:14)

   In Stephen's speech:

    They killed those who foretold the coming of the Just One (*ho dikaios*). (Acts 7:52)

   In Paul's speech after his arrest in the Temple:

    The God of our ancestors has chosen you to know his will, to see the Just One

As a Just One he was expected to heal. This would explain the emphasis in the texts on his healing activity around the Sea of Galilee in the villages such as Capernaum. In order to understand this healing ministry in the Second Temple environment we need to accept a close link between sickness, demons and sinfulness and to understand that the cosmos was under the control of the powers of evil, forces that were commonly depicted as demons. These demons were responsible for certain natural phenomena such as sudden storms, responsible for illness, responsible for sinfulness and that obduracy of mind that resisted pious instruction.

The practice of exorcism, casting out demons, the practice of healing and prolonged religious debating were identical in their purpose - they were forms of combat against the demonic world of evil. The Just One was the outstanding righteous person who stood between the people of God and these evil forces, and organised the battle against them. As such it is easy to see how he might have been acknowledged as a Messiah, particularly if the tradition about his Davidic origins was known.

Apart from a healing ministry, Jesus also performed miracles in the text of the gospels. In the Israelite tradition the consistent working of miracles was confined to Moses, Elijah and Elisha. The latter two were northern prophets. Only Elijah and Elisha raised people from the dead. The links with the Jesus stories are palpable. Only Elijah was expected to return and to restore Israel. Jesus either saw himself or was seen by others in this way.

Elijah is identified at the end of the Hebrew canon as YHWH's envoy but in conjunction with Moses.

> Remember the teaching of my servant Moses, the statutes and ordinances that I commanded him at Horeb for all Israel. Lo, I will send you the prophet Elijah before the great and terrible day of YHWH comes. He will turn the hearts of parents to their children and the hearts of children to their parents, so that I will not come and strike the land with a curse. (Malachi 4: 4-5)

(*ho dikaios*). (Acts 22:14)

In 1 John 2:1 we are shown how the Just One could be linked with another term 'advocate/ intermediary', *ho parakletos*:

> My little children, I am writing these things to you so that you may not sin. But if anyone does sin, we have an advocate (*parakletos*) with the Father, Jesus Christ the Just One (*ho dikaios*)

Earlier, in Malachi (probably a collection of prophetic oracles rather than a designated person), there was a less specific mention of a 'messenger of the covenant' and the implication in the postscript is that this messenger is identified as Elijah:

> See, I am sending my messenger to prepare the way before me, and the Lord whom you seek will suddenly come to his temple. The messenger of the covenant in whom you delight —indeed, he is coming says YHWH of Hosts. (Malachi 3:1)

Elijah was seen as the successor of Moses, just as Joshua had been. Later Rabbinic tradition would stress the priestly origin of Elijah. In other words Elijah becomes the ideal future priest who will interpret the *torah* as it should be interpreted.

One of the other prominent aspects of the Jesus ministry in the gospel record is his promotion of table fellowship. His communal meals, the gospels make clear, were open to all. This included women, even prostitutes, sinners and the tax-collectors. The company comprised the outcasts of society, the marginalised, to whom Jesus offered hope and forgiveness by means of his table fellowship, outside the normal ritual channels. These meals had been prefigured in the stories of Elisha who provided food for his followers.

When we take this evidence into account, is it possible to identify the Historical Jesus? Could he, for example, have belonged to one of the known sectarian strains within Second Temple Judaism: Pharisees, Sadducees or Essenes?

The Pharisees were religiously committed lay people, usually more urban than rural, disgusted by the corruption of the ruling elite and the priesthood of Jerusalem. They sought reform through their personal commitment to the will of God and through a thorough ordering of their daily life. Their teaching was broad based and they accepted oral tradition. They were open to new ideas such as apocalyptic notions concerning a coming judgement, a future resurrection of the dead and the existence of intermediary angels. They also enjoined a rigorous ritual purity. Jesus may have been similar in outlook to the Pharisees in many ways, open to new apocalyptic thinking but he would have placed less emphasis on ritual observance and cleanness. While he was more lenient than the Pharisees as regards Sabbath observance, he was more rigid as regards divorce. Certainly, later tradition made it quite explicit that Jesus was never recognised as a Pharisee.

Nor did he move in the circles of the Sadducees, the privileged Temple elite. Nor is there sufficient evidence to link him with the Essenes. He shared many of their ideals, much of their thought world and some of the Essene rituals coincided with later Christian rituals. But there were differences. Essene interest was more concentrated on the restoration of the legitimate priesthood, on ritual observance and was more intensely apocalyptic than that of Jesus.

There seems to be no evidence that he belonged to any of the known major sects. It must be remembered that the majority of Jews in the Second Temple period did not formally belong to them. The total Jewish population at the time of Jesus would have been in the vicinity of 2–2.5 million people. Josephus gives the figures of only 6000 Pharisees and only 4000 Essenes who were said to have lived in many cities and villages.

We are left with the simple identification of Jesus known as the Just One and the Messiah. In other words, he was identified as a local saint in rural Galilee, an advocate or *parakletos* of the people before their God. He was dedicated to the overturn of evil. As an individual Just One, his ministry of healing, of miracle working, exorcism and table fellowship was a prolonged ritual that dramatised as well as effected God's progressive victory over the forces of evil. Evil was being conquered and human barriers were being dismantled by the Messiah.

In Luke 6:27-36 we get a second level description of Jesus the Just's program of local group renewal. These would not be his actual words but would probably reflect the broad content of his preaching.

> Love your enemies, do good to those who hate you, bless those who curse you, pray for those who abuse you. If anyone strikes you on the cheek, offer the other also; and from anyone who takes away your coat do not withhold even your shirt. Give to everyone who begs from you; and if anyone takes away your goods, do not ask of them again. Do to others as you would have them do to you.
>
> If you love those who love you, what credit is that to you? For even sinners love those who love them, If you do good to those who do good to you, what credit is that to you? For even sinners do the same. If you lend to those from whom

> you hope to receive, what credit is that to you? Even sinners lend to sinners, to receive as much again. But love your enemies, do good, and lend, expecting nothing in return. Your reward will be great, and you will be children of the Most High; for he is king to the ungrateful and wicked. Be merciful, just as your father is merciful.

He wanted to revitalise the local group, to restore the values of a covenantal way of life.

This identification of Jesus as a Messiah and Just One makes sense of the accounts of his death. There was, as a corollary to the notion that the Just One stood between the people of God and the evil forces, the idea that the Just One suffered on behalf of others. With the eventual death by execution of Jesus this was incorporated into his image. Jesus the Just, having established a following of disciples from Galilee, went on a pilgrimage to Jerusalem for Passover. It is most unlikely that this was his first venture into Judaea or Jerusalem. John's gospel seems to indicate that, while still under the tutelage of John, he had actually ministered there.

The Jews in Galilee had remained faithful to Jerusalem. They attended festivals in the Holy City, they supported the Temple. It was not easy to do these things; for a Galilean to make the pilgrimage to Jerusalem meant running the gauntlet of the Samaritans who remained hostile to the mainstream Jews. Jesus is shown to have been part of this show of loyalty, but how many times he went to Jerusalem we cannot say.

However, we perceive in the stories a strong reaction to the holy city of Jerusalem. Dismayed at the display of commerce and power in the Temple, he was involved in some sort of demonstration over the rank commercialisation and worldliness of the Jewish cult. He would have been like a pious, rural monk of the Renaissance period visiting Rome and being religiously affronted by the sale of indulgences. He was arrested. Jerusalem, at festival time, was a tinder-box, waiting for the disruptive spark. While Jesus might have been allowed to cause sparks in Galilee with audacity, the authorities would not allow him to do so in Jerusalem at Passover.

He would have been executed for a civil offence against public order. However, his death was seen by his followers in the Jesus-movement as that of a Just One, who was the *parakletos* for his people; his death was interpreted as a religious martyrdom authorised by mainstream Jews who had drifted from their ideals.

The four gospels are replete with contradictions and inconsistencies concerning his arrest, trial, condemnation and death. It is impossible to determine the role of Judas, the denials of Peter, the order or timing of the trials, the witnesses to his execution, the sequence of actions accompanying the death, the disposal of the body and so forth. What seems to be historically reliable is that he was arrested by Romans on the charge of causing insurrection against the Roman *imperium*, perhaps with some collusion by local Jewish authorities.

If there was historical Jewish cooperation in his death, it would have been comparable to the isolated instances of Jewish collaboration with German authorities against their own people in the ghettos and camps during World War II. The final legal responsibility for the charge and his condemnation rested with Rome and the Roman imperialistic system. Any Jews implicated in the process would have been self-seeking collaborators or more likely either unwilling agents or passive bystanders.

It came about that by the time of the written gospels there was a growing tendency to place the blame for Jesus' death not on the Romans but on the Jewish authorities. Christians wanted to exonerate Jesus from any civil charge that raised questions about his innocence in gentile circles. The civil offence was excised from the tradition; the charge of insurrection was replaced by the charge of blasphemy. It would have been at this stage that Annas and Caiaphas, whose roles in the complex politics of High Priesthood were not later understood, came into the narrative with the stories of one or more meetings of the Sanhedrin court.

Whether Pilate would have been involved directly in what would have been a rather mundane administrative procedure of executing an insurrectionist is also questionable. By the time the gospels were written the formula was determined: 'Jesus had died under Pontius Pilate'. This meant neither more nor less than that Jesus had died at the hand of Roman imperial authority, represented at that time by Pontius Pilatus.

Pilate was presented as a vacillating judge, offering to release Jesus and washing his hands of responsibility for his death, before he caved in to Jewish demands for his execution.[7] The whole scenario made sense in the later constructed picture: Jesus before Caiaphas became an assertion of

7. The end point of the trajectory from Pilate's personal historical involvement to his theological role in the Jesus narrative can be seen in the *Acta Pilati* (an expanded version is contained in the *Gospel of Nicodemus)* dating from the fifth century in which Pilate is absolutely exonerated of any responsibility for Jesus' death. He even consults Jesus for advice on the sentence he should impose, and the burden of guilt is laid on the Jews. In the *Paradosis Pilati*, contained in the text of the *Acta*, Pilate explains to the emperor Tiberius that he allowed Jesus to be crucified 'because of the unlawful insubordination of the lawless and godless Jews'. The destruction of Jerusalem in 70 CE was interpreted in the text as God's punishment of the Jews for deicide.

his High Priesthood; Jesus before Pilate became an assertion of his royal Messiahship.

Any historical involvement of Pilate or the Jews in the civil trial of Jesus can be contested and scepticism should be shown regarding the gospels' description of a religious 'trial' before Annas and Caiaphas. The three figures of Pilate, Annas and Caiaphas would have been historical characters drawn into a fictive narrative that was designed for the purposes of a Literary Jesus.[8]

I would think that the gospel writers knew virtually nothing of the circumstances of the actual death of Jesus apart from the brute fact of his crucifixion. The words spoken from the cross, his being offered vinegar, the division of his garments by lot, his mockery by Jewish authorities, the words spoken at his death are all theological statements and not historical recollections. They are taken from texts from the Hebrew Scriptures and Psalm citations describing the plight of the suffering Just Ones.

The theological discourse describing his death referred to aspects of the Literary Jesus: Jesus taking on the sinfulness of his people and dying for others. While this was never an aspect of the Messiah, it was very much part of the image of the Just One. We see a clear coalescence of the two images of Messiah and Just One at this point.

What historically can be said about the resurrection from the tomb? It needs to be stated unequivocally that the resurrection statement, 'Jesus is risen from the dead', refers uniquely to the Literary Jesus. It has no relevance for the Historical Jesus. But we can vaguely trace how it came to be applied to the Literary Jesus.

In common with Mesopotamian beliefs, life after death was earlier restricted by the Jews to some great cavern under the earth. In the Jewish tradition it was called *she'ol*. Normally, *she'ol* was a dead-end; there was no exit point. However, there were some who had gone to *she'ol*, but had an expectation of returning: Enoch, Eliezer, Methusalah, Hiram of Tyre, Elijah, Rabbi Jeshua ben Levi are just some of these.

Hence there was nothing highly unusual in an account of Jesus' return from the dead. It might even have been an historical fact that early Christians believed that he had returned from the dead. The tradition that he had returned would have originated with vision stories. Jesus, who had gone to *she'ol*, was said to have appeared to a select few of his followers after that time. The visions were not accorded randomly to individuals or

8. Unfortunately, the literal acceptance of this non-history has led the Western world to wreak vengeance on the innocent Jewish people at repeated times.

without purpose. The visions were intended to indicate succession among Jesus' followers and to ensure that the movement that Jesus had initiated would continue beyond his death. However, there was competition as to whom Jesus had appeared with the intention of indicating succession.

We will briefly cover the history of this competition insofar as we can. It impinges on the Historical Jesus.

The successors to Jesus

My work in anthropology had convinced me that succession in the establishment of a religious tradition was of utmost importance. There needed to be some way by which the original experience could be replicated. That often required the nomination of a successor.

There was a tradition within Jewish writings that a religious leader nominated a successor. Thus each Ancestor nominated a son, Moses nominated Joshua. Sometimes, this nomination required the leader to appear after death in a vision.

Who had been nominated by Jesus? That was the big question. There was a well-established claim later on that Jesus had nominated Peter during his lifetime and, in addition, that after his death he appeared in a vision to Peter. This is the story to be found in the three Synoptics.

In the gospel of John it was Mary Magdalene who was the first to see the risen Jesus. Certainly, there were some Christians who looked to Mary as the successor.

However, James, known in both biblical and non-biblical sources as the 'brother of the Lord', must have claimed that Jesus had actually appeared first to him. This would have made him, not Peter, the successor to Jesus. The account of this vision is recounted in the context of a meal in the now lost *Gospel according to the Hebrews*. It reads:

> (Jesus) took bread and gave thanks and broke it, and then gave it to James the Just, saying to him: 'My brother, eat your bread because the Son of Man has risen from those who sleep'.

It is possible that this appearance to James is the tradition underlying the Emmaus story in Luke 24, James being originally the unnamed disciple in that text. His name would have been excised by the Peter followers. By the time of 1 Corinthians 15, Paul could give an official listing of many visions.

> For I handed on to you as of first importance what I in turn had received: that Christ died for our sins in accordance with the scriptures, and that he was buried, and that he was raised on the third day in accordance with the scriptures. And that he appeared to Cephas, then to the Twelve. Then he appeared to more than five hundred brothers and sisters at one time, most of whom are still alive, although some have died. Then he appeared to James, then to all the apostles. Last of all, as to one untimely born, he appeared also to me.

It is interesting to note that often the context for these visions was also specified—Jesus appeared usually at meals, at the table fellowship that had been the hallmark of his ministry in Galilee. He broke bread, he ate fish. In the Synoptics, the Last Supper became the all-important final meal, the final act of table fellowship in his ministry and the prototype of the context for his future visions. It was a construct, symbolically situated between the meals taken during the ministry and the ritual meals shared after his death. But the question really was: who was the nominated successor—whether in the Synoptic description of a meal on the eve of his death or the *Gospel to the Hebrews'* version after his death?

Peter, Mary Magdalene, the 'Beloved Disciple' mentioned in John's gospel and James were all contenders. After Jesus' death, competing leaders continued to host communal meals in his memory. The participants were convinced that Jesus was present at the meals and the visions became more widespread.

But another aspect of the tradition was adding a new and significant dimension to the Jesus-visions. This was increasing apocalypticism, the impending expectation that The End was coming and there were obvious signs of it. Jesus would have shared the common Galilean expectation of a future and final divine intervention in the world order that would introduce God's final kingdom. But, after his death, his followers became more apocalyptically minded. Apocalyptic thought looked forward to the final day at the end of the world when the tombs would open and the dead would rise. It would have been clear to this apocalyptic mentality that if there was a living Jesus after his death, there must be somewhere a corresponding empty tomb. Hence, an empty tomb tradition was combined with the earlier Jesus-visions which focussed on the identification of successors to Jesus.

Thus Matthew, Mark and Luke have a common tradition of an empty tomb discovered by women and later reported to Peter, and of visions to Peter and the Twelve. John introduces the Beloved Disciple into the discovery and has visions to Mary Magdalene at the tomb as well as to the Twelve. Scattered throughout the Gnostic texts there are other references to visions of the living Jesus (who, according to the Gnostics, did not actually die)—to James the Just, Thomas, Judas, Peter and others. Such was the complex growth in resurrection belief: Jesus appeared to certain followers to nominate a successor, therefore his tomb had been opened and he had emerged as the first of many who would return to life according to apocalyptic expectation.

Since The End did not come immediately, the resurrection of Jesus would have required an ascension and an enthronement. Philo described Moses' ascension of the mountain at Sinai as his entering into the divine realm and becoming himself divine. He is said to have become 'God and king of the whole nation'. Luke has constructed a very literal depiction of the ascension into the sky. In John the resurrection and an account of a more spiritual ascension are seen as simultaneous. The resurrected Jesus entered at once into the realm of divinity and it was an easy step from there to regard him as divine from the very beginning, as the Johannine tradition would do.

There were many accounts of visions after Jesus' death and they cloak the fact that there were many competing groups of 'Christians', Jewish sects that followed the lead given by Jesus. There was the Peter group, there was the James group, there was a John group (which eventually linked up with the Peter group), there were the Hellenists led by Stephen and there were Gnostic groups who looked to a variety of successors of Jesus.

The forms taken by the gospels were determined by the social and religious context of these groups. The Synoptics were all devised within the Peter group. The gospel of John was devised within the John group but it later was accepted into the Peter group with some deft additions. Gnostic gospels had their form determined by the thinking, practices and values of their attendant groups. Other gospels came and went just as their communities came and went.

We could write a stark outline of the biography of Jesus, the Historical Jesus, based on facts gained from the summary references in pagan histories and from reading between the lines of the Christian Scriptures as has been attempted above. The outline would, in broad strokes, detail some facets of his early life and development, make much of his relationship to and division from John the Baptist, pass comment on his ministry as a Just One and Messiah, and then account for his execution and the circulation of the story of his resurrection. We can also, as seen above, describe broadly what happened in the generation after the death of Jesus. This latter would be nothing like the version in the Acts of the Apostles.

This historical work may have some indirect influence on interpretation of the written Christian Scriptures. It is not essential to that interpretation. The historical work does not prove or disprove anything to do with the Christian Scriptures. The Christian Church should rely only on the Literary Jesus.

We now turn to the Literary Jesus, the more detailed story that circulated after his death and which was written large in the gospels.

The Literary Jesus

The Literary Jesus is the Jesus of the canonical gospels. In fact, there are four Literary Jesus-es. They have their own stories (admittedly with significant overlaps) and they have their own line of argument.

We begin then with certain broad slices of the four canonical gospels. Instead of trying to mine the earliest stratum from the gospel tradition, as the Jesus Seminar participants have attempted, each gospel is taken as a whole and separately, just as it is. When does this latest stratum date from? Perhaps 70-100 CE, perhaps much later. Any chronological sequencing would be conjectural in a final analysis and unimportant. We can disengage from the slices of gospel material a number of synchronic stages. These are phases that are essential for the progress of the story of the Literary Jesus: the opening statement on Jesus (the infancy narratives in Matthew and Luke; the prologue in Mark and the Hymn in John); the ministry of Jesus; his final ministry in Jerusalem, culminating in his arrest and execution and the resurrection.

In many ways Rhetorical Criticism, the method of the second revolution, has continued to guide this research on a Literary Jesus derived from the gospels. Hence, what had been achieved earlier in the second revolution could be transported into the third revolution. But the third revolution places the outcomes into a very different context.

We have already seen the Literary Jesus of Mark in detail. After a Prologue identifying Jesus as the Messiah, succeeding to John the Baptist who has come to confront evil in the world, Mark describes the ministry of the Messiah. Within a journey in Galilee, he performs the works expected of a Messiah: he gathers followers and makes them into a new 'Twelve', a New Israel; he teaches, heals and debates with enemies in the manner of the Messiah and finally he is met consistently with hostility and rejection. The Literary Jesus calls for the Twelve to make an affirmation of faith in him and together they make a new journey to Jerusalem where he fulfils the role of the Messiah by dying and rising from the dead.

Matthew's Literary Jesus, even more clearly than Mark's, is presented as a Moses-like Messiah in an infancy narrative peppered with references to Moses taken from the Hebrew Scriptures. Jesus' public ministry, reusing the material from Mark, is divided into five books of Stories/Sayings, parallel to the Five Books of Moses in the Hebrew Scriptures. The Five Books culminate with Jesus' Jerusalem ministry and the account of his death, parallel with what Matthew would have received from his source—Mark. His death is the death of a suffering Messiah.

Matthew's resurrection consists of the combination of a vision from Jesus *redivivus* in Galilee and the empty tomb in Jerusalem. His final exhortation is: 'I am with you'. It corresponds to the title of *Immanuel*, 'God with Us', used of Jesus in the opening infancy narrative and is intended to form an *inclusio*, a connection between the beginning of the gospel and its end. In all, the gospel explains how the Messiah-model works.

The Literary Jesus of Luke's gospel was, as with Matthew and Luke, a Messiah but Luke has depicted his Messiah-Jesus in the mould of an eschatological prophet. The Prophet-Messiah prepares the first stage of his ministry in Galilee. Then begins a remarkable journey to Jerusalem, replete with sayings, stories and good works. It covers some ten of Luke's twenty-four chapters in length. Material that Matthew had derived both from Mark and the Q source is interwoven into this travelogue. At the culmination of the journey Jesus reaches Jerusalem, where he is rejected by mainstream Judaism and condemned to death.

Tellingly, as Jesus dies on the cross in Luke, a Gentile centurion announces: 'Truly this man was a Just One'. The Literary Jesus is interpreted as a Just One. Luke has a more extended resurrection section with appearances to women, then to two disciples on the road to Emmaus and finally to the group of disciples. The gospel concludes with an ascension story.

However, in order to appreciate Luke's full message, the Acts of the Apostles should be read as the second volume of his opus. It shows how the disciples, having been instructed and prepared by Jesus, in turn continue to spread God's word. Jesus is with them and they are filled with the Spirit of God, God's powerful presence. Telling once again the story of the ascension, the Literary Jesus in Acts appears to the disciples and says:

> It is not for you to know the times or periods that the Father has set by his own authority. But you will receive power when the Holy Spirit has come upon you; and you will be my witnesses in Jerusalem, in all Judaea and Samaria, and to the ends of the earth. (Acts 1:7-8)

This is the divine plan which follows immediately after the events of the gospel of Luke. The Acts begins in Jerusalem, where wondrous things occur through the ministry of the disciples, and then the disciples move outwards first into Judaea and Samaria and thence, through the ministry of Paul, to Asia Minor and Europe, 'the ends of the earth'.

Luke thus has shown, while remaining faithful to the sources he received from earlier Christians (particularly the gospel of Mark), that God's work which had begun in Israel with the Jews, had been taken over by the Christians, who were both Jews and Gentiles, and had now spread to 'the ends of the earth'. Luke and the Acts, when read together, give the official account of what Christianity has achieved.

The Literary Jesus, according to Luke's gospel, was not a revolutionary but the Prophet and Messiah of Israel. Christianity was not a revolutionary organisation, which the Romans should fear, but a group of loving and caring followers of the Prophet-Messiah. What had begun among the Jews had now spread beyond Israel to the whole world.

Matthew, Mark and Luke—the three synoptics—had substantially the same Literary Jesus, but with some variation. In each case Jesus was the Just One and Messiah, but the experience of the group associated with a particular gospel must have coloured the presentation of each of the Literary Jesus-es.

The Literary Jesus in John's gospel is presented differently to the other three canonical gospels. In the opening Hymn, the Son is a divine being, The Word, or Logos, who took on the human form of Jesus and then acted as a human mediator, later returning to the divine realm. John presents a Literary Jesus based on this premise. It is very close to a Gnostic Jesus.

To understand the events in the public ministry of this Johannine Literary Jesus, it is necessary to interpret a series of what John calls 'signs' in order to perceive the outlines of the human-divine being. A 'sign' in John is human activity in which the Literary Jesus reveals his true purpose and mission. The first 'sign' is the changing of water into wine at the wedding feast of Cana. Jesus' action shows that the old order (water) is being replaced by a new order (wine). There are seven of these 'signs' (Cana, the cure of an official's son, the cure of a crippled man, the feeding of 5000 people, the cure of a blind man, the raising of Lazarus and the final sign is the Death and return to the heavenly realm of Jesus) and the astute reader is led inexorably from one to the next and expected to deepen in faith as the plot progresses.

The gospel of John insists that it is the Literary Jesus, who reveals The Son, that is ultimately important, not the human form of the Historical Jesus. This is definitively explained in John's resurrection story. This story in John 20 has a different function by comparison to the parallel stories in the synoptics. It contains the final definition of the Literary Jesus. It states that just as the Historical Jesus of Galilee, in a limited time and space, was a human mediator for a restricted group of followers who lived side by side with him, so the Literary Jesus identified by details from the Hebrew Scriptures and proclaimed by the believing group, acts as a mediator for all those willing to open themselves to him. This latter 'Jesus' is the important factor for humankind, not the historical Jesus of Galilee.

Hence, the purpose and meaning of the well known Johannine texts becomes clearer: 'Do not continue to hold on to me (the Historical Jesus), because I have not yet ascended to the Father', as spoken to Mary Magdalene, and 'Blessed are those who have not seen (the Historical Jesus) and yet have come to believe', spoken to the obtuse Thomas. The access to the Literary Jesus is the only way of salvation for latter day believers and this contact takes place via the Scriptures and Christian preaching, wherein the Literary Jesus is re-presented.

In each of the four canonical gospels, the Literary Jesus is variously depicted as the Just One, the Messiah and the Son of God, (which has ambiguous overtones). Above all else, he is the mediator. The Just One in the synoptics has been overlaid with the trappings of the Moses-like Messiah. This meant that a complex form developed with elements from the stories of Moses, Joshua, David, Elijah and Elisha being inserted into the narratives.

Academic literature on the gospels has uncovered texts and images related to all these figures from the Hebrew Scriptures and there has been conjecture as to the relevance of the parallels. Did Jesus set out to emulate these ancient predecessors? Was it some sort of coincidence that Jesus performed miracles similar to Elijah and Elisha? The simple answer is that these parallels have nothing to do with history. The texts refer to the Literary Jesus, a complex figure who is implicated in complex activities to carry a message. The Literary Jesus never existed as such. He is an amalgam of historical snippets with an overlay of later religious thought and insight.

Conclusion on the Historical and Literary Jesus-es

There was undoubtedly an Historical Jesus. The many attempts, particularly during the course of the Third Search, to re-find the Historical Jesus demonstrates the difficulty, and I would insist the impossibility, of achieving anything more than a general and conjectural outline. I could not concur with any of the Historical Jesus-es put up with confidence by the scholars involved in this Search. More than that, apart from legitimate historical curiosity, the only purpose in such an endeavour would be to clarify aspects of the development of the Literary Jesus. John's gospel makes it clear that the Historical Jesus is a distraction for Christian believers.

The Search for the Historical Jesus is as valid as the Search for the Historical Julius Caesar. It can tell us many things about our past and how we all came to be the sort of people we are. However, the sources must be carefully assessed. The gospels are not primarily historical documents contributing to this historical search; they have been manipulated. They can only be used by historians with the greatest care and in this case very little can be said about the Historical Jesus.

It is the Literary Jesus that is of importance. It is of importance to Christian believers in the first instance. This is the figure that challenges them, determines their faith, that controls their belief. The Literary Jesus never existed but this construction of a mediator is common practice for all religion. Christian believers, from their leaders to the people in the pews, must give up the conviction that their religion relies on history. It has no historical foundation. It is based on a story, a very clever story. Importantly, the sacred story will only work if its basis is accepted as a story and not mined for history.

But further, Christian believers must give up the claim that their religion is exclusively valid. It is one religion among many among the peoples of the world. It may be best for this person; it need not necessarily be best for all.

The Literary Jesus is of great importance also for historians of religion. Each of the Literary Jesus-es gives a blueprint for how an early Christian community operated. It explains their view on ultimacy, how they fashioned Jesus into a focus on ultimacy. There is no other way that the historian of religion can find access to understanding how a particular Christian group began, how it then developed. The four canonical gospels, originally belonging to separate groups, each with its own Literary Jesus, were amalgamated into the religious thinking of the Church at Rome and given legitimacy after the time of Constantine. It was a mammoth effort. The historian of religion needs to conjecture about the original groups, their coming together, their change over time.

The Literary Jesus, found in multiple forms in the canonical gospels and in other forms in the apocryphal gospels, is capable of reinterpretation. It is the role of tradition to reinterpret and to bring one or other of the Literary Jesus-es up to date. Sociologists of religion could follow the path taken by such new Literary Jesus-es as they structure new communities of Christians.

Each community will undoubtedly maintain that their Jesus is the correct one, that their Literary Jesus was in fact the original one. Often they will maintain that their Literary Jesus is a replica of the Historical Jesus. On all counts they are mistaken.

The Biblical Jesus

What of the Biblical Jesus, the so-called historical figure derived from the gospels who not only was born in a stable in Bethlehem (with details combining the disparate stories of Matthew and Luke), then walked the earth, cured or exorcised people and worked nature miracles and raised humans from the dead, was executed and was himself resurrected out of a tomb? Was he a peasant, a prophet, a Cynic, a character from the Dead Sea Scroll texts? Like the Biblical Israel, the Biblical Jesus should never have been constructed. It is an impossible hybrid brought about by inserting the conjectures about an Historical Jesus into the storyline of a Literary Jesus or vice-versa. The Biblical Jesus distorts history; it also distorts the whole religion of Christianity.

The third paradigm, to which I finally became attuned, has upturned the study of both Judaism and Christianity and the interpretation of their Scriptures. It has not disproved them; it has not suggested that they do not proclaim good ways of living. The third paradigm looks at the Christian Scriptures from the point of view of the study of culture, of tradition, of religion in general. The third paradigm is pluralist: all religions, including

Judaism and Christianity, provide a way of finding ultimate order in life. None of them has an exclusivist hold on this technique. All religions have a human history and, if they survive, they perform an essential human function. This is true of the religions as a whole, it is also true of their sacred writings.

The Christian Scriptures are one of the phenomena of literate Christianity. They are not history. They are intended to control the sacred story and ritual of Christian groups, to give them authentic direction towards forming a Christian experience. They do not have any validity beyond or above the sacred writings of any other religious group.

Note

There is an enormous literature on the so-called Third Search for the Historical Jesus. The following general texts are useful:

Chilton, B and Evans C (eds) (1994), *Studying the Historical Jesus: Evaluations of the Current State of Research,* Brill: Leiden

Martin, R (2000), *The Elusive Messiah. A philosophical overview of the Quest for the Historical Jesus,* Westview Press: Boulder, Colorado

Particular interpretations mentioned in the chapter were:

Borg, M (1994), *Meeting Jesus Again for the First Time,* HarperCollins: San Francisco

Crossan JD (1993), *The Historical Jesus: the life of a Mediterranean Jewish Peasant,* Collins Dove: Melbourne

Horsley, R (1987), *Jesus and the Spiral of Violence,* Harper and Row: San Francisco

Mack, B (1988), *A Myth of Innocence: Mark and Christian Origins,* Fortress: Philadelphia

Meier, J (1994), *A Marginal Jew: Rethinking the Historical Jesus, vol 1: The Roots of the Problem and the Person of Jesus.* Doubleday: New York.

Schussler Fiorenza, E (1994), *Jesus: Miriam's Child, Sophia's Prophet,* Continuum: New York

On the question of the religious successors of Jesus, see my own article and its bibliography:

Crotty, R (1996/3), 'James the Just in the History of Early Christianity', *Australian Biblical Review* , *44*, pp 42-52

and there is a good collection of articles in

Byrne R and McNary-Zak, B editors (2009), *Resurrecting the Brother of Jesus: the James Ossuary Controversy and the Quest for Religious Relics*, University of South Carolina Press: Chapel Hill.

CONCLUSION

And so I have now described the effect of the third revolution on my thinking and its methodology within the new paradigm.

I do not now believe, in the first place, that there is any historical intent in the Hebrew Scriptures apart from extraneous nuggets of historical fact, usually handed on by chance, that have no importance for the final product.

Similarly, I do not believe that there is any historical intent in the Christian Scriptures apart from extraneous nuggets of historical fact, usually handed on by chance, that have no importance for the final product.

I do not believe that there is any validity for an exclusivist attitude with regard to the Hebrew Scriptures or the Christian Scriptures. I do not think that either Judaism or Christianity can claim exclusivist validity as religions.

Searching for history in the Hebrew and Christian Scriptures should be seen as a distraction as far as the believer is concerned. There is nothing wrong if the intention of the research is historical. The historian however is quite separate from the committed biblical interpreter, even if sometimes the same people undertake the two pursuits. The committed biblical interpreter, searching for religious meaning and direction, should not in any way be concerned with historical facts.

The interpreter is confronted by a set of symbolic discourses. They have deep meaning, but they are not historical. The historian should not be looking to deepen Christian faith (or Jewish faith) or find deep religious meanings in ancient texts. History is a formal method of recreating the past so that it throws light on the present. It has nothing to do with religious faith.

The Hebrew Scriptures and the Christian Scriptures are phenomena of two religious movements that have continued to the present day. They are obviously esteemed by the adherents of those religions. They will perform their role so long as the adherents do not misuse them. Making them into history is misusing them. They need to be read as sacred literature which still has all the characteristics of ancient literature.

I will now summarise where I have reached with the two main topics with which this book's discussion began.

Hebrew Scriptures

To begin with, the Hebrew Scriptures as we now have them were put together mainly during the Persian period in the fourth century BCE for the purposes of giving cultural identity to a group of newcomers to the land. These writings established the newcomers' continuity with a past, glorious Kingdom, that was fashioned out of memories, some historical remnants and imaginative invention. The newcomers positioned themselves within this Kingdom. This past glorious Kingdom was Literary Israel, a state and a people. It never historically existed.

The biblical writings, based on the narrative of Literary Israel, would not have been written in their more or less final form until the Greek period, under the control of the Hasmoneans in the second century BCE. They saw the culmination of Jewish history in their glorious takeover and restoration of Jerusalem.

Just to be very clear, I will summarise. There was never a period in which Adam and Eve sired Cain and Abel, there was no Flood Generation and no Tower of Babel. There were, however, clever stories gleaned from the Mesopotamian culture that were cleverly woven into a tale of creation marred by sinfulness. They are Sin Stories. The stories described, possibly as well as any discourse ever has, a reflection on the human state. We humans are thrown into the world. We do not achieve the great things we are enabled to envision. We so often see ourselves as failures. Where can we turn for assistance?

There were no historical Ancestors—Abraham, Isaac or Jacob or their wives, at least in the particular detail in which the stories depict them. There were stories of possession of the land by outsiders, making use of some traditional materials and names of past people (who may or may not have been historical). These stories would eventually be fashioned into an explanation of the beginnings of Literary Israel. The Bible reader, dispirited by the Sin Stories, is confronted by the wandering Abraham, a literary person who provides a ray of hope.

The Ancestor stories lead down to Egypt. The transition is cleverly described in the novella of Joseph. In Egypt, the reader comes upon Moses; Moses was not an historical character. There was no Exodus out of Egypt, at least not as it is described in the Hebrew Scriptures. It was a literary creation that made use of town names and dim memories to tell of a Great Suffering and a Great Journey under a leader Moses whereby the newcomers came back into the Land.

There was no martial conquest of the land of Palestine by newcomers. Again, town names and dim memories of long past battles were used to tell of the Taking of the Land. Beneath this literary creation, a generation of newcomers probably in the fifth century defined themselves as rightfully taking over the satrapy of Yehud.

There was no United Kingdom of David and Solomon that eventually divided and broke down into two kingdoms, both of which were eventually destroyed by world powers. This was the way in which the newcomers to Yehud explained the previous magnitude of a Great State in a fictional past from which they claimed to derive. The elements of this story of Suffering, Exodus and Life in a new Land were then arranged into a story that gave self-identity to the Hasmoneans in the second century before the Christian era as they repossessed the city of Jerusalem. The history of this late period during the Greek occupation of Judaea becomes vitally important.

The texts of the Torah, the Prophets and the Writings were being gathered, edited and expanded in the immediate centuries prior to the Christian period to give cultural meaning and direction to the Judahites. The final form of Literary Israel we now have is that imposed by the Hasmoneans. The collection of writings became the cultural and religious blueprint for the Hasmoneans. It became their Bible. Since that time, tradition has interpreted and reinterpreted that Bible.

Hence, there have been many Literary Israels. One of the roles of the religious interpreter is to trace them and document them. The earlier work on JEDP was of this type. It discovered that there had been a number of editorial attempts to put order into the presentation of a Literary Israel. The interpreter can compare whether a modern presentation of a Literary Israel, say in the twenty-first century, is within the confines of those early, foundational Literary Israels. Not that there would be anything wrong in going beyond the original ones, but then the question of whether the modern interpreting community was still Jewish could be raised. Tradition allows later communities to reinterpret the past for the purposes of the present.

Christian Scriptures

The first Christians inherited this story of Literary Israel. No doubt they unquestioningly accepted it, just as I had instinctively accepted biblical stories in my youth. They did not know about academic history and its protocols; they had no need to know. They also believed that Jesus was a new Moses and a new David and a new Elijah and Elisha, come to revitalise a people that had lost hope in the promises within the biblical narrative. The revitalisation was taking place in the context of long periods of Greek and Roman oppression, of a distant YHWH approached by the Jewish rituals. This was tradition at work.

Stories about Jesus developed in much the same way as had the traditions behind Literary Israel. Eventually stories of his wondrous deeds—preaching, healings, exorcisms—were linked with the story of his death which they claimed took place as an expiation for the sins of all and the story of his return from *she'ol* in order to appear to significant people. These stories were formed into the narratives of the gospels.

Some of these stories may have been historical in our sense, others would have been later constructions. In a number of Christian centres, some decades after his death, the stories and sayings took on a formal structure. They became orderly gospels depicting a series of Literary Jesus-es. They were never histories; they were literary constructions meant to stimulate belief in those who read them. They may have employed historical reminiscences; they certainly employed elaborations and fictions for a good purpose.

The Literary Jesus was interpreted against the background of Literary Israel. There is a link between the two. Scholars of a Literary Jesus are obliged to do their prior study on Literary Israel.

Some Final Musings

I have now documented my life journey from the time I accepted the Hebrew Scriptures and the Christian Scriptures as Dreamtime stories. Then I was overwhelmed by the evidence that showed the anomalies—there were human-author features in them, there were discrepancies. The first revolution in my thinking was the introduction of the historical-critical method. It provided balance and direction but it eventually generated its own anomalies: history could not be integrated into the narrative process. The second revolution was accepting the Bible as Literature and, specifically, using the methodology of Rhetorical Criticism so as to see the full value of the literary strategy within the texts. But the study of anthropology and secular history raised further anomalies. These religions and these sacred writings needed to be set in a broader context of religious pluralism and the sacred writings of both Judaism and Christianity reinterpreted accordingly.

What do I see as the consequences of accepting the three revolutions through which I have passed?

In the first place, the search for history, so much a part of the first revolution, needs to be abandoned in the study of the Bible by those who are not primarily interested in history. This will be hard to accept for many Jews and Christians. History is an academic occupation, taken up particularly in the Western world since the Enlightenment, and used to understand the past and its interactions and the influence of those interactions on the present. Historical study is a noble occupation. But history is not what religion is about. In the case of Judaism and Christianity, what we are left with are not accounts of historical events in the sense of real past happenings; we are left with two collections of texts that were cleverly designed to stimulate belief, instruct believers and guide believers.

Secondly, the third revolution would see both Judaism and Christianity as religions alongside other religions of many kinds. They both have a sacred story and their own rituals. These are protected by their sacred writings. They both give rise to a religious experience that allows the devotees to have a focus on ultimacy. Thereby, those devotees are able to cope with the most profound questions and experiences of life. How do these religions of Judaism and Christianity compare to other religions? They are options.

Thirdly, in this context, the role of the interpreter of the Christian Bible needs to be rethought and this is of importance. The interpreter can certainly search for the original meaning and context of these biblical texts. That would be an interesting task and it should be granted that sometimes it is achievable: this is what the text would have meant when it was first presented in this format. The value in doing so would be to check whether the present Literary Israel or Literary Jesus, as proclaimed and handed on in a religious community, is really based on these original forms. Whether that is a concern, however, will depend on the religious community. Both Judaism and Christianity certainly changed, sometimes subtly and sometimes drastically, in earlier times. No doubt they are still changing.

Interpreters might want also to follow the changing meanings that the text has had as it progressed through the life of a community or compare different meanings given to the one text by different contemporary communities: this is what the tradition means and how the tradition moved forward. This would be interesting and might be valuable.

If we take the gospel of Mark, for example, it may be possible for the interpreter to use literary techniques and interpretive assiduity in order to ascertain what the text meant to the original hearers, who might have lived in Rome or elsewhere and might have been Roman nationals or other. It may also be possible for an interpreter to ascertain the meaning that the text of Mark had when a particular medieval community received it and reinterpreted it or even misunderstood it. However, if the interpreter wants to serve a religious purpose and minister to a modern Christian constituency, then that interpreter's prime task is to go one step further and determine what the text could mean for the community at this particular time. Does this meaning compare with the meaning in the past? Is this community's belief still recognisably Christian? These questions may mean much or little.

In so doing, the Christian interpreter defines what the Literary Jesus means for this group. This is not at all the same as searching for an Historical Jesus. The Literary Jesus is the mediator for any Christian group and accepting this fact is the definition of 'Christian'. The Literary Jesus is thereby the focus or lens by which the community sees beyond the here and now to ultimacy. This Literary Jesus can have a myriad number of forms. The interpreter could propose a better-defined Literary Jesus for this present group, presumably based on the original Literary Jesus of the gospels, and it can be accepted or rejected by the group.

And there is a final consequence. If we define the Christian God (*'abba*, Father) as the symbol of ultimacy, the means whereby a Christian community finds ultimate purpose and direction in human life, then the Literary Jesus is the focus or lens by which access is gained to that ultimacy by those Christians. Human life, at least for some people, can presumably be better lived with such an ultimate direction. But in this discourse, 'God' is by definition beyond human understanding, otherwise a focus would not be needed.

At some point the question will be raised not only about Jesus, the Literary Jesus or the Historical Jesus, but also about God, about ultimacy, about whatever symbol has been used for ultimacy.

The Existence of God

Does this 'God' of Judaism and Christianity really exist? This has been a perennial conundrum. The arguments of Thomas Aquinas and Anselm of Canterbury during the later Middle Ages still convince certain people.

Aquinas argued, for example, that we are able to perceive things in motion. No-one denies motion as a reality in the world. But, if a thing moves it must be moved by something else. And that mover must itself be moved by another. This process cannot regress forever and ever. We must come to the Unmoved Mover, who is God. Aquinas had four other similar proofs of this type.

Anselm's Ontological Argument runs thus:

- God, by definition, is 'The One greater than whom cannot be conceived'.
- But if something exists not only in the mind but in reality as well, that is greater than something that exists in the mind only.
- Therefore, if God is greater than anything else, God must exist both in the mind and in reality.
- Therefore, God exists (that is, God exists in reality).

I will not run through the arguments supporting or denying these proofs (and I can only commend them for cultivating philosophical subtlety). I simply want to say that, as far as religion is concerned, it does not matter if there is a God in reality or not. It is the actual idea of 'God' that is all important. It is whether God (or any other symbol reflecting ultimate meaning) is there in the mind of the human, not whether there really is a God out there. The Literary Jesus acts as a focus on the Christian God and gives people meaning and direction. That meaning and direction is there, whether in reality there is a God out there or not.

Perhaps there is a need to revise. Studying anthropology, I became more and more interested in other religions. Which religion is the true religion? They are all true if they work for the believing adherent in the way I have described. They work if they function so as to provide a focus on ultimacy. None are the same; all are nevertheless equally valid. Hinduism uses its myths of many gods and its colourful rituals to focus the adherent on *brahman*. Buddhism uses its myths of the Buddha and its ritual of meditation to focus its adherents on *nirvana*. Islam uses the reading of the Qu'ran and its practices of *islam* ('submissiveness') to focus its adherents on Allah. In these ways humans find ultimate meaning and direction.

Going further, the Humanist who has strong beliefs about humanness and the environment in which the human lives and achieves, who sees ultimacy through the focus of the Ideal Human, also finds meaning of life. The Green who sees the natural world in symbiosis with the human species and perceives ultimacy in the symbol of some form of Gaia, through the focus of symbolic nature, likewise finds that meaning. Who is left out? In my opinion, as stated earlier, only children who have not reached the age of discretion and those adults who are intellectually challenged do not possess this need and this facility to find ultimacy through a focus.

Are all people 'religious'? It depends on whether you like that terminology. I would call them religious but others might prefer 'spiritual' or 'psychic'.

Judaism uses its myths of Literary Israel and its rituals, reinforced and protected by its Hebrew Scriptures, to focus practising Jews on YHWH. Christianity uses the myths of the Literary Jesus and its rituals, reinforced and protected by its Christian Scriptures, to focus believing Christians on The Father. If the system works and believers experience ultimacy through a workable focus, then nothing further needs to be said or done.

Culture and religion, the structure of religion, a pluralist view of religious truth, the rejection of academic history as a valid prerequisite for religious meaning, an openness to religious agnosticism or atheism—these are the parameters of the third revolution and the latest paradigm.

The third paradigm has advantages. It abhors with due ridicule the whole idea of violence stirred up in families and communities over religious allegiance. Religion is a matter of personal preference. Should my children be Buddhist or Christian or a religious amalgam they concoct for themselves? That question is of the same order as: should they become a homely and happy carpenter or a dedicated Third World medico or perhaps just peaceably wander the world?

Let us however be quite clear: the paradigm that has resulted from the third revolution has its disadvantages.

- It does not explain the problem of evil. Of course, no other approach to religion convincingly explains it either, apart from a religion that posits a Good God and an Evil God. Why should the innocent child suffer? It is part of the world order; I will do all I can to alleviate such suffering, but in the end I have no explanation and I have no universal remedy.
- It does not explain what happens after death. I presume (since my knowledge is finite and limited) that my body returns to matter, that my intellectual spirit, bound inseparably to the bodily processes, ceases to function and that I live on only in memories and in any good that I might have achieved. Stories about a specific afterlife may act as mental analgesics to quieten apprehension about the inevitability of death; they may have the function of pointing to the fulfilment of a life well lived. In the end, death is the moment when we return to where we came from; we came into the world quietly and peaceably at conception, mysteriously and peaceably we pass from it. We may have trauma after conception and before death, but these two borders of life are themselves nothing to dread or fear.

Is that enough? Is that all that results from a lifetime of studying the Christian Bible, the Hebrew Scriptures and the Christian Scriptures?

Is that due return for so long spent on studying languages, interrogating texts, evaluating endless theories?

It has to be; after the third revolution and after thinking in the third paradigm, that is all there is.

For me, it is sufficient.

INDEX

9 781921 817489